WHO'S AFRAID
OF PHILOSOPHY?

MERIDIAN

Crossing Aesthetics

Werner Hamacher

& David E. Wellbery

Editors

Translated by
JPlug

Stanford
University
Press

Stanford
California
2002

WHO'S AFRAID
OF PHILOSOPHY?

Right to Philosophy 1

Jacques Derrida

Stanford University Press
Stanford, California

© 2002 by the Board of Trustees of the
Leland Stanford Junior University

Printed in the United States of America

Assistance for the translation was provided by the French Ministry of Culture.

Who's Afraid of Philosophy? Right to Philosophy 1 was originally published in
French in 1990 as pp. 9–279 of a book entitled *Du droit à la philosophie,*
© 1990, Editions Galilée.

ISBN 0-8047-4294-4 (alk. paper)
ISBN 0-8047-4295-2 (pbk. : alk. paper)

Original Printing 2002

Last figure below indicates year of this printing:
11   10   09   08   07   06   05   04   03   02

Typeset by James P. Brommer
in 10.9/13 Garamond and Lithos display

Contents

Translator's Note

Who's Afraid of Philosophy? is the first part of a massive work entitled *Du droit à la philosophie* (*Right to Philosophy*). That larger work consists of essays, interviews, and talks given by Jacques Derrida between 1974 and 1990 concerning philosophical research, the teaching of philosophy, and the relation between philosophy and institutions, in particular, the university. Its second half will appear in English as a subsequent volume entitled *Eyes of the University*.

Many chapters in the work make reference to or take up directly the Groupe de Recherches sur l'Enseignement Philosophique (Greph), the Collège International de Philosophie (Ciph), and the Etats Généraux de la Philosophie (Estates General of Philosophy), in all of which Derrida played a key role.

Founded in 1974, Greph conducted research on philosophy and its teaching and became engaged in concerted struggles against measures to restrict the teaching of philosophy in French schools. Named after former minister of education René Haby, the Haby Reform in particular set out to curtail the teaching of philosophy in French secondary schools.

Held on June 16 and 17, 1979, the Estates General of Philosophy brought together more than twelve hundred people from diverse backgrounds, including teachers (of philosophy and other disciplines), scholars, and non-academics, all concerned about the fate of philosophy, in particular in the wake of the Haby proposal. The proposal was never implemented.

The Collège International de Philosophie was to a certain extent an outcome of such efforts not only to preserve but to extend the teaching of philosophy. Part of a mission concerning the possibility of such a college formed by the Socialist government that came to power in 1981, Derrida circulated a call for proposals for potential research projects and received an overwhelming response. The Collège was founded on October 10, 1983, and is funded by the state, though autonomous in its operation. Its mission is to provide a place for "philosophical" research that existing institutions either forbid or marginalize. To this end the Collège does not require the same kind of teaching or research accreditation demanded by other institutions.

While the difficulties in translating Derrida are multiple, as is well known, one in particular deserves mention here. Derrida often refers to *l'enseignement philosophique*, literally "philosophical teaching" or "philosophical education." I have most often translated this term as "the teaching of philosophy," since in the context of the struggles detailed above, it is specifically philosophy as a discipline that is most clearly at issue.

For their generous and insightful interventions, I would like to express my deep gratitude to Helen Tartar, Haun Saussy, and, most of all, Elizabeth Rottenberg, friend never lost through many a league.

WHO'S AFRAID
OF PHILOSOPHY?

Privilege: Justificatory Title and Introductory Remarks

To Jean-Luc Nancy

Title, chapter, chapter heading, heading, capital, capital letter: questions of title will always be questions of authority, of reserve and right, of *rights reserved*, of hierarchy or hegemony. The title "Right to Philosophy,"[1] for example, keeps in reserve a multiplicity of possible meanings, capitalizing them in its folds, ready to bring them out, and more.

We should begin by *decapitalizing*. It would be necessary to employ or deploy these significations. But if this form, *Right to Philosophy*, can remain as it is, here, *folded up*, it is to the extent that it remains the form of a title: that which gets its authority, thus its power, its prestige—and its *privilege*—from being able to dispense with forming a sentence and making itself explicit.

Its privilege, which it gets from its unicity as much as from its place, is to be able to keep quiet while making us believe, rightly we assume, that it has a lot to say. This privilege is always guaranteed by conventions that regulate the use of titles, whether the titles of works or social titles, in our society. In the case of what we call works [*oeuvres*], the free choice, the singular virtue of every title is a privilege that is legal and authorized, if one can put it this way. One receives the title of doctor, but, by right and in principle, one sovereignly chooses the title of a talk or book one signs— which alone carries that title.

The moment one forms a sentence with these words, *Right to Philosophy*, the moment one develops, exploits, or lightens the equivocation, the power of the title begins to dissolve and discussion begins. Democracy too, no doubt, and in a certain manner philosophy. How far can this movement go? For philosophy (this will be my hypothesis) *clings to the privilege it ex-*

poses. Philosophy would be what wants to keep, by declaring it, this ultimate or initial privilege that consists in *exposing* its own privilege: to danger or presentation, sometimes to the risk of presentation.

Let's make some sentences. If I say, for example, and this is the first meaning of my title, "How does one go *from right to philosophy*?," we get involved in a certain problematic. It will be a matter, for example, of the relations permitting one to go from juridical thought, from the juridical discipline or practice, to philosophy and the *quid juris* questions that have long worked at its heart. It will be a question, more precisely, of the relation of the juridical structures that implicitly or explicitly support philosophical institutions (teaching or research) *to* philosophy *itself*, if such a thing exists outside, before, or beyond an institution. In this first meaning, the title *Right to Philosophy* announces a program, a problematic, and a contract: we will deal with the relations between right and philosophy. What is more, every contract implies a question of right. And a title is always a contract. That, in the unique case of philosophy, this contract be destined to more than one paradox is here our privileged theme, privilege as our theme.

In this first type of sentence, only one of the five words [in *Du droit à la philosophie—Right to Philosophy*], in fact, the single letter *à* [to], carries the entire semantic determination. Meaning here pivots on the different values an *à* can carry. We have in effect just evoked the relation of right *to* philosophy as that of an *articulation* in general: between two areas, two fields, two structures, or two institutional mechanisms. But with the same semantic determination of the *to*, with the same value of *a relation to*, another sentence announces another program—and another problematic. One can in fact rightly note that, to analyze these problems (institutional right and the philosophical institutions of research and teaching), we have to talk about right [*droit*] to philosophers. We have to talk about right [*droit*] *to* philosophy. We have to recall the questions of law [*droit*], the enormous continent of the juridical problematic about which philosophers in general—and especially in France—talk too little, even if and no doubt because, law [*droit*] talks through them so much: we have to talk about right [*droit*] to philosophy. We have to talk to philosophy about right [*droit*], have to talk to philosophy and philosophers about the immense and ramifying question of right [*droit*]. The "to" still says *articulation*, but this time in a different sense, that of the speech articulated in the *address*, of the word that is addressed or intended for: we have to talk about right to philosophy.

But this articulatory mode does not exhaust the entire relation of the "right to philosophy." The French syntagm *du droit à* can signify something else and open another semantic access. One says "to have the right to" [*avoir droit à*] to indicate the access guaranteed by the law, the right of way, the pass, the *Shibboleth*, the authorized entry. Who has the right to philosophy today, in our society? To which philosophy? Under what conditions? In which private or public space? Which places of teaching, research, publication, reading, discussion? Through which instances and filterings of the media? To have the "right to philosophy" is to have a legitimate or legal access to something whose singularity, identity, and generality remain as problematic as what is called *Philosophy* [la *philosophie*]. Who, then, can lay claim *legitimately to philosophy*? To think, say, discuss, learn, teach, expose, present, or represent *Philosophy* [la *philosophie*]?

This second value of the "to" (the relation no longer as *articulation* but as *address*) deploys another possibility. To recapitulate, to this point we have three typical sentences:

1. What is the relationship of *right to philosophy*?
2. We have to talk about *right to philosophy*—and thus to philosophers.
3. Who has *the right to philosophy* and under what conditions?

If we now further circumscribe the syntagm "right to philosophy," which allows us to make an *adverb* as well as a *noun* of the word *right*, we engender or identify the space of another sentence and thus of another regime of questions: is it possible to go *right to philosophy*? To go *straight* to it, *directly*, without detour? This possibility or ability would at the same time guarantee the immediacy, that is, the universality and naturality, of the philosophical exercise. What can that mean? Is it still possible, as some believe, to philosophize *straightforwardly*,[2] *directly*, immediately, without the mediation of training, teaching, or philosophical institutions, without even the mediation of the other or of language, this or that language? By citing in this way, putting between quotation marks, the expression of a "right to philosophy" in which the word "right" is adverbialized, we have the matrix of a fourth sentence, a fourth type of sentences, but also the title of another problematic. It will come to enrich and overdetermine those we have just identified.

Certain people are always impatient to *access-the-things-themselves-*

directly-and-reach-right-away-without-waiting-the-true-content-of-the-urgent-and-serious-problems-that-face-us-all-etc. Thus, they will no doubt judge an analysis that deploys this range of meanings and possible sentences playful, precious, and formal, indeed futile: "Why be so slow and self-indulgent? Why these linguistic stages? Why don't we just speak directly about the true questions? Why not go right to the things themselves?" Of course, one can share this impatience and nonetheless think, as I do, that not only do we gain nothing by immediately giving in to it, but that this lure has a history, interest, and a sort of *hypocritical* structure, and that one would always be better off to begin by acknowledging it by giving oneself the time for a detour and analysis. At stake is precisely a certain right to philosophy.

The analysis of the potential values that sleep or play at the bottom of the idiom "right to philosophy" must be an exercise in vigilance and must only "play" to the extent that the question of the "game" is here of the most serious kind. For at least two reasons. One stems from the question of the *title*, the other from that of *language*.

1. "The right of . . . ," "the right to . . . ": The Institutional Presupposition

To have the right of, the right to, is to be entitled, justified in doing, in saying, in doing by saying, this or that. A title *authorizes, legitimates, gives value*, and *brings together*. This is true for *something*, which therefore is never a simple thing, or for *someone*, who then becomes "somebody." For something that is never a thing: the title of a talk or work, of a talk *as work* [oeuvre], or of an institution that in its own way is at once talk and work, since it has a history that withdraws it from the so-called natural order and since it depends upon a speech act. The title is the name of the *work*, in whatever sense one takes this word (work of art, political work, institution).[3] It brings the work together by naming it and allows it, thus identified, to assert its right to existence and to be recognized—legalized or legitimated. What holds for the work (that thing that is not a thing and that does not belong to nature in the modern sense of the word) also holds for someone, for someone's entitlement—to say, to do, to say by doing this or that: doing "things" with words. But the title given (or refused) someone always supposes, and this is a circle, the title of a work, that is, an institution, which alone is entitled to give (or refuse) it. Only an institution (the title of the body entitled to confer titles) can give *someone* his or her title.

This institution can no doubt be incarnated by people, even by a single person, but this incarnation is itself guaranteed by some institution or constitution. That a title is given (or refused) someone by an institutional body means that guarding over titles, as much as guaranteeing them, falls to that which, as institution, already holds the title. *The origin of the power to entitle or accredit can thus never be phenomenalized as such.* The law of its structure—or the structure of its law—*demands that it disappear.* This is not merely a circle. The thinking of such a "circle" at least forces one to re-form the immense questions that are already "filed" under the classic titles of "repression," "suppression," or "sacrifice."

Each of the texts collected here in its own way attempts to account for this paradoxical topic of the *institutional presupposition.*[4] Such a topic also affects the structure of the institution as archive (nothing less than what historians, in short, call history): an institution remembers, to be sure. It is made for that. It monumentalizes names and titles, those it has given, those from which it has received its own.

But something else can always happen *against its will,* affecting the structure of its very space. It can, first of all, *forget* its own elect: we know that it sometimes loses their names in ever more inaccessible depths. This selectivity no doubt signifies, first of all, the finitude of an institutional memory. The paradox lies elsewhere, however, even if it is *also* the effect of an essential finitude: what we call an institution must sometimes remember what it *excludes* and selectively attempts to doom to being forgotten. The surface of its archive is then marked by what it keeps outside, expels, or does not tolerate. It takes the inverted shape of that which is rejected. It lets itself be delineated by the very thing that threatens it or that it feels to be a threat. In order to *identify itself,* to be what it is, to delimit itself and recognize itself in its own name, it must espouse the very outlines of its adversary, if I can put it thus. It must wear its adversary's features, even bear its name as a negative mark. And the excluded thing, whose traits are deeply engraved in the hollows of the archive, imprinted right on the institutional support or surface, can end up in turn becoming the subjectile that bears the memory of the institutional body. This is true for the founding violence of states and nations and the peoples it never fails to suppress or destroy. And this never takes place once and for all, but must necessarily continue or repeat itself according to diverse processes and rhythms. But this is also true, on an apparently more modest scale, of academic institutions, philosophy in particular. What is more, the academic example supposes, structurally, the politico-state example. To remain outside of France and in the past, the University of Frankfurt is not only the institution that refused to confer the title Doctor of Philosophy upon Walter Benjamin, but it is *also* that. This university of course stirs memory, attention, or admiration, for other reasons. But if we remember this university—and certain exclusions by which it has, precisely, identified itself—that is *also* thanks to a note in the complete works of Benjamin. Would so many of us recognize Hans Cornelius's name if a certain editor's note at the end of Benjamin's complete works were not dedicated to this event, exemplary in so many ways—the rejection of *The Origin of the German Mourning Play* as a thesis for the *Habilitation*?[5]

Like every publication, a teaching—for example, a seminar on the question *of the right to philosophy*—can, I will even say should, always *problematize*, that is, put forward, its own limits and conditions in order to draw attention to them, to make them the theme of research: What entitles us, what gives us the right to be here, already assembled, even if to experience disharmony or discord, even if to observe that the premises for a discussion have not been met or that we cannot even agree on the meaning and terms of such an observation? What entitles us, what gives us the right to be here, you and I, I who take or keep the floor for the moment, without *apparently* having asked for authorization? That is, to a certain extent at least, an *appearance*: in fact, we know very well that a long and complicated process of *authorization* (implicitly requested of several—academic, editorial, media, and so on—agencies or instances, and more or less willingly granted by this or that among them) has preceded this act, in as far from natural a fashion as possible.

There is nothing to assure us that this space (seminar, preface, or book), the place where this act takes place, belongs to philosophy and that it is entitled to carry that title. As its title indicates, the question dealt with here can carry beyond or stop short of the philosophical—whose meaning, for the moment and on principle, should not be given. Does the question "What is the philosophical?" *belong* to philosophy? Yes and no: a formally contradictory response, yet anything but a null or evasive one. To belong to philosophy is certainly not to be *part of a whole* (a property, a state or nation, a multiplicity, a series or group of objects, a field of knowledge, the body of an institution, even if these are open totalities). Upon the necessity or possibility of this "yes and no," upon the trembling limit that traverses or institutes it, upon the *thinking of the philosophical* it seems

to call for, upon all that depend today the most serious stakes and responsibilities. According to philosophers, when it is posed concerning a science
or art, the question "what is . . . " always belongs to philosophy. It belongs
by rights to philosophy. Therein lies the right of philosophy. Since philosophy alone retains this right, according to philosophy, it is also a privilege.
Philosophy would be this privilege. It would not receive it, but would be the
power of granting it to itself. The oldest theme of philosophy is found
here once again: the question "What is physics, sociology, anthropology,
literature, or music?" would be philosophical in nature.

But can the same be said about the question "What is the philosophical?"? This is the most and least philosophical of all questions. We will
have to take it into account. It is in all the institutional decisions: "Who
is a philosopher? What is a philosopher? What has the right to claim to be
philosophical? How does one recognize a philosophical utterance, today
and in general? By what sign (is it a sign?) does one recognize a *philosophical* thought, sentence, experience, or operation (say, that of teaching)?
What does the word *philosophical* mean? Can we agree on the subject of
the philosophical and of the very place from which these questions are
formed and legitimated?"

These questions are no doubt identical with philosophy itself. But in accordance with this essential unrest of philosophical identity, perhaps they
are already no longer completely philosophical. Perhaps they stop short of
the philosophy they interrogate, unless they carry beyond a philosophy that
would no longer be their ultimate destination.

A question addressed *to philosophy* about its identity can respond to at
least *two dominant figures.* Other approaches are no doubt possible, and
here we are working to engage in them in a preliminary way. But the two
figures that have won out in the tradition seem opposed to one another as
essence and *function.* On the one side, that of essence (which also happens
to be that of history, the origin, the event, meaning, and the *etymon*), one
attempts to think philosophy *as such,* as what it *is,* what it *will have been,*
what it *will have anticipated being* since its origin—and one will do this
precisely by placing oneself at the point of an event that establishes itself,
in the experience of a language, on the basis of the *question of being* or of
the *truth of being.* This is the figure of Heideggerian "destruction," defined
as schematically as possible.[6] On the other side, that of function, and in a
style that is apparently more nominalist, one begins by denouncing such
an originarism: it would teach us nothing about a *pragmatic* truth of phi-

losophy, that is, about what it *does* or what is *done* under its name, about
the use [*parti*] we make of it, the part [*parti*] or the stands [*parti*] we take
in it, in speech acts, discussions, evaluations, social, political, and institutional practices, whose difference, above all, must be grasped, rather than
the genealogical thread that would reconnect them to some forgotten emer-
gence. This functionalist pragmatism is the model, at least implicitly, for
numerous modern interrogations *on the subject of* philosophy, whether
they are deployed by philosophers, sociologists, or historians.

Beyond all their differences and oppositions, and they are anything but
negligible, these two figures of the question *on the subject of* philosophy
(What is it? What does it do? What does one do about or with it?) always
presuppose one another, to begin with or in the end. Nominalist prag-
matics must give itself a rule in advance in order to set its own operations
under way and recognize its objects. That rule is always a *concept of philosophy*, which itself demands that one *presuppose a sense or essence*, the being
on the basis of which the being-philosophical of philosophy is thought.
The originarist approach (and this is also true of that of Heidegger) itself
must presuppose an event, a chain of events, a history in which a philosophical thinking is no longer distinguished from a "speech act" made possible by an arche-conventional or quasi-contractual condition in a given
language. It must therefore presuppose the performative moment of a social and institutional "function," even if more appropriate names are given
to these "things" after having put them through "destruction."

If we were to invent and adjust another type of questioning, if that were
to be possible, we would have to start by understanding and formalizing
the necessity, if not the fatality, of this common presupposition. It is on
this path that we find ourselves. All the debates evoked in this book recall
this, whether they concern the inaugural proposals of Greph,[7] the Introduction to the Estates General of Philosophy, the founding of the Collège
International de Philosophie, or the Report of the Commission on Philosophy and Epistemology. Each time, I joined vigorously and unequivocally
in struggles to ensure and develop what is often called the threatened "specificity" of the discipline of philosophy: struggles against its fragmentation,
and even its dissolution into the teaching of the social or human sciences,
sometimes (the more traditional risk in France) into that of languages and
literatures. But at the same time, it was necessary to remind those who
would make a merely defensive and conservative, sometimes narrowly dogmatic, even corporatist use of this just argument that this "specificity"

must remain of the most paradoxical kind. Its experience is also that of an aporia across which an uncertain path must continually be reinvented. It is not only the specificity of one discipline among others (even if it should be recalled that it is *also* that), with its field of objects and its stock of transmissible rules. If philosophy must remain open to all interdisciplinarities without losing itself in them, that is because it does not lend itself as one discipline among others to the peaceful and regular transaction between kinds of knowledge with established borders or objects that can be assigned to given territories. What has been called "deconstruction" is also the *exposure* of this institutional identity of the discipline of philosophy: what is irreducible about it must be exposed as such, that is to say, shown, watched over, laid claim to, but in that which opens it and ex-propriates it, as what is proper in its properness distances itself from itself in order to relate to itself—first of all, in the least of its questions about itself. Philosophy, philosophical identity, is also the name of an experience that, in identification in general, begins by ex-posing itself: in other words, expatriating itself. Taking place where it does not take place, where the place is neither natural, nor originary, nor given.

Questions of title and right always have a *topological* dimension. No institution does without a symbolic place of legitimation, even if assigning this place can be overdetermined at the intersection of empirical and symbolic, physico-geographic and ideal givens within a homogeneous or heterogeneous space. A seminar can take place in a specific institution (physically but not without drawing from it a symbolic benefit that sets the stakes for the transactions and contracts), a seminar given by someone who does not belong to that institution (Jacques Lacan at the Ecole Normale Supérieure for several years, for example) or by someone who, a former student of the Ecole Normale Supérieure, teaches there under the auspices of that other public establishment that is the Ecole des Hautes Etudes en Sciences Sociales, or even of an institution having no physical place proper that, like the Collège International de Philosophie (Ciph), founded in 1983, is by right a private association (governed by the so-called Law of 1901), autonomous in its operation and orientations, although its board of directors includes, by statute, the representatives of four ministries! The map of these "places" calls for an exact description and the interferences of these paths favor a turbulence quite auspicious for reflection on the historicity of institutions, notably philosophical institutions. If the latter are thoroughly historical, that means that neither their origin nor their solidity is natural, and especially that the processes of their stabilization are always relative, threatened, essentially precarious. The apparent firmness, hardness, durability, or resistance of philosophical institutions betrays, first of all, the fragility of a foundation. It is on the ground of this (theoretical and practical) "deconstructability," it is against it, that the institution institutes itself. The erection of the institution *betrays* this ground —signals the ground as a symptom would, and reveals it, therefore, but deceives it as well.

2. Horizon and Foundation: Two Philosophical Projections (the Example of the Collège International de Philosophie)

Let us take the example of Ciph and limit ourselves to the question of titles. A private institution, though it is supported, which is to say indirectly authorized de facto if not de jure, by the state that encouraged its founding, Ciph claims to be autonomous. It indicates in its very constitution that no title as such is required to participate in its research. That is, no academic title, no institutional accreditation. This disposition is not original. It characterizes other French institutions, such as the Collège de France or the Ecole Pratique des Hautes Etudes, which, moreover, were often founded to provide a place for research, knowledge, and people that the current criteriology, titlology, and procedures of legitimation (notably in universities) censored, marginalized, or quite simply ignored. In this respect the originality of Ciph stems from at least two characteristics: its declared and statutory internationality and the absence of chairs or permanent positions. However, not to require an already coded academic title is to renounce neither the title nor even the notion of the academic title in general. The logic of the title, of legitimation or accreditation, follows rules that are more difficult to identify, but that are just as discriminating. It is possible for rules not to be registered in a charter, and, moreover, they can change along the way. One of the rules declared by Ciph appears at once strict, singular, and seemingly exorbitant: in all the "areas" with which "philosophy" can enter into relation, priority should be given to directions in research, to themes and objects that *currently* are still not *legitimated* in French and foreign institutions. (The word *legitimate* appears often, sometimes accompanied by precautions, in the report that prepared the founding of the Collège and became its regulating charter.)

Taking many forms and admitting of many degrees (exclusion, misunderstanding, marginalization, inhibition, insufficient development), this nonlegitimation in itself calls for refined analyses, ones that are at once preliminary and interminable. To be able to claim also to be philosophical, such an analysis must not be merely operative. In principle it must include in its space the treatment of its own conceptual instruments, beginning with the concept of *legitimation*, which is so useful and which, with its often careless reference to right, law, legality (positive or not), dominates the social sciences, notably when they concern culture, education, and research. To borrow a convenient distinction from Fink (even if its pertinence is bound to be essentially limited), we would have to make a *thematic* concept of the *operative* concept of legitimation, de-instrumentalize it as much as possible (it is never possible purely and absolutely) in order to interrogate philosophically its genealogy, scope, and conditions of validity. We will see the limits of thematization re-imprinted in those of objectification.

To submit an operative concept to philosophical thematization is not only, in this case, to submit scientific efficacy to epistemological or philosophical reflection. It is not to fold knowledge back into speculation. In the best of cases, precisely the one that must be sought out, this amounts to reviving, enlarging, or radicalizing scientific conceptuality, methods, and practices themselves. The concepts of legitimation or objectification, for example, are fruitful and effective, notably in the work of Pierre Bourdieu, because they can also, in a given situation, correspond to a sociologically determined figure of the social sciences in their relation to all kinds of instances, in particular to the history of discourse and philosophical institutions, whether it be a question of the legality (or legitimacy) of the law or the objectivity of the object. We will return to this.

To give priority to the unlegitimated, thus to legitimate by privilege what at a given moment appears illegitimate: what a strange rule for an institution! This might appear incredible, paradoxical, impractical. It can hardly have the form and status of a rule. And since, in the case of Ciph, this process must have an essential relation to the answer to the question "What is philosophy?," it is a matter of nothing less than doing justice to what is deprived of its rights. Nothing less than instituting the right to philosophy where that right appears null, denied, forbidden, or invisible. But is that not philosophy itself? In action and at its indefinitely resumed origin?

And yet, is what I just called exorbitant, "incredible, paradoxical, impractical" not also the most widespread thing in the world? No matter how conservative it is, every institution claims to be legitimating. It therefore claims to create titles. It is destined to produce legitimations where people, objects, or themes previously had none. An essential difference, of course, in principle remains between this normal legitimation, the customary task of classic institutions, and the legitimation proposed by Ciph. The latter presupposes no predetermination of any type of object, theme, or field, and therefore no competence; it does not identify in advance a "comparativity" or the "interdisciplinarity" whose classic concept supposes already-established disciplines, each like a separate state, in the security of its constitution and boundaries, in the recognized limits of its rights and axioms; and it gives privilege or priority to what is supposed to be known to be excluded. But since the relation to philosophy remains the rule and title of the Collège International *de Philosophie*, it indeed had to imply a stable, stabilizing, unifying reference to the philosophical. Not necessarily to an essence of philosophy, but to a certain *experience* of the question "What is philosophy?" Is this experience already philosophical? And, above all, is it essentially, in the last or first instance, an experience of the question?[8]

The question of right, here of the right to philosophy, is subject to the law of a distinction that certain people might find subtle, artificial, or speculative. But in its consequences and implications, this division controls, today, an immense territory, by dividing it. The organization of philosophical *space*, as such, is delimited in at least *three ways*. We can think (1) that the right to philosophy already belongs to philosophy, completely and by right; it would presuppose the memory and task, the essence or unity, of the project, and thus an answer to the question "What is philosophy?," which is formulated, as I suggested above, either in a logic of the originary event or in that of pragmatic function. We can also consider (2) that this belonging by right implies no identification of philosophy, no accepted or stabilizable answer to the question "What is philosophy?" in any form whatsoever, but only the participation in the "community of the question,"[9] a possible question on the subject of philosophy. Community would here be constituted as and from the question *of* philosophy, by the "What is philosophy?" A question can be formed, resonate, or give rise to the discourse it appeals to, it can *appeal* in general, only by instituting or presupposing the community of a certain interlocution. (If it is too early at this point to locate this interlocution in "intersubjectivity," we also cannot not accord it a memory, a genealogy, and a project: a "project" before the "subject.") But we can, finally, (3) admit the thinking, practice, and experience of a "right to philosophy" without presuppositional recourse to either a given essence of philosophy (the answer to the question "What is philosophy?") or even the supposedly originary possibility of the question "What is philosophy?"

In this third move, we would thus not give ourselves or demand the right to presuppose either the answer to, or the formulation of, the question "What is philosophy?" (therefore considered as events whose genealogical possibility remains to be thought) nor even the possibility of a question in general, even the question as the ultimate form and final entrenchment of a community, here of a community of *thinking*. The question (and with it all the forms of negation, research, critique) envelops in itself an affirmation, at least the "yes," the affirmation with no other content than the other, to whom, precisely, a trace is addressed, even if in the dark. The thinking of this "yes" *before* philosophy, *before* the question even, *before* research and critique, does not mean a renunciation of philosophy, of what might follow it or follow from it. This thinking *can*, one can even think that it *must*, lead precisely to philosophy. It can do so from the moment that, in the form of duty or debt, it already finds itself *committed*, inscribed in the space opened and closed by this *pledge*—given to the other, received from the other. But it traces a form of strange limit between all the determinations of the philosophical and a deconstructive thinking that, while undertaken *by* philosophy, does not belong to it. Thinking is faithful to an affirmation whose responsibility places it *before* philosophy but also always before there *was* philosophy, thus short of and beyond philosophy, identifiable figures of philosophical identity, the philosophical question about the subject of philosophy, and even the question-form of thinking. Deconstruction, as it appears to be required by or, rather, as it appears to require thinking, is involved in this third possibility. All I can say, at this point in a preface, is that the common aim of the texts gathered in this collection does not consist in recalling works published elsewhere under the title of deconstruction but in better indicating how deconstruction forces us to *think* differently the institutions of philosophy and the experience of the right to philosophy. Here less than ever is *thinking* opposed to science, technique, calculation, and strategy. Now is the time to indicate once again that the line I am drawing here between thinking and philosophy, thinking and science, etc., has never taken the form and function Heidegger gives it.[10]

To give right *to* philosophy is not to give right *over* [*donner droit* sur] philosophy, at least in the sense of the authority exercised over or with regard to—for we will be interested later in the idiomatic play between the adverb and the noun: "to give right onto" [*donner droit sur*] can simply mean *opening onto*, with or without authority, power, or surveillance: a window or a door "gives" right onto the street, yard, forum, classroom, prison courtyard. To "give" right onto philosophy, where this right does not yet exist, whether it is ignored or misunderstood, inhibited, refused, or forbidden, is a banal task, since it resembles the legitimating or "entitling" function of every institution. But the form it was assigned by Ciph remains of the most paradoxical kind: it seems to assume the foreknowledge of what is still forbidden. (I privilege for the moment the form of the "forbidden" over the other modes of the nonexistence of philosophy in order to emphasize that philosophy can always be interpreted and is in no way "natural." It always has a meaning; it betrays a counter-force, an always already "symbolic" force.) A singular institution, for example, Ciph, should therefore locate, within institutions or outside of them, in their margins or their interinstitutional space, what every other institution cannot or does not want (*cwan't*) to legitimate. For that to happen, a beginning of legitimation must, in a certain form and under certain conditions, have permitted the approaches forbidden by existing institutions, or at least by what dominates in them (for they are always heterogeneous and worked through by contradictions), to be detected, tracked, and to take shape, virtually or implicitly. This simple fact is enough to threaten the very concept of legitimation to the core: it has no opposite. Nonlegitimacy can appear as such, be its signs ever so discreet, only in a process of prelegitimation. In other words, in order for that which is not yet established elsewhere to take shape through a theoretico-institutional analysis that would do justice to it, a new institution must take advantage of a certain capacity to access what is forbidden (repressed, made minor, marginalized, even "unthought") elsewhere. It must therefore access a certain knowledge still deprived of all institutional manifestation. Who can claim that such a thing, such a knowledge or foreknowledge, exists?

To the extent that it is a question of philosophy, an institution that likes to think it is this "new" ought to take advantage—this would be its very right—of an access to philosophy that is still made impossible or regarded to be so elsewhere. A claim one would be right to consider exorbitant, especially if it comes together in a single person or in the unity of a homogeneous discourse. That this is not the case and that this very hypothesis is structurally untenable already complicates the very idea of such a claim, but not without also and at the same time compromising the identity, unity, and assembling of an institution founded upon such a project. But is it not the example of the untenable hypothesis, the impossible project, that we are evoking? Does Ciph not expect its unity, the unicity of its Idea, at least, to come from the exorbitant? (All my questions in this regard, and especially the most incredulous ones, can only come from a place that remains external to Ciph, regardless of the part I might have taken in founding it. But I have always thought that participation in or belonging to Ciph ought to be like no other.) The exorbitant is immediately contaminated or compromised. It selects using the most reassuring norms. If Ciph claims to discover new and necessary paths, new possible legitimations, that is because it is already inscribed in a network of legitimacy or a process of legitimation: by the form of its project and the discourse that presents it, by the people who support the project and speak for it, by those who argue for its foundation, directly or through intervening allies. Ciph had every title to be founded; it responded to numerous, diverse, interrelated, and overdetermined interests. Their analysis would be difficult, but it is possible in principle.

Despite the privilege of its apparent unicity, despite the fact that, in the general configuration of all its characteristics, Ciph is perhaps like no other institution in the world, it still retains some resemblance to many other modern places of research. It responds to scientific, political, technical, and economic imperatives. What is more, while leaving aside already classified academic titles, it does not give up considering all titles; and its criteriology or titlology is no less discriminating. In its selection it considers unsanctioned titles, which are more numerous and more mobile, but which can be perceived and evaluated by a community that institutes itself and comes together in this experience. A community (being-with, being-together, meeting, gathering, convened by convention) is always presupposed in the value of the word and concept "title." The reason for this is not only etymological, but the roots of the word would give us a hint that would confirm it. Rightly or wrongly, certain people take the etymology of *title*, through *titulus* (inscription, title of nobility, certificates of genealogy), back to a present radical in the Greek *tiō* or *timaō* (to estimate, evaluate, honor, valorize), from which comes *timē* (evaluation, estimate, the price attached to something or someone, dignity, reward, honorary office, worth, civil service). Some take this properly axiomatic or axiological register of the economico-politico-juridical evaluation of *tio* all the way back to the Sanskrit root *ci*, where the game of meanings unfolded is folded back and *re-connected* in the very idea of *connection*. It is gathered up in the idea of gathering or co-adjoining. It contracts in the idea of a contract. Whence con-vention, consent, re-union, colligation, co-institution in spirit, in the closure or enclosure made possible by said synagogal convention; whence also the sense of mark and re-mark, the research, the recognition, that seeks to know while venerating and honoring, knowledge as the recognition of a right and an authority.

Now, one of the remarkable and paradoxical structures of the *philosophical* title, as of everything that legitimates a contract and authorizes a *so-called* philosophical institution, is that for once nothing should be posited in advance. Nothing should be presupposed by this alliance or convention: no object or field of objects, no theme, no certitude, no discipline, not even the so-called philosopher who would give himself that title on the basis of his training, research identity, or horizon of questioning. *Philosophy has no horizon*, if the horizon is, as its name indicates, a limit, if "horizon" means a line that encircles or delimits a perspective. This is precisely not the case, by right, for other disciplines or regions of knowledge. As such, and this is the very status of their identification or delimitation, they can indeed think their object in an epistemology, transform it by transforming the founding contract of their own institution; but, at least in the institutional act of their research or teaching, they cannot and must never doubt the pregiven and preunderstood existence of an object or type of identifiable being. Interdisciplinarity and the institutions that practice it never put these *horizontal* identities into question. They presuppose them more than ever. This is not, this *by right should not be the case for philosophy, since there is no philosophical horizontality.*

There is a privilege there, an excess and a lack of power, that complicates principially all of philosophy's undertakings in an interdisciplinary space that it calls for but that, more than any other discipline, it must resist. Those who gather in the name or on account of philosophy in fact presuppose, of course, traditions and the knowledge of questioning. They always have, *in fact*, horizons. And numerous and diverse ones, which never simplifies things. But by right, they must always, *at every moment* (and the reference to the moment signals here the always possible rupture or interruption of a discursive or historical continuum), claim to be *justified* in putting into question not only every determinate knowledge (which researchers in other fields can also do) but even the value of knowledge and every presupposition regarding that which receives the name "philosophy" and gathers them into a so-called or self-styled philosophical community. Not even the *self* of *self*-styling, like self-jurisdiction, is ensured, at least not before the performance of its *vertical* self-institution; and *everyone* (a word under which the name *subject* would already constitute a philosophical thesis that could be debated in a very narrowly determined horizon) in principle has the right to question, in addition to all the modes of discourse (of which debate represents but one example) in which this questioning is brought into play, the very idea and the forms of "presupposition" in general, that is, of the concept or word I have for the sake of convenience been using for a while in order to determine the implications of the implicit. The implicit does not always fall back into the thetic, hypothetical, or prethetic form of a presupposition.

Hence the extreme difficulty, in fact, the aporia in which we become entangled the moment we attempt to justify the title "philosophical" for an institution or community in general. Of course, not every community will be called philosophical from the moment it practices *skepsis, epochē*, doubt, contestation (pacifist or violent, armed with discourse or other powers), irony, questioning, and so forth, regarding its constitutive bond, and thus the properness of what is proper to it. But no community will be called philosophical if it is not capable of reexamining, *in every possible fashion*, its fundamental bond (title, contract, convention, institution, acquiescence to a particular being-with, being-with in general never awaiting a particular commitment).

This aporia can still be read in the report we presented to the government in 1982 to justify the founding of an International College as the Collège International *de Philosophie*. The title of one chapter of the report is "Titles," plural, and it begins with that of philosophy. The first sentence reads: "By now justifying the titles of this new institution, beginning with the name we propose to give it, we want to emphasize its titles to exist. Why philosophy? Why philosophy today? And why would this new College be first of all a College of Philosophy?"[11]

The whole chapter that opens thus will signal the aporia of a community that proposes to found itself on an unprecedented contract, a dissymmetrical contract inscribing in itself nonknowledge and the possibility of breaking the contract at any moment, of deforming or displacing not only its particular terms but its constitutional axiomatics or essential foundations, including the idea of a contract or institution. No doubt, self-foundation or self-institution always proceeds thus, notably when states are being formed. But the fiction of constative knowledge and irreversibility are always and structurally indispensable to it.[12] Here, on the contrary, it is out of fidelity to an absolute quasi-contract with no history, to a pre-contractual commitment, that the presupposition, even the essence as contract, of the institutional contract could be put into question. It is always in the name of a more imperative responsibility that the responsibility before an established instance (for example, the state, but also the specific figure of philosophical reason) is suspended or subordinated. It is not irresponsibility that is demanded, then, but the right not to have to account —in the final analysis—to this or that apparatus of judgment, before this or that regime of appearing.

Such would be the *double bind* of the philosophical commitment or *pledge*, as it remarks or reentitles itself everywhere: in the social, institutional, disciplinary phenomena of the philosophical, in philosophical contracts, foundations, or legitimations, in the philosophical right to philosophy. For if right can always be read as a philosopheme, it is submitted to the same paradoxical "law" of the double bind: unstable, precarious, and deconstructible, it always precedes itself and calls for an indestructible responsibility. Indestructible because always revived in an anxious raising of stakes that makes it unappeasable and, above all, that makes any good conscience impossible. The philosophical determination of this responsibility, the concepts of its axiomatics (for example, "will," "property," the "subject," the identity of a free and individual "I," the conscious "person," the self-presence of intention, and so forth), can always be debated, questioned, displaced, critiqued, and, more radically, deconstructed. This will always be done in the name of a more demanding responsibility, one more faithful to memory and the promise, one always beyond the present. In the name of this responsibility, yet more will be demanded of the "right to philosophy," yet more right to philosophy will be demanded.

3. The Name "Philosophy," the Interest for Philosophy

The name "philosophy" is thus submitted to a kind of torsion that folds it back toward an excessive, unbounded, inexhaustible place. It recognizes itself there without recognizing itself, is at home there and away from home. The thing or concept "philosophy," that is, what this word entitles at a given moment and in particular discourses, always remains unequal to the responsibility that, in its name, carries beyond its name or the names available for it. In its rhetoric or logic, this torsion can look like a laborious contortion. It can appear useless or avoidable, even comic, especially to those who are always sure they can smooth or flatten out the space of discourse, efface its "performative contradictions" with a sigh of impatience and distinguish in good conscience between the philosophical and the nonphilosophical on either side of a straight and indivisible line. In the report I just cited, on the contrary, when it comes to the title "philosophy," belonging to the "philosophical" is designated as a problem, even a problem that is still "brand new," a philosophical problem, perhaps, but not only and necessarily. The dividing line is not given. Perhaps it is not a line. It takes shape as the experience of a paradoxical responsibility that others are invited to share, to give themselves the means of sharing. This is done in the language of a report that is not intended for professional philosophers (a situation in which our entire problem is reflected and concentrated) and that does not hesitate to emphasize the "provisional" recourse to certain nonetheless decisive words, all the while retaining a formal reference to the "need of philosophy" (Hegel) or to the "interest of reason" (Kant), an *interest* that, as long and as much as possible, would have to be kept sheltered from all preinterpretation. That this last precaution already gives itself a certain right to philosophy is the paradoxical provocation in whose singular space we find ourselves and attempt to come to an agreement:

> Therefore, if we propose the creation of a College *of Philosophy*, it is not first of all to signal that this institution belongs integrally to what we might believe we can determine in advance as the *philosophical* destination or essence. It is, *on the one hand*, to designate a place of thinking in which the *question of philosophy* would be deployed: the question *about* the meaning or destination of the philosophical, its origins, its future, its condition. In this regard, "thinking" for the moment only designates an *interest for philosophy*, in philosophy, but an interest that is not philosophical first of all, completely and necessarily. It is, *on the other hand*, to affirm philosophy and define what it can be and do today in our society as regards new forms of knowledge in general, technique, culture, the arts, languages, politics, law [*droit*], religion, medicine, power and military strategy, police information, etc. The experience of thinking *on the subject of the philosophical*, no less than philosophical work, is what might be the task of the Collège. A task at once classic (what philosophy has not begun by seeking to determine the essence and destination of philosophy?) and re-

quired today to deploy itself in singular conditions. Later, we will say the same for the values of research, science, interscience, or art.

Right [*droit*] is indicated twice in this passage. Once literally and specifically (it is a matter of the juridical science or discipline), another time implicitly and co-extensively with what claims to *justify* the entire project, the interest for philosophy as the *right to philosophy*. This latter right therefore gives itself the right to think right philosophically as institutionalized discipline. The choice of the word "thinking" to designate what exceeds the particular modes of thought that would be philosophy and science is only justified strategically and provisionally in this context. It of course indicates the necessity of a certain "having it out with" Heidegger, a reference that to me seemed, and still seems, absolutely indispensable in this context, but, as I have explained elsewhere, and again right here a moment ago, in the form of listening and thinking, which is also to say, of debate and deconstruction. Moreover, the moment we translate a certain gesture by Heidegger into our language, we must consider the consequences of the fact that "thinking" belongs to a lexical system (which is always more than itself) in which we no longer find the semantic network that Heidegger associates with *Denken*. We find another lexical system, we find ourselves in another place of meaning—and, the moment we *also* read German and other languages, *in the space and time of a translation of* pensée [*thinking*]. If, at least, one takes translation seriously and as something other than a peaceable recoding of already-given meanings, I see no other or better definition for what we are speaking about here: the time of a translation of "thinking."

Which puts in motion the essential instability of that community or collegiality, the indecision of its title, the scruple with which it demands its right to philosophy, in the name of philosophy, its difficulty in founding itself as philosophical. In a word, its difficulty in founding itself, if the values of founding and foundation are also philosophemes through and through, and philosophemes essentially associated with values of right. (We find a simple indication of this in the fact that in its predominant contexts *Begründung* means, above all, justification.) Under the name of the Collège International de Philosophie is found, therefore, an institution that has been quasi-founded for seven years, but on the open and still gaping question of the subject of founding power and its own self-founding power. The day of the official inauguration of Ciph (legally we should really say *in the presence of* three ministers rather than *by* Mr. Fabius, Mr. Lang, and Mr.

Schwartzenberg[13]), the Minister of Culture insisted upon remarking that, despite the presence of this governmental pomp, it was indeed a matter of "self-foundation." Taking the floor to improvise a brief response, I of course followed him in emphasizing the jealous will for independence of the founding members of Ciph, in particular in regard to the state. But I immediately added that it was not possible, under those conditions, to improvise a rigorous discourse on this problematic value of self-foundation; and that I did not *know* if there had ever been any self-foundation and whether, at any rate, that could ever be known, give place to knowledge, belong to the order of knowledge.

The concept of self-foundation is eminently philosophical. For this reason, and one must recognize a philosophical structure or era in it, it becomes a theme or problem. (What is a self-foundation? Is there any? How must the question be determined? etc.) It becomes a theme and a problem, in any case, for Ciph, about which we are too quick to say that it founded itself. Moreover, even if we took this philosophical concept as a rule by confining ourselves to a philosophical space that could be closed off (*concesso non dato*), *we will never be sure there has ever been self-foundation*. Less than ever in the case of a private and/or public institution, such as Ciph— which in this regard still today remains in the and/or (thus the neither/nor) public and/or private. The status of such an institution supposes, de facto if not de jure, the (de facto) support, but consequently the (de facto, thus de jure) authorization, of the state. In order still to speak of self-foundation in such a space, a theory of the state and civil society would have to be elaborated in all rigor, and would especially have to be implemented in conditions that are so new that they in fact appear to be unimaginable and even inconceivable.

However, if no foundation has ever been able to authorize itself rigorously in the inaugural moment of being installed, in the present of some originary event, does that exclude all fundamental autonomy? Can an autonomy not be conceived that, without being purely given in an initial present, remains an experience, a work, and a crossing, in short, an impure process that, while never presenting itself as such, would however not be heteronomous and subjugated? Another question follows: must this self-foundation that is destined to be a process more than it is given from the beginning be conceived under the regime of a regulative Idea, of an Idea in the Kantian sense, which would come to orient an infinite progress? At times more visible than others, this question traverses all the essays collected in this work. And it is always redoubled by the question of its own translation into Kantian language, whether that of the infinite Idea or of right. At this point we can say that a self-foundation could not be a present event. It cannot *exist*, in the strong sense of this word that implies *presence*, at the moment of installation or institution. Individuals, *subjects*, in the strong sense of this word that implies *presence*, or the community of subjects apparently responsible for foundation, rely directly or indirectly on a network of powers, on legitimating forces and "interests" of all kinds, on a state of things and on the thing the state. This is very clear for Ciph, which, however, seems very close to self-foundation and to the subject we have been able to speak about without worrying too much about it. It is even clearer for all the other public and private foundations. If, however, across the obvious limits of hetero-foundation, the idea of an absolute self-foundation takes shape (without literally presenting itself), this promise is not nothing. In certain conditions the promise constitutes a "performative" event whose "probability" remains irreducible—even if the promise is never kept in a presently certain, assured, demonstrable fashion. If something like *Ciph* is habitable, it is as the experience of this space of the promise. To this extent, the affirmation of a concern for independence, autonomy, and self-legitimation is not necessarily, and in anyone's mouth, a "mere word," even if no institutional reality is or can be adequate to it. The self, the *autos* of legitimating and legitimated self-foundation, *is still to come*, not as a *future* reality but as that which will always retain the essential structure of a promise and as that which can only arrive as such, as *to come*.

4. The Democracy to Come: Right of Language, Right to Language

Right to philosophy: if the meanings enveloped in this title have to be unfolded, it is not to play upon them, but for reasons that stem first of all from the question of the *title*, which we have just looked at, and then from that of *language*, which we are coming to.

Let's consider the overlaid multiplicity of meanings in the artificially isolated expression "right to philosophy," insisting now on the adverb, now on the noun "right." This multiplicity comes together, it is articulated and therefore plays inside an idiom, a lexicon, and a grammar. This immediately recalls the problem of the connection between the exercise of philosophy and a national language—and re-marks it in language itself, in *this* language. Instead of taking it up directly, straight ahead, head-on, as I have often tried to do elsewhere, let's take another detour. What is at stake in the expression "right to philosophy," in which, this time, "right" would be an adverb and not, as was the case in the preceding pages, a noun?

Imagine someone, you perhaps, who, at wit's end, ends up losing his or her temper: When are you going to stop beating around philosophy? Instead of philosophy itself, which belongs to and interests everyone, why do you content yourself with speaking about philosophical institutions? The socio-political conditions of possibility of teaching and research in philosophy? All the juridical protocols preliminary to the possible access to the philosophical thing? Go right to philosophy! Right to philosophy!

Certain journalists are not the only ones who formulate this demand, even if it sometimes takes the form of being put on notice or of threatening pressure: we are thus reminded of their "every right" ("We have the right to demand immediate intelligibility"), of our obligations ("You are held responsible for providing it"), and of the sanctions ("You will be judged negatively, or, worse, passed over in silence—we have the means of doing so—if you do not grant our legitimate request"). This is the premise of those who make themselves the representatives of a "public opinion" or rather of the specter of a readership they project and sometimes constitute even before appealing to it. Such a demand is not first of all that of the media. It reproduces a traditional denial in the discourse of the academic institution. In substance, it says: "Philosophy is more than and different from its 'supports,' its 'apparatuses.' And even its language! Whoever wants to philosophize can do so immediately and directly. The shortest path, the best path, toward philosophy is *straight ahead*, as great philosophers, among them Descartes, have said. Philosophy is the most easily shared thing in the world. No one can forbid access to it. The moment one has the desire or will for it, one has the right to it. That right is inscribed in philosophy itself. The effect of institutions might be to regulate, even to limit, this right *from the outside*, but not to create or invent it. This right is first of all a natural right and not a historical or positive one."

I schematize thus the principle of a logic that no doubt corresponds to a profound and continuous tradition. It dominates from Plato to Descartes and Kant, despite their significant differences. The ultimate justification: the idea of a right to philosophy is a philosophical idea, a philosopheme that assumes that philosophy has already entered the scene or has at least taken shape as such. One is already in philosophy the moment one asks the institutional or juridico-politico-technical question of the right to philosophy. This—absolutely short, straight, direct—path has *already* been traveled. To philosophize, one essentially has need of no writing or teaching apparatus. School walls are as *external* to the act of philosophizing as publication, the press, the media. No interdiction, no limitation can touch philosophy itself, no censure, no marginalization. Acts of aggression can of course reach the public phenomena of philosophy, publications, the educational apparatuses (the academic, the scholastic, or the doctrinal), but not the interest for philosophy. At most, these can threaten the (public) exercise, but not the experience, of philosophy, which has nothing to do with the limit between the private and the public. This philosophy would not be afraid of any attack. It does not need to be justified or defended, not, at any rate, by anything other than itself. It is *proper* to philosophy to say what is *proper* to it, and thus to ensure its *proper* defense and justification. Even if outside struggles or work come to help it in this task, it will be as an auxiliary, a supplement, and even a suppletive; and the limit between internal property and external supplementarity must remain as clear and indivisible as the limit between the inside and the outside.[14] One recognizes here a "logic"—and thus a strategy—open to the most insistent and formalized deconstructionist questions.

What does such a "logic" imply? This at least: to forbid everyone or certain people the school of philosophy would not be to bar *one's own path* to philosophy. The story of Theophrastus of Eresus, who was forbidden to *preside over a school* of philosophy on pain of death, is well known. Diogenes Laertius tells the story. A student of Leucippus, a disciple of Plato, Theophrastus left the latter to follow Aristotle, whom he one day succeeded as the head of the "school." So many titles: from Aristotle he not only received his teaching; he also inherited control and authority over the school. He also got his name, actually his nickname, from him. His first name was Tyrtamus. Aristotle called him Theophrastus (he who speaks like a God) "because he was divinely eloquent." La Bruyère adds, in his *Discourse on Theophrastus* (*Discours sur Théophraste*), that Aristotle had first called him Euphrastus, "which means he who speaks well. Since this name did not correspond enough to the high regard he had for the beauty of his genius and expressions, he called him Theophrastus, that is, a man whose language is divine." This genealogy of titles taken at their word, so to speak, is complicated further: Eu-Theo-phrastus loved the son of his master or stepfather. Diogenes Laertius: "It is said that he loved this philosopher's son, Nicomachus, although he was his disciple." This man of gentle and divine speech had hordes of disciples, among them Menander, the comic poet. Over two thousand disciples, it is said, which indicates, especially at the time, a true "popularity." What is a popular philosopher? This question will be raised again more or less directly in the essays that follow.[15] Theophrastus, at any rate, was "popular" enough among the Athenians to risk losing his life there as much as his adversary did when Agonides dared accuse him of impiety, just as Meletus had accused Socrates. In one form or another, has impiety not, from time immemorial, and thus still today, been the indictment against every disturbing thinker? The fundamental category of every accusation? And doesn't impiety most often consist in taking the uncertain, chance, fortune, *tukhē* seriously? Cicero reports (in *Tusculanae Disputationes* V, 9) that Theophrastus was accused of having said, "Fortune is queen of the world." Sophocles, the son of Amphiclides, had a law passed: philosophers could not preside over a school without the "consent of the people and the senate, on pain of death." It was then that Theophrastus and a few other philosophers left. They returned when Sophocles in turn was accused of impiety: "The Athenians repealed the law, condemned Sophocles to a fine of five talents, and voted for the return of the philosophers."

A vote for the return of the philosophers! Must philosophy wait to be given votes publicly? Does it need majorities (democratic or not)? In the logic of classical discourse, such as I have reconstructed it here, the answer would not be long in coming: no, the interdiction applies only to the right to education, teaching, the discipline, even the doctrine, but in no way to philosophy *itself*, to the thing itself, *die Sache selbst*, "philosophy," the "business" of philosophy. If from the point of view of positive right, laws, or the police, one can make a dent in the right to the philosophical institution, this violence would not reach a natural right to philosophy: Theophrastus, in his retreat, can continue to exercise this right, can go right to philosophy without statutory mediation, alone or within a community, even if it is "unavowable" or "inoperative" in the sense Blanchot and Nancy give these concepts. Such a community should not be confused with that of the city-state or receive its legitimacy or authorization from it. Not that it would be secret or at work clandestinely. Not that it is necessarily composed of "members," "conspirators," "plotters," or even "dissidents." It would simply remain heterogeneous to the public law of the city, the state, as well as civil society.

This logic has richer resources at its disposal than those I expose schematically and principially here. But it can always inspire a protest of this type: "Why the devil do you need to burden yourself with new public or private philosophical institutions? Why try to have them legitimated by the state, society, the nation, or the people? Why these detours? Be philosophers right where you are, you yourselves, either in silence or by speaking to those who can understand you, who you can understand, with whom you can come to an understanding. You do not need a social contract for that. You might not even need anyone . . . "

A very strong temptation: such a discourse is not only seductive, it will, precisely [*justement*], just barely [*de justesse*], never be lacking in justice [*de justice*] and legitimacy. It has on its side, by right, the absolute of right, every right. However, without challenging this discourse, we can nonetheless fold it back toward its presuppositions. Without even catching it in the "performative" trap of its own pronouncements, of its own discursivity, for which it would indeed have to assume philosophical responsibility, a particular philosophy can be detected in it. It is first of all a philosophy of *langue* and *langage*. Two apparently opposed and irreconcilable concepts of language [*langue*] can share the same "presupposition" and the same interpretation of the right to philosophy, that is, that of a sort of natural right that is rigorously dissociable from an institutional right.

Let's reduce these concepts to their most typical characteristic. It would be a matter, *on the one hand*, of a techno-semiotic, purely conventionalist and instrumental concept of language [*langue*]. Everything that derives from these formalizable signifiers belongs to technique and the institution. But since there is in principle no indissoluble affiliation between philosophical thought and a natural language [*langue*], this formal language [*langage*] is accessible to everyone and itself remains, like the institution, external to a kind of natural, that is, original and universal right. This technologism assumes, as is often the case, a kind of originarist naturalism from which it emerges. *On the other hand*, to separate language [*langue*] from semio-technique, the originarity of idiom from its instrumental contamination, is to end up at the same result. Every speaking being, before any institution, can have access to philosophy, one would therefore say. That philosophy be originally linked by privilege to this or that language (Greek, German) can then have several consequences: such privileged idioms are themselves foreign to instrumentalization, conventional translation, and the institution; they are quasi-natural, "naturalized," even if their originarity is that of an inaugural event or founding institution. And if we consider that there is no philosophy outside these languages, translating oneself into them is an experience to which, in principle, every speaking being must have access. My limited intention is to describe this second hypothesis in terms of a very general typology: one could attempt to verify it in the texts of Fichte, Hegel and Heidegger, Benjamin, Adorno, and many others. In both cases, an originary (natural, universal) right is separated from an acquired (positive, institutional) right because it is believed that, in language, the originary and the technical can be separated. The *law of iterability* that, I have tried to show elsewhere, limits (structurally and definitively) the pertinence of such a concept of the origin and of technique goes unrecognized.[16]

According to this great, typical opposition (nonlanguage/language; originary/technical language), only the first right, natural right—or more radically, a "right" before the opposition *physis/nomos*—would be immediately linked to the essence of the philosophical or, more radically, of a thinking according to originary *logos*; the other right would be derived, contingent, and variable according to the historico-political vicissitudes of societies in their positive right and juridico-scholarly—or more radically, *epochal*—apparatuses. This logic prohibits any "fight for philosophy" that would not in itself be purely philosophical, the "business" of philosophy, and that would not subordinate the juridico-political to the philosophical. In a word: philosophy would have the right to speak of right and not the reverse. I must insist upon this point since most of the texts collected in this volume claim to participate in such a "fight." Will they have done so in the name of philosophy? Or in the name of something else that could be the affirmation of a thinking that is still or already foreign to philosophy and even to the question about philosophy? The very form of these questions no doubt deserves the most guarded, patient, suspended, we might even say unresolved attention. A *singular* irresolution (this one, at this point) that I believe to be neither negative nor paralyzing, no more contrary to thinking than to philosophy, and for which I therefore believe I must assume responsibility beyond certain stands I have taken, beyond my argumentations, discussions, and firmest commitments. More than once, the trace of this will be found here.

If philosophy is neither "natural" nor "institutional," if it speaks neither in an originary language nor, just as immediately, through all languages or every system of signs constructed to this end, is thinking (and "acting") beyond these oppositions, yet without disqualifying them, still philosophical? Is there a right to think philosophy that carries beyond philosophy? With the right it seems to open to itself, and properly, does philosophy exceed a narrowly determined instance of the juridical? What philosophy, what right, what law (*nomos*) did Socrates refer to when he protested, as Diogenes Laertius tells us, against Lysias's apology? "Your speech is very beautiful, Lysias, but it does not suit me [*ou men harmottōn g'emoi*]." Diogenes comments: "It was indeed obviously more juridical than philosophical [*to pleon dikanikos ē emphilosophos*]." When Lysias asked, "If my speech is beautiful, how is it that it doesn't suit you?," Socrates responded, "Cannot, in the same way, a piece of clothing or shoes be beautiful and yet not suit me?"[17] The meaning of this exchange remains enigmatic, and Diogenes' commentary even more so. He seems to imply, at any rate, that what was unsuitable, even unseemly, discordant, for Socrates, was an apology too concerned with right (with juridical wrangling, *dikanikos*, legalist or legitimist ratiocination), when a more properly *philosophical* defense would have been necessary, that is, a defense better suited to what Socrates was and said, more in tune with the "business of philosophy," with the philosophy in him and beyond him, responding and corresponding to the voice, to the sign (*semēion*) that spoke in him like an innate, natural demon to make of him the philosopher he was destined to be.

Here the "question of language" concerns not only what is in the main called "natural" or "national" language but also, no doubt more discriminatingly, the linguistic subgroups, dialects, codes, and subcodes that, before every other institutional jurisdiction, condition the effective access and thus the real right to philosophy. What *happens* if, to go "right to philosophy," one must at least *pass through* a language and a large number of *subcodes* whose dependence on a "root"-language is at once irreducible and overdetermining, this overdetermination being none other, precisely, than the very process of philosophy? What if this passage, while not on the order of a simple detour or instrumental mediation, necessarily disappoints all desire to go *right to philosophy*?

Even if one could bypass all institutions, all academic apparatuses, all schools (in the Greek or modern sense of the word), all disciplines, all (public or private) media structures, recourse to language is indispensable for the minimal practice of philosophy. This massive and trivial evidence must be remembered not for itself but for the conclusions to which it should lead, and which we do not always draw. What is more, what I just called "conclusions" perhaps deserve another name, for precisely the order of derivation is in question here. Beyond the great, canonical questions about translation and the originary privilege of a natural language (Greek or German),[18] the problematic that interests us here affects more pointedly what, producing itself "inside" a language upon the arrival of philosophy, no longer has its *topos* "between" different so-called natural languages. If it were asserted, as has often been done, especially in Germany, that because of its "founding concepts," indeed, its original lexical and syntactic possibilities, the exercise of the right to philosophy, even to thinking *tout court*, is conditioned by competence in and, more generally, the experience of a language (for example, Greek or German), if it were added, as has often been done, especially in Germany, that competence does not consist here in acquiring some available techniques; then the adventure whose risks and end remain incalculable no longer concerns one or two languages among others. It involves itineraries of translation that lead toward or away from the aforementioned languages at the same time. It involves *translations even "inside" these languages.*

This last necessity is enough to displace the entire stakes. If one says there is no philosophy without Greek or German (etc.), that neither only *nor first of all* excludes those for whom these languages are not their "mother tongue," but also the Greeks and Germans[19] who do not speak or write their own language *in a certain manner*, which is called philosophy, this manner of speaking and writing being of the most singular kind, marked by a shrouded history, strangely interwoven with other histories and other threads from the same language or other languages. Philosophy is not only linked to a natural language. The serious and massive question is not only that of the eurocentrism, the helleno- or germano-centrism of philosophical language. Within every language, European or not, what we call "philosophy" must be linked regularly and differently, according to eras, places, schools, social and socio-institutional circles, to distinct discursive procedures among which it is often difficult to translate. The life of philosophy is also the experience of these "intralinguistic" translations, which are sometimes as perilous or prohibited as other translations. To have access *effectively*, in effect, to these discursive procedures and thus to have the right to the *philosophical such as it is spoken*, for philosophical democracy, democracy in philosophy, to be possible (and there is no democracy in general without that, and democracy, the democracy that remains still to come, is also a philosophical concept), one must be trained in these procedures. One must be trained to recognize connotations, so-called stylistic or rhetorical effects, semantic potentialities, virtual folds and bends, a whole economy at work in what is perhaps, under the name of philosophy, only the most economical practice of natural language.

This concern, which is also that of the democracy to come, traverses all the institutional debates this book will evoke (notably around Greph, the Estates General of Philosophy, the foundation of Ciph, and the Commission on Philosophy and Epistemology). If a possible philosophy *in French* were to be accepted or wished for, if one were to think a philosophy *in French* (I am not saying French philosophy) were possible without already being pregnant, I mean made pregnant with translations (from Greek, Latin, German, English), asserting that this French idiom is a philosophical idiom[20] would not suffice to conclude that every French person, every immigrant born in France, and so forth, has an effective right to philosophy and that, once having passed through "elementary" training (what is that?) in the language, he or she could have the right to go right to philosophy. The practice (academic or not) of philosophy is hand in glove with a *certain French*, that of certain groups or social circles (let's not say "classes" so as not to go too quickly) and professionals, with their dialects, subcodes, that is to say, over-codes, academic apparatuses, in each instance linked to particular places of so-called general culture. Obvious and trivial facts, objects of analysis, which today are numerous and refined, to be sure. But everyday experience shows that they must be remembered, in particular by many teachers of philosophy. Some of them deny this situation, which philosophy should, on the contrary, have trained them to identify. Failing to recognize in particular the effects of discrimination that it engenders, they want to protect a state of things by conserving at any price rhetorical models, forms of control, and social rules of the philosophical exercise, whose genealogy, however, is so particular, so marked, sometimes so easy to analyze. In order to oppose all questions and change, some are ready to accuse those who worry about this discrimination (out of philosophical as much as political concern) of wanting to "adapt," "adjust" (read "reduce") philosophy to a "social demand." I believe more or less the contrary: in this area as in others institutional conservatism closely serves a social demand that it disclaims. The transformations for which some of us are working—and which will often be at issue in this book—certainly suppose taking into account mutations of all kinds (social ones in particular, in this country and in others), but not in order to adjust "philosophy" to them at its own expense: rather, in order to improve its chances, its rights, or the rights it gives, which it can allow to be thought differently.

5. Border Crossing: Declaring Philosophy

Up to this point, some will say, the question entitled "right to philosophy" has been treated or justified formally, apparently without real content. In this lexic of justification or jurisdiction, legitimation or foundation, as it immediately intersects with the opposition between form and content, we recognize an inevitable *topos* in every problematic of right. One of the most insistent criticisms regarding juridicism, like that regarding a certain "return of right [*droit*]" today, is aimed in particular at its formalism. These criticisms have often been Marxist in inspiration. Let's recall this as a sign and the beginning of a new stage in this introduction: while claiming to root itself in a natural right in order to produce a positive and international one, the Universal Declaration of the Rights of Man has of course been carried into a rich and striking history, at least since 1789 and notably since the Second World War. Through multiple reelaborations, this history seems to be moving in the direction of an increasing specification of its contents, notably of "social rights," and among these (the rights to work, rest, safety, leisure) are found the rights to instruction, culture, and education. About the latter, we must ask ourselves: (1) whether they include, and in what sense, a right to philosophy, a universal right that carries beyond national, but also social differences; in other words, if philosophy is one "discipline" among others, with the same rights and limits, in what is so confusedly called culture; and (2) whether a thinking (philosophy or not) that gives itself or demands the right to question, in one way or another, the authority and foundations of juridical discourse, even the discourse of the rights of man, is still teachable and accessible, if it can claim to be the object of a universal right of access. While accepting, up to a certain point, the distinction form/content, one ought first to signal that a right to philosophy can only become effective, in its definition and exercise, if all the concrete conditions are met. And what we just said about language is indissociable from all of existence, in its historical, social, and economic dimensions in particular. Nothing in all that can be the object of, and confer an absolute privilege upon, any one discipline.

We must of course ask ourselves (question 1) if something like philosophy, if there is any and any that is one, is a content that would be one part

like any other of teachable knowledge, of culture and everything understood under the titles "culture," "instruction," "education," and "training."
But these concepts do not overlap one another; they have a history, a genealogy (*paideia, skholē, cultura, Bildung*, etc.), and a highly complex structure: the jurists, the actors or writers of the declarations, have few doubts
about this subject when they formulate the universal right to culture. We
can maintain, without threatening or denigrating either one, that philosophy does not belong completely to culture. No more so than science, or
than philosophy, belongs to science, and so forth.

Another fold, another preliminary complication: as speech act, as a performative utterance that disclaims itself, to the extent that it produces the
force of law by claiming to describe or observe a "nature" that everyone is
supposed to be familiar with and share, a declaration of rights always remains paradoxical. It cannot posit and justify a right to instruction and in
it, hypothetically, a right to philosophy, without already implying a philosophy, an instruction, in particular an intelligibility determined by its
concepts and language. As speech act, such a declaration has always been
a group of philosophical statements. Even if it does not mention this discipline, it thus prescribes a priori the teaching and propagation of philosophy, of *a* philosophy, in particular of *the* philosophy of language that it
itself supposes in order to produce itself.

Although the conceptual couple performative/constative, with the entire
theoretical apparatus it puts in play, at a certain point seems of limited relevance, it still remains invaluable for an analysis of the philosophical and
juridical statements we are dealing with here. Because of its essential claim
to found itself on a natural right, a declaration of the rights of man inter-
prets itself as a descriptive statement. It claims to found its prescriptive
statements (for example, "the law must be the same for everyone . . . ")
upon observations. The "must" gives way to "is" or "can," words within
which the limit between essence, possibility, and having-to-be, between
natural and positive law, between natural and conventional necessity, lets
itself be crossed surreptitiously. *Being natural or, rather, having to be natural,
to man,* the access to titles ("dignities") or to speech and freedom itself *must*
be exercised: "All citizens being equal [or rather, even thereby, *having to be
equal*] in the eyes of the law, they are equally eligible for all public dignities, places, and employments, according to their ability and without any
distinction other than their virtues and talents." Or again: "The free communication of ideas and opinions is one of the most precious human

rights; every citizen can therefore speak, write, and print freely, but must answer for the abuse of this freedom in the cases determined by the law."[21]

In what way does this discourse legitimate itself by denying its performative power and rooting it in a constative self-representation, the very self-representation of philosophy that has always claimed it is the language of being stating what is? The proponents of this discourse, those who offer it, support it, and bring it out, must claim they describe what each person (everyone) knows to be and to be true. For them it is only a matter of recalling that, of making it explicit, thematizing it in the element of philosophical consensus. This element is transparent—or destined to transparency. But it is indissociable, noncontingently, from the practice and understanding of language, here of the French language. On July 11, 1789, La Fayette declared to the National Assembly that the merit of a declaration of rights consists in "truth and precision; it must say what everyone knows, what everyone feels." It must, therefore, it *must*, but it must only state. It must, by submitting itself to a theoretical prescription, to the prescription of being theoretical and not prescriptive, take note of (by showing) what everyone knows or feels. It is supposed to add nothing to this knowledge other than its explicit stating. The imperative concerns the act of saying alone: but it must still be "well" said, that is, "truthfully and precisely." The problems of composition are no longer extrinsic. The Declaration of the Rights of Man implies a philosophy, a reminder that will surprise no one, but also a philosophy of philosophy, a concept of truth and its relations to language. And the access to the declaration, to the content of what it says, which gives the right to all rights, assumes instruction and the knowledge of language. Only instruction, and first of all instruction in language, can make one aware of right, and in particular of the right to instruction. The two "competencies" envelop one another. They are folded onto one another.

Considering what we said above about the philosophical over-coding or subcoding "inside" a natural language, one can easily understand that the debates on language and education, at the time of the composition of the rights of man, were not simply about form any more than the "composition" debates were. When we "talk philosophy" we must always (this is the beginning of a prescriptive statement) attempt to evaluate, for example, the number and place of all those who would understand nothing or little of all these potential or actual stakes: billions of human beings, all but a few thousand, and among the very few who read me at this very moment, the passage of information, of meaning, and the effects of interpretation or persuasion are very unequal. These differences are irreducible. They define the very field of political struggles for the progress of the rights of man and of democracy, and they have an essential relation to the experience of language, to education and the teaching of philosophy (philosophical teaching, the teaching of or about philosophy, debates on the subject of philosophy). On July 27, 1789 (fifteen days after La Fayette), the archbishop of Bordeaux, Champion de Cicé, spoke in the name of the "founding committee." He reproached the first draft by Sieyès for being too abstract, too profound, too perfect. It assumed "more wisdom and genius than can be expected from those who must read and understand it; and everyone must read and understand it."

This remark presupposes a distinction between the semantic content of the rights of man and their expression in language. The former being what they are in their integrity, adapting the most appropriate formulation of them to their addressees or beneficiaries is a distinct and posterior task. That task, Champion de Cicé assumes, can and must take as its rule a statistically evaluable (by a kind of spontaneous sociology) state of the capacity to understand this text. And, first of all, the "everyone" to which he refers. Is it a matter of all the French? Of the French "people," an entity that coincides neither with the sum of all the citizens (among whom certain might not speak the language) nor all those who speak the language (and are not necessarily citizens, part of the French people)? Or rather, another dimension of the philosophical presupposition, all those, French or not, who, speaking another language, could receive this semantic content intact through an unequivocal translation? What is at stake in the sentences I just cited can be better measured when one considers the linguistic and academic politics of the French Revolution in certain of its phases or projects,[22] the violence of an imposition of language that accentuated the imposition initiated in the sixteenth and seventeenth centuries. On August 19, 1789, Rabaud Saint-Étienne deployed the same logic. The consensus here is deep enough to give these declarations the value of an example or type. What does he demand other than a "simple, clear declaration in a style that would be within the reach of the people, that would encompass all the maxims of a bond and freedom that, taught in the schools, would train a generation of free men, capable of resisting despotism"?

Who, already, can understand this sentence? And what do words like "people" or "within the reach of the people," "taught" or "would train" cover? Is the people only those citizens considered to be in a state of culture, instruction, or minimal education, which is within its "reach," having to be within everyone's reach? Is the people a given or the horizon of a training? As the syntax, modes, and tenses of these statements indicate, this is a matter of demands or wishes. What is demanded is a "simple, clear declaration in a style that would be within the reach of the people," of a people assumed to be known and whose linguistic and hermeneutic competence could be evaluated at the moment of the declaration; even the technical conditions of the people's access to the text of this declaration, a direct or indirect access through the mediation of representatives (politicians, men of the law, or teachers who were to be sent to "Frenchify," as it were, villages in which the "people" did not speak French) should be ensured. The moment it is a question of wishes, these imply that the aforesaid ideal declaration remains to come. But the "maxims" exist already. The "maxims of a bond and freedom" are already there, formed, thinkable, knowable, in short, by everyone, and known from the moment they are taught in the schools. "Taught in the schools": the syntax should not give us any illusions. It means: such as they *will have to be* taught in the schools. We will have to decide to teach them in these schools if we want to train free men, men who would be what they are and who *would know*, no, who *know* what they are. Men *are* "free," naturally, *are* "capable of resisting despotism." But they are not yet this; they are not yet what they already are; they know it but do not yet know that they already know it, that is, that they do not yet know it. The time of teaching as time of training lodges itself in the fold between the *already* and the *not yet*, the indicative and the future or subjunctive, to which logical grammar (the grammar taught in general) has difficulty submitting. The word *maxim* seems to have a rigorous meaning here. The maxim is not the law. In Kantian terms, it is the formulation of the subjective relation to the law, the rule of action in conformity with the law. Teaching and training would be given on the level of the maxim, the place in which the consistent and "synthetic" rules of a subjective action in conformity with the law have to be deployed. The latter, as "natural" or "a priori" law, does not, *stricto sensu*, have to be taught. Its teaching, if it takes place, would remain not a "formative" but a purely philosophical teaching. Analytic, maieutic, it would consist in revealing, disclosing, or making explicit what is already known—or assumed to be so.

The *knowledge* of these laws, these rights, and this natural justice would therefore be the philosophical precondition to every intelligible declaration of the rights of man, as to every institution of positive laws: and, first of all, to the constitution of a state founded on this knowledge. One of the ambiguities of the Declaration of 1789 is that it does not content itself with stating or "recalling" the principles of natural right. It also posits elements of constitutional law concerning the separation of powers, for example. What is important here is that constitutional law should be founded on a philosophical knowledge of natural right. This is what Mounier tells the National Assembly: "For a constitution to be good, it must be founded on the rights of man, and must obviously protect them; to prepare a constitution, therefore, the rights that natural justice grants to all individuals must be known; all the principles that must form the basis of every kind of society must be *recalled,* and every article of the constitution must be the consequence of a principle." I have emphasized the word *recall.* He claims to recall that the essence of a constitution (and especially of the declaration of the rights it supposes here) consists in a declarative act that contents itself with bringing to the light of memory what is already known in principle (at its origin and by rights). This, at the time of the French Revolution, entails referring to a very specific concept of the declaration. It will be difficult to make it coincide with the definition that Guizot will give this concept in his *Nouveau dictionnaire des synonymes de la langue française,* to limit ourselves to this one indication: "To declare is not only to make known what is unknown. It is to say things expressly and with intent, in order to instruct those to whom one does not want them to remain unknown."

The figure of the fold, explicitation, or complication often imposes itself upon us. It is not, we know, incompatible with that of a circular band or invagination.[23] The right to teaching assumes the knowledge and teaching of right. The right to, as right of access (to whatever, teaching, philosophy, and so forth), assumes the access to right, which assumes the capacity to read and interpret, in short, instruction.

The circulation of this circle is inscribed in the great and old concept of *ability* [pouvoir]. It is indicated in the grammar and semantics of the verb *can* [pouvoir], as it can be read in jurisdictional declarations, in the statements that pronounce the law. In the famous article 11, for example: "The free communication of thoughts and opinions is one of the most precious rights of man; every citizen can therefore speak, write, and print freely, but must answer for the abuse of this freedom in the cases determined by the law." The word "can," the verb *can* in the third person singular of the present indicative, can and must be readable. One has the right to interpret it, in two ways, simultaneously and indissociably. On the one hand, "can" means "must be able": not "every citizen can" at this moment (is capable of), but must be able (permitted) to speak, write, print (teach?) freely. Even if he cannot do so *in fact* today (and this is indeed why we *posit*, even if to *recall*, this normative or prescriptive law), he must be able to do so in principle and by right. But on the other hand, as citizen he can do so without delay: if he is recognized as a citizen, the state ensures the present effectiveness of this ability. State power [*pouvoir*] should guarantee that the citizen's ability or power [*pouvoir*] does not remain formal, that it no longer belongs solely to the order of the possible, of the abstract wish or simple prescription. But how can one ensure the passage between the two meanings or modalities of power or ability? Through an ability-to-interpret, speak, write, decipher. This latter passes by way of the practice of language and, to the extent that it is a matter of universal principles, by way of philosophy. By way of the training of ability as linguistic and philosophical competence. This latter ability is of course inscribed in the circle, but it is also the condition of the circulation of the circle. It is the becoming effective of right, as *right to*.

This expression, "right to," with which we have already made a lot of sentences, marks a sort of mutation in the history of right. It is difficult to date rigorously, but it announces a difference in regime in the relations between the citizen and the state, if at least, as has been the case from Kant to Kelsen, right, distinguished from morality, is understood as a system of norms in which the state manifests itself by exercising sanction or coercion.[24] This difference in regime makes the passage from the *right of* to the *right to*, even if a *right to* remains virtually implied in the *right of*. In the history of the declarations of the rights of man and their corollaries over the last two centuries, much more has been said about the *right to* when the aim has been to determine the contents of the social rights that should fill in the abstract formality of the rights of 1789. Far from contenting itself with not impeding the exercise of the *right of* (right of property, rights of speech, writing, publishing, resisting oppression), the state must also intervene actively to make possible the exercise of the *right to* and to prepare conditions favorable for it. The example of the "right to work" must be capable of being extended to the rights to instruction and culture. It must be capable of this. It must by right, but we encounter here a structural—and structurally double—difficulty from the moment we consider right and philosophy. On the one hand, as I suggested above, we cannot speak of a *simple belonging* of philosophy (and thus of right, as of any knowledge insofar as its axiomatic is philosophical) to culture, general instruction, the disciplines formerly said to be basic (the list of which would never end, within a distinction between basic and applied research[25] that is more difficult than ever to make). It is not enough, then, to "extend" the right to (for example, the right to work, the right to philosophy), as one would progressively enlarge a homogeneous field. That is why so many states and societies allow themselves not to do everything to ensure this right, without stirring up big protests, even in regimes that are said to be democratic. But on the other hand, and inversely, the right to philosophy and to right should not expect an extension of right precisely because it is a priori, principially and by right, implied in the meaning and simple understanding of every "right to." One cannot offer the discourse of the right to work, for example, without having already accepted, legitimated, even demanded, in principle and by right, the right to philosophy and to right.

In both cases, following one or the other of these logics, the state must undertake to create the necessary conditions for the exercise of a right to philosophical training. How can one determine these conditions? Where are the limits of what a state must or can do in this regard? Where does the responsibility of the social body, of "civil society," begin and end? Concerning the right to health or work, one can pretend to content oneself with certain generalities or obvious facts: every citizen or, rather, every inhabitant must be able to receive professional training, practice a profession, participate in social insurance contracts, and so forth. Even if this determination remains too formal (What professional training? What professions? What care? How can one justify the massive inequality among citizens and the categories of inhabitants?, etc.), we know approximately what is being named. But right? But philosophy? What does the state or society designate under this title? Let's take the example of what used to be called the "philosophy class," today the Terminale,[26] the only place in France where everyone seems to agree that "some philosophy" is taught. Some think it already takes up too much space there, France being one of the rare countries in which "some philosophy" is present as such in secondary education and the only one in which it is present in such an identifiable and specialized fashion. Others think this space is very insufficient, that it should not be reduced to the space and time of one "class" and one year. Let's not enter into this debate yet—it will take up almost this entire work. Let's note just one of the dimensions of the disagreement. It is also a matter of a disagreement about the name of philosophy and of the philosophical discipline. Those who remain content with the little philosophy that is taught in the Terminale, like those who think that it is still too much, can respond to those who speak of the "right to philosophy": at any rate, to the extent that it is implied everywhere (and first of all, I have said, in the reading, understanding, or critical interpretation, thus in the exercise, of all rights), we find *some* philosophy everywhere, in particular in the other disciplines, and from the moment we learn to speak the language. This philosophy need not be confused with a specialized discipline. This argument has great titles of nobility in the philosophical tradition, and we will speak about them later.[27] On the contrary, and for this very reason, those who demand that "philosophy," as specialized discipline, be present as such *before* the Terminale fear that in the absence of a rigorous, critical, and explicit discipline, other contents (moral, social, and political ideology, etc.) will insidiously and dogmatically occupy the place of what they consider "philosophy."

In all these hypotheses, should the state or the social body do more or less than institute a "philosophy in the Terminale," formally—very formally—ensuring each citizen the chance of encountering one of those things that are called philosophy at least once in his or her life? Or rather, must this go further? How far? Does that mean training the largest possible number of teachers of philosophy? Who will determine the extent of that possibility? According to what criteria? Why would it not be the right or duty of the teachers of other disciplines—as some demand—to include philosophical training in their own education? And why would this training be reserved to future professional teachers?

These are concrete, current questions often debated beyond the circle of those who "militate" for respecting the rights to philosophy. Whatever their seriousness or complexity, they all envelop another question that might be called more "radical." If the declaration of a right hides a performative under a constative, its "convention" always assumes a philosophy. It at the same time assumes that its own meaning is accessible to everyone "interested" (or assumed to be, for this community is not yet given; it is never given, but rather is to be constituted by this very right). The access to the meaning of this declaration (made possible by literacy, the introduction to a certain type of hermeneutic, that is to say, to so many other things) is at the same time, in one and the same movement, the access to the meaning thus *authorized* of *this* philosophy, of *the philosophy that* implies itself in it.

One therefore has the right, *a priori*, to demand of the state or social body that signs this declaration, thus taking responsibility for it and claiming to give it the force of law, that it make effective the exercise of *this right to*, of the right of access to the philosophy of this declaration, to the discourse that is supposed to found or legitimate it. First difficulty. Second difficulty, still more formidable but just as inevitable: this philosophy, that of the declaration of the *right to*, is no doubt a great philosophy, but it is but one philosophy and is not sheltered from all questioning—philosophical or not. Philosophy stands under the law that demands that the right to philosophy never end, and that it never suspend questioning, irony, *skepsis*, *epochē*, or doubt when facing any philosopheme, even the philosopheme that seems to found in a determinate fashion a given declaration of rights, for example the terms of a Declaration of the Rights of Man, including the right to philosophy. The Universal Declaration of the Rights of Man naturally involves training, through "instruction," subjects capable of understanding the philosophy of *that* Declaration and of drawing from it the strength necessary to "resist despotism." These philosopher subjects should be capable of taking on the philosophical spirit and letter of the Declaration, that is, a certain philosophy of natural right, of the essence of man, born free and equal in rights to all other men, which is also to say, a certain philosophy of language, the sign, communication, power, justice, and right. This philosophy has a history. It has a specific genealogy. Its critical force is immense, but its dogmatic limits no less certain. The (French) state should do everything, and it has done a great deal, to teach (let's not necessarily say "inculcate") this philosophy, to convince citizens of it: first, through education and across all the educative procedures, well beyond the old "philosophy class." That this undertaking would still today encounter all sorts of resistance is a massive fact. That all these resistances are not inspired by reactionary dogmatisms or obscurantist impulses, that certain of them do not remain within but carry beyond a certain state of Enlightenment or *Aufklärung*, is also a fact. It is certainly less massive. It is open to equivocations, which are sometimes grossly exploited by obtuse ideologues who calculate their interest in it. But it announces even more pointedly a difficulty and a necessity of thinking.

The logic of what we call, in short, the Declaration therefore involves making effective the right to a philosophy, its own, but it tends to make minor, to marginalize, to censor (by every means, and the means are some-times subtle and always overdetermined) other philosophical discourses or other discourses *on the subject of* philosophy, in particular when their ques-tioning exceeds the philosophico-juridico-political machinery that sup-ports the state, the nation, and its pedagogical institutions.

From this angle, one realizes that a right to philosophy could not be one right among others. One can, no doubt, no doubt one even must en-trust the conditions of its implementation to a state, which, as state of right, is qualified to make effective the very right that posits or constitutes it. But these conditions of implementation should remain *external* to the philosophical as such. Is this possible, in all rigor, in all purity? No, but *external* would here mean tendentially, ideally extrinsic: once the state is obligated to ensure the technical, material, professional, institutional, and so on, conditions of a right to philosophy, no contract would bind phi-losophy itself and institute this philosophy as a reciprocal and responsible partner of the state. If this were demanded of philosophy, even implicitly, philosophy would have the right, a right it only gets from itself, this time, and in no way from the state, to match wits with the state, to break uni-laterally every agreement, in a brutal or cunning, declared or, if the situa-tion demands, surreptitious fashion. This irresponsibility toward the state can be demanded by philosophy's responsibility to its own law—or the re-sponsibility of what I above called *thinking*, which can, in analogous con-ditions, break its contract with science or philosophy. Despite appearances, this is not to reconstruct the essential interiority of a philosophy whose "business" would be to justify itself. On the contrary, it is to carry its re-sponsibility still further: to the point of giving itself the right—or privi-lege—to go on questioning, without trusting too quickly, the limit between the inside and the outside, the proper and the improper, what is essential and proper to philosophy and what is not.

If we follow this kind of argumentation, the right to philosophy can be managed, protected, facilitated by a juridico-political apparatus (and de-mocracy, insofar as its model is already given, remains in this regard the best one); it cannot be guaranteed, still less produced, through the law as a body of prescriptions accompanied by coercion and sanction. Jumping some steps, let's say that the philosophical act or experience takes place only once this juridico-political limit can be transgressed, or at least ques-tioned, perturbed, in the force that will in a certain sense have naturalized that limit. As for what would link this transgression to the production of a new right, "thinking" (which "is" that very thing) must be able to pronounce its right beyond philosophy and science. *Through* philosophy and science, as I might have said a moment ago: *through* the state. There *is no* pure instance. "Thinking," a word that entitles only the possibility of this "no," must even, in the name of a democracy still *to come*[28] as the possibility of this "thinking," unremittingly interrogate the de facto democracy, critique its current determinations, analyze its philosophical genealogy, in short, deconstruct it: in the name of the democracy whose being to come is not simply tomorrow or the future, but rather the promise of an event and the event of a promise. An event and a promise that constitute the democratic: not presently but in a here and now whose singularity does not signify presence or self-presence.

6. Of a "Popular Tone"—or of Philosophy (in) Direct (Style) (Directives and Directions: Straight, Rigid, Rigorous, Rectilinear, Regular)

How have we arrived here?[29] To justify a title, *Right to Philosophy*, we have ventured a few sentences intended to give it a meaning. Inasmuch as a title is not a sentence, it has no meaning. It has only the meaning that virtual sentences could give it. While every sentence can also function as a title at the heart of a discourse, only juridico-conventional devices can introduce order into this situation, and to an always limited extent. Austin reminds us that a word never has meaning by itself, but only in a sentence. That is the first proposition of a text whose title[30] is not an actual sentence and thus has, "properly speaking," no meaning. "Properly speaking, what alone has a meaning is a sentence." Only a sentence has meaning, but a sentence is a sentence (only) on this condition. Properly speaking, if it has no meaning, a title reminds us that it is, properly speaking, the "properly speaking" that risks making but little sense, for a title, in the situation of a title guaranteed by laws, capitalizes the entire meaning of the virtual sentences that it at once evokes and silences, that it summons and represses in the same movement. It gets all its authority from this movement—an authority at once silent and inexhaustible. This is the truth of the title, of every title, the efficacy of the title, the stroke [*coup*] of the title: it retains the sense it does not have, all the sense it does not have, some sense it does not have. It makes sense. That is its *privilege*.

"Right" figured as a noun in most of the sentences we have formed to this point to give the title the meaning it retains but which it does not have and to articulate all the relations of right to philosophy. But we have not yet treated the segment of the title between quotation marks, which, we noted above, permits (more or less artificially, but a title is the most artificial and deceitful place in language) "right" to be considered as an adverb, in the sense of "directly," as in "go 'right to philosophy.'" What can "right" mean here as adverb or adverbialized attribute? What significant or relevant sentence can one make with it in the syntagm that would articulate it with philosophy? Instead of responding to this question by opening a new series of arguments, let us rather try to analyze a logico-semantic crossing between the two groups of sentences. The site of this crossing seems to me to suggest a certain privilege of the reference to Kant. There are many reasons for this, both historical and systematic: (1) because Kant tells us something about the opposition straight/curved or straight/oblique in the problematic of right (*Recht, Jus*); (2) because of the very obvious and close communication between a discourse of the Kantian type and the moment of the French Revolution or the event of a Universal Declaration of the Rights of Man; (3) because the discourse that certain social sciences bring to pedagogical institutions, notably to the teaching of philosophy, itself gives the Kantian heritage a paradoxical predominance. This happens in diverse ways, notably, among the most striking and remarkable works, through the role given to the problematics of objectification (and of the objectification of objectification) or legitimation, even licitation. Through numerous and complicated relays, notably that of Weber, these problematics undeniably *have it out with*[31] a Kantian heritage, whether they assume it or not, and to assume here does not mean to accept or adhere to. I think naturally of the analyses of Pierre Bourdieu and of those they have made possible.

Within the limits of this preface and to situate several of the essays that will concern Kant directly in this work, let us recall the question of "popular philosophy" as it is posed in the Preface and Introduction to *Metaphysics of Morals*.[32] The critique of practical reason must be followed by a system, that is, the metaphysics of morals, which is divided into the doctrine of virtue and the doctrine of right. The latter, another name for the metaphysics of right, must take a pure concept of right as its rule, even if it relies on the practical and is applied to cases that are presented in experience. Empirical multiplicity cannot be exhausted, and cases are presented only in the form of examples. They do not belong to the "system," which therefore can be approached but in no way reached. Thus one must content oneself, as was the case with the metaphysics of nature, with the "first metaphysical principles of the doctrine of right." What is here called "right" is what, Kant tells us, derives from the system outlined a priori and is inscribed "in the text" (*in den Text*), that is, the principal text, while the rights linked to experience and particular cases find themselves relegated to the Remarks and other annexes to the corpus.

Here, then, the question of the language of the philosopher, or rather of his discourse, imposes itself. Must he remain "obscure" or make it his duty to become "popular"? We should not be surprised to see this question arise concerning right or the metaphysics of right. The philosopher's language (the discursive implementation of a language within language) must in fact become popular, Kant responds to a certain Garve, unless this imperative were to lead the philosopher to neglect, fail to recognize, or, worse, lead his readers to ignore, rigorous distinctions, decisive divisions, essential stakes for thinking. Kantian rigor and prudence appear so exemplary— and so appropriate to our modern debates on philosophy and the media— that a long citation imposes itself here. It is a supplementary complication that the major, strategically determining distinction, the distinction that cannot and must not in any case let itself be "popularized," is, in Kant's eyes, that of the sensible and the intelligible, the very distinction that so many deconstructive approaches have tracked down for a long time, in itself and in the extreme diversity of its effects. It must be taken into account today if one wants to reconcile the responsibilities of philosophical and "deconstructive" rigor, new orders of public or media space, and the imperatives of the democracy to come. The strategy of public discourse must be more cunning than ever—and incessantly reevaluated. Although "popularity," as Kant, who speaks elsewhere of a "popular tone,"[33] suggests, can today no longer mean, if it ever could have, "to be sensible," we can draw a formal and analogous lesson from the response to Garve—and in advance to all the Garves of modernity:

> Philosophical treatises are often charged with being obscure, indeed deliberately unclear, in order to affect an illusion of deep insight. I cannot better anticipate or forestall this charge than by readily complying with a duty that Garve, a philosopher in the true sense of the word, lays down for all writers, but especially for philosophical writers. My only reservation is imposed by the nature of the science that is to be corrected and extended.
>
> This wise man rightly requires (in his work *Vermischte Aufsätze*[34]) that every

philosophical teaching be capable of being made *popular* (that is, of being made sufficiently clear to the sense to be communicated to everyone), if the teacher is not to be suspected of being muddled in his own concepts. I gladly admit this with the exception only of the systematic critique of reason itself, along with everything that can be established only by means of it; for this has to do with the distinction of the sensible in our knowledge from that which is supersensible but yet belongs to reason. This can never become popular—no formal metaphysics can—although its results can be made quite illuminating for the healthy reason (of an unwitting metaphysician). Popularity (common language) is out of the question here; on the contrary, scholastic *precision* must be insisted upon, even if this is censured as hair-splitting (since it is the *language of the schools*); for only by this means can precipitate reason be brought to understand itself, before making its dogmatic assertions.

But if *pedants* presume to address the public (from pulpits or in popular writings) in technical terms that belong only in the schools, the critical philosopher is no more responsible for that than the grammarian is for the folly of those who quibble over words (*logodaedalus*). Here ridicule can touch only the man, not the science.[35]

Several times in this work, the consequences and implications of such a declaration will be analyzed, as will the "socio-pedagogic scenography"[36] in which it is inscribed. How is one to go from the principles of this philosophical pedagogy (as philosophical pedagogy of principles) to a doctrine of right? How to go, more precisely, to this value of "right" constructed on the analogy between what the noun designates (*le droit, jus,* "right," *das Recht*) and what the adjective or the adverb means (direct, rigid, rectilinear)? Kant alludes to this analogy and attempts to justify it in a Remark (that is, let us remember, in what does not belong to the principal "text" of the metaphysics of right, not being inscribed "in the text"). The Remark to paragraph E of the Introduction to the Doctrine of Right deals with and claims to justify the analogy according to which right (*das Recht, rectum*) is opposed (*entgegengesetzt*), as that which is right (this time in the sense of direct or rectilinear, *gerade*) to what is curved (*krumm*), on the one hand, and oblique (*schief*), on the other. *Krumm,* curved in the spatial or physical sense, also means, according to a psychological or moral figure that encompasses or revives the whole question, crooked, deviant, deceitful. Likewise, *schief* ("oblique, slanted, tilted, gauche") can have an analogous value: false, erroneous, out of place, improper, awkward.

This Remark follows paragraph E (of the Introduction to the Doctrine of Right), which concerns "strict right [*das stricte Recht*]." Right is only strict, only attains its proper stricture, to the extent that it is constraining, exacting, but also to the extent that it links a "reciprocal universal coercion" with the "freedom of everyone," and does so according to an "external universal" law, that is, a natural one. This value of exteriority distinguishes pure right from morals. Right has no internal depths; its "objects" (*Objekte*) must be shown in actions. It is a domain of visibility or theatricality without fold. Even when a certain interiority is summoned or called to appear (questions of veracity, remorse, deep conviction, motives, etc.), it is assumed that it can be exposed completely—in a discourse or in expressive gestures. This exteriority of strict and pure right is in no way "mixed up" with "some prescription relative to virtue."

But exteriority is not enough to *found* right. It does not justify it. According to a sort of logico-transcendental *factum* (whose wake is found in Kelsen), the foundation of right is not juridical but moral. "This is indeed based [*gründet sich*] on everyone's consciousness of obligation [*auf dem Bewußtsein der Verbindlichkeit*] in accordance with the law [*nach dem Gesetz*], which also means everyone's being *before the law*, Vor dem Gesetz, a being-before-the-law that is at once moral and juridical, therefore, and thus also anterior to this distinction between the two laws]; but if it is to remain pure, this consciousness may not and cannot be appealed to as an incentive to determine one's choice in accordance with this law. Strict right rests instead on the principle of its being possible to use an external constraint that can coexist with the freedom of everyone in accordance with universal laws."[37]

This consciousness (excluded as a "motive" for right) is nonetheless the consciousness of strict right. Is it a moral or a juridical consciousness?[38] The consciousness of obligation is already juridical and still moral. It is what "founds" strict right. But Kant suggests that it does not belong to the order of what it founds. The founding of strict right would not be juridical. Not in the sense in which one could say, in a Heideggerian gesture, that the juridicity of right or the essence of right is in no way juridical (with all the didactico-institutional consequences that follow), but in the sense in which the being-right of right is its (moral and juridical) right to be right: the order of the law and not of being. A question of stricture.[39]

The possibility of an analogy between right and rectilinearity is closely related to pedagogy, even if this relation appears principal and virtual. What is at stake in fact is the presentation (*Darstellung*) of a concept, its presentation in a pure and a priori intuition, but following an analogy.

Kant defines (before the Remark, precisely) "strict right": "the possibility of a complete, reciprocal constraint in accordance with the freedom of everyone following universal laws" (25). Let us again recall this important point: only a perfectly *external* right deserves the name of strict (narrow) right, even if this right founds itself on the consciousness of an obligation before the law. But such a consciousness is not the motive for a juridical arbitration that must rely on the possibility of an *external* constraint, at least to the extent that it can be reconciled with the freedom of everyone following universal laws. If we have the *right to demand* the settlement of a debt, it is not to the extent that we can persuade the debtor's reason, but to the extent that we can constrain him, in a manner that is compatible with the freedom of everyone "following a universal external law": "right and the faculty of constraining are one and the same thing."

It is in order to construct this pure concept of right, that is, to present it in a pure *a priori* intuition, that the question of analogy is posed. At issue is the analogy between this pure concept of right and the possibility of the free movement of bodies under the law of the equality of action and reaction. The analogy between pure right and pure mathematics is announced by a "just as, so too [*sowie*]." "But, just as" in pure mathematics, the properties of its object cannot be derived immediately, directly, from a concept (hence the necessity of "constructing" the concept), "so too" the presentation of the concept of right is not made possible directly by the concept itself, but only by reference to a reciprocal and equal constraint under universal laws. This first analogy remains too formal and belongs to the order of pure mathematics. That is still not enough, therefore, to explain the recourse to analogies with the "right" (*gerade*, rectilinear), the curved, or the oblique. A supplementary argument, another analogy, must ensure the mediation—and Kant must allude to the care shown by reason, to the concern (*Versorgen*) it offers, a reason that is providing, providential, giving: to put at our disposal, within reach of our understanding, as far as possible, a priori intuitions that help us construct the concept of right. Without such solicitude from reason, without the system of limits that it procures, guarantees, and crosses *at the same time*, no "presentation" would be possible, and we can say, skipping some steps, no properly philosophical rhetoric, pedagogy, communication, or discussion:

> But, just as a purely formal concept of pure mathematics (for example, of geometry) underlies the dynamical concept [of the equality of action and re-

action], so too reason has taken care to furnish the understanding as far as possible with a priori intuitions for constructing the concept of right. Straightness or rectitude (*rectum*) is opposed to what is *curved* on the one hand and what is *oblique* on the other. In the first case, it is a question of the *inner property* of a line such that there can only be a single *one* between two given points, inclining no more to one side than to the other and dividing the space on both sides equally. Analogously to this, the doctrine of right wants to determine that *what belongs* to each has been determined (with mathematical exactitude). Such exactitude cannot be expected in the *doctrine of virtue*, which cannot refuse some room for exceptions (*latitudinem*). (26)

We cannot measure here everything at stake in this difficult Remark, notably in the allowance it makes for *exceptions* in the order of virtue. We must, however, add another reason to those we have given above to justify this recourse to Kant. Along this long digression, it will perhaps not be impossible to take into view, obliquely, and not straight on, what we are *doing* on this journey: what we are saying, the form of this discourse, the privilege accorded to Kant, the justifications given for it. In short, it would be a matter of reflecting on laws, norms, a situation of which these introductory Remarks would *also* be an example, treated as such ("objectivity"?), as an example—I don't dare say as an exercise. I emphasize *also* because it is perhaps not impossible even thereby to say and to do something else as well.

7. Drawing One's Authority Only from Oneself— and Therefore, Once Again, from Kant

As justified as it might be in itself, the reference to Kant and to the Kant of the *Doctrine of Right* is not the only one to impose itself here, as will have been suspected. To what have I given in? To what does one give in when according such a privilege?

What does it mean to refer to Kant in order to draw authority from him, even if the authority of an objection to Kant? What benefit do we still derive from a discussion or explication with Kant?

The meticulous analysis of Kantian discourse regularly imposes itself, to be sure, as a major and authentically philosophical gesture. But this gesture is not only necessary and interesting from a philosophical point of view in the *strict* (proper, internal, intrinsic) sense. It also guarantees, authenticates, legitimizes the philosophical dignity of an argument. This gesture presents itself as "major." It signals "great" philosophy. It raises to the level of the canon. Whatever the supposedly intrinsic necessity of this reference to the Kantian discourse on right, morals, politics, teaching in general, the teaching of philosophy insofar as it is not one teaching among others, etc., our relation to this necessity, the interest or pleasure we take in recognizing and exposing it (which happens to me every time I read Kant, and it is always for the first time), all that implies a program and a repetition. For many of "us" ("us": the majority of my supposed readers and myself), the authority of Kantian discourse has inscribed its virtues of legitimation to such a depth in our philosophical training, culture, and constitution that we have difficulty performing the imaginary variation that would allow us to "figure" a different one. Better, the "relation to Kant" signals the very idea of training, culture, constitution, and especially "legitimation," the question of right, that is, the element in which we see the situation I am describing at this moment take shape. Even in the expression "relation to," a "French philosopher" over-hears or infers the translation of the "relation to [*Beziehung auf*]," of the relation to the object or to "something in general," a Kantian syntagm.

The Kantian heritage is not only the Kantian heritage, a thing identical to itself. Like every heritage, it exceeds itself to provide (or lay claim to) the analysis of this heritage and, better, the instruments of analysis for every heritage. This "supplementary" structure must be taken into account. A heritage always surreptitiously bequeaths to us the means of interpreting it. It superimposes itself a priori on the interpretation we produce of it, that is to say, always, to a certain extent, and up to a line that is difficult to determine, that we repeat of it.

Yet whoever says this (here me, for example) does not need to specify "I am a Kantian" or "I know Kant well." It is as though the "relation to Kant" were tattooed on. It is the privileged inscription of an absolute privilege, one quasi-naturalized right in the training, and by that training, in its programs, its values and implicit evaluations, the modes of argumentation and discussion it authorizes, the kinds of sanction and reproduction it codifies, the genres of exercise it favors (the essay, the thesis, the dissertation), the rhetoric, the "style," the experience of language it privileges. This is no doubt due in large part to the "figure" of Kant, to this philosopher's public image in the *doxa* of a socio-cultural circle determined by the French schooling that for a long time included a "philosophy class": all young French bourgeois are supposed to have heard of this severe, difficult to read, bachelor, civil servant philosopher. There again, let us read or reread *Le Discours de la syncope*. Beyond the baccalauréat and everything that remains of it in all the circles where this diploma is a certificate of culture, Kant is, so to speak, in all the programs and on all the juries of philosophy. Whether we follow him or distance ourselves from him, Kant is the norm.

One would therefore *have to* (an imperative that appears to me to be dictated here although I dictate it) question and displace this norm, if possible and if that is thinkable, if thinking demands it. But to question the laws and determinisms that have put such a privilege in place, one still has to read Kant, turn toward him, thematize the phenomenon of his authority, and thus super-canonize him. Can this paradoxical effect of capitalization be avoided? If one contented oneself with "turning the page," with skirting Kant, with no longer naming him, with acting as if he were not there, himself, that is to say, his heritage, one would risk reproducing it even more efficiently, naively, clandestinely, unconsciously. For the irrigation of common philosophical discourse with Kantian philosophemes, words, procedures, axioms most often occurs underground. It goes unseen, so complicated and roundabout are its paths. Therefore, at the risk of returning again to Kant to accumulate the surplus value of the critical bids that are raised, is it not more *worth*while, *must* one not try to read and thus situate Kant differently? Must one not at least begin by bringing to light those effects of authority that are already, strictly, "within" (if one can put it this way, for this language is still Kantian) his oeuvre, by studying its hierarchizing, canonizing, marginalizing, and disqualifying procedures, the "internal" structuring of the text, the exclusion (that is, the externalizing) of the Opuscules, Parerga, or Remarks? A brilliant example of this is found in what Kant proposes on the subject of Remarks in the Preface to the *First Metaphysical Principles of the Doctrine of Right*, that is, that everything that does not issue from the system outlined a priori is not worthy of belonging to the principal "text" and finds itself relegated to the Remarks. Where, in this respect, does a Preface that declares, pronounces, and in fact posits the law it declares find itself? What is the place of jurisdiction? To elaborate this type of question, one must no doubt read Kant differently, but one must not stop reading him.

A few other *remarks* in the margin of the Remark on paragraph E.

Whether we adopt or critique it, the Kantian model exercises its authority over all the philosophical (that is, European) mechanisms of teaching across the most diverse (Hegelian-Marxist or Husserlian-Heideggerian) relays. This fact is no doubt unique, but we can take it up from at least *three angles.* The question of its singularity, that is, its absolute privilege, will only be more pointed. Kantian critique and metaphysics are inseparable from modern teaching. They "are" this teaching, that is to say that they "are" teaching forms untried until now.

1. They propose a pedagogy. They situate the moment and necessity of the pedagogical: outside the pure thinking of principles, but as the necessity of an ascent to pure principles for the "people" as "unwitting metaphysician." I have insisted, and will do so again (later, in the chapter entitled "Popularities"[40]), on this topic of pedagogy and what it assumed about metaphysics (the construction of the concept of the people and the "popular" on the basis of the distinction between reason and understanding, imagination and sensibility, the opposition of the intelligible and the sensible, the pure and the impure, the inside and the outside, the strict and the nonstrict).

2. Let's move quickly to the fact that Kantian philosophy is elaborated and structured as a teaching discourse. More precisely, that of a professor in a state University. This can be seen not only in the well-known fact that Kant wrote essays and theses, that he led the life of a civil servant, and that he had all kinds of debates with the royal power upon which he depended, the echo of which we find in particular in *The Conflict of the Faculties* and *Religion Within the Limits of Reason Alone.* This was the case, in this form and to this degree, of no philosopher before him. On the other hand, after him, rare were the noteworthy philosophers who did not find themselves in an analogous situation. These "facts" being well known, it would no doubt be more interesting and difficult to identify the marks of that situation in the logico-rhetorical form and even in the very "content" of Kantian philosophy. This philosophy was homogeneous and predisposed to the becoming-public-teaching of philosophy in given socio-political conditions: classrooms, programs, evaluations, and sanctions within a system (the school and the university) holding not only a power of the transmission and reproduction of knowledge (which might have been considered secondary by certain representatives of professional philosophy) but above all a power of judgment, evaluation, and sanction, that is, the power of a jurisdiction, of an instance pronouncing the law, accompanying its declarations with an objective constraint (this is the very definition of right according to Kant), and deciding on the legitimacy of a discourse or a thinking, on relevance and competence, by conferring upon it a title, indeed, a professional right.

3. This *possibility* of Kantian discourse is as much a symptom (and there are so many others) as a determining factor. It would be naïve to choose here between the two terms of such an alternative. It would be better to attempt to think this singular "history" (the only privilege there is) in such a way that the discourse, critique, and metaphysics of a certain Immanuel Kant could be read at once as "cause" and "effect," meaning and symptom, production and product, origin and repetition, so many distinctions formalized by a graphics of iterability,[41] inscribed in it as "effects" that it in turn relativizes without, however, disqualifying them. "Kant" is the name of something "possible": made possible and making possible in turn. Something possible that is no doubt produced, carried by the birth of the modern state and its teaching systems, whose limits and precarity it therefore shares; like the modern state, this something possible is of course also carried and produced by the history of earlier philosophies, as by so many other preexisting forces, drives, and pressures. But this symptomal formation is powerful, gathered together in its formalization, overdetermined and overdetermining. It therefore *possibilizes*: *in turn*, but it is destined to this *turn*. Through numerous relays of potentialization, it participates in the most structuring, the most productive, *and* the most destructive operations in the history to come of discourses, works, and European institutions. It informs European "culture," which is also to say European "colonization," wherever it operates.

The possibilization of this power can also be read in the "internal" organization of Kantian discourse. It works on the critical idea itself, in its rhetorical-conceptual armature, architectonic motif, system of limits, and machinery of semantic oppositions. What could be more indispensable than such an architectonics for a philosophical institution charged, if one can put it this way (although charged in complete freedom respecting academic autonomy, of course), by the state, even by any civil or clerical power whatsoever, with assuming the mission of judging, of telling the truth (but also, and even thereby, of authorizing those who distinguish competences, confer titles, produce and propagate legitimacies), of pronouncing the law or, more radically, the truth[42] and metaphysical principles of the doctrine of right, of providing the very criteria for distinguishing the strict from the nonstrict, of deducing according to rigorous and specific rules the possibility of "equivocation" or "illegitimacy" in the order of right?[43] What could be more efficient in this regard than a discursive machinery of the Kantian type with its principial and cutting oppositions between the sensible and

the intelligible, phenomenon and noumenon, internal and external phenomenon, the pure sensible and the empirical sensible, the transcendental
and the empirical, the pure and the impure, the *a priori* and the *a posteri-
ori*, the objective and the subjective, sensibility, imagination, understanding, and reason. As for the "internal" difficulties of this machinery, when it
has the most difficulty maintaining the purity of these oppositions (the theory of schematism, the critique of judgment, and so many other "composi-
tions" or "mixtures" that give delight—and increased authority—to the
great Kant experts or drill coaches, beginning with Hegel or Heidegger),
they have also become canonical. Not only do they not jam the process of
propagation, but they endow the canon with a surplus of power, authority,
and longevity.

(Let this remark between parentheses suffice here. Deconstruction, which
produces itself first of all as the deconstruction of these oppositions, therefore immediately concerns, just as much and just as radically, the institutional structures founded on such oppositions. *Deconstruction is an institutional practice for which the concept of the institution remains a problem.*
But since, for the reason I am in the process of pointing out, it is not a
"critique" either, it destroys no more than it discredits critique or institutions; its transformative gesture is other, its responsibility is other and consists in following as consistently as possible what I have above and elsewhere called a graphics of iterability. That is why the same responsibility
rules at once philosophy (the struggles for the recognition of the right to
philosophy, the extension of philosophical teaching and research) *and* the
most vigilant practice of deconstruction. To consider this a contradiction,
as certain people do, is to understand as little about deconstruction as
about philosophy. It amounts to considering them terms foreign or opposed to one another. As for the responsibility to which I am referring
here, it is no longer purely philosophical, in fact, nor can it be determined
by philosophical concepts of responsibility (the freedom of the subject,
consciousness, the I, the individual, intention, voluntary decision, etc.),
which are still *conditions* and thus *limitations* of responsibility, sometimes
limitations in the very determination of the unconditional, the imperative, and the categorical. If, therefore, the responsibility we are calling for
(or rather, which is recalling itself to us here) exceeds the philosophical as
such, we will call it, for obvious reasons, neither "higher" nor "more profound" than philosophical (or indeed moral, political, ethical, or juridical)
responsibility, nor simply foreign to it. It is even *engaged* in philosophical

responsibility, which does not mean thoroughly inscribed in philosophy, for it is also engaged by injunctions that command at once more imperatively and more gently, more discreetly and more uncompromisingly: among other things, that one "think" the philosophical determinations of responsibility, the imperative, or the unconditional, which is also to say, their socio-institutional determinations.)

8. The Hypersymbolic: The Court of Final Appeal

It will be objected, not without some semblance of correctness: well before Kant, every philosophy will have proceeded by systems of conceptual delimitations and oppositions; is that not the essence and normal functioning of metaphysics? Can one not say of Plato what one says of Kant? No doubt, and to this extent pre-Kantian discourses play an *analogous* role in their relation to politico-institutional structures. The study of this analogy is a vast and necessary program, in order better to specify the originality of the Kantian site and know where the analogy finds its limit. Kantianism is not only a powerfully organized network of conceptual limits, a critique, a metaphysics, a dialectics, a discipline of pure reason. It is a discourse that presents itself as the essential project of *delimitation*: the thinking of the limit as the *position* of the limit, the foundation or legitimation of judgment in view of these limits. The scene of this position and this legitimation, of this legitimating position, is structurally and indissociably juridico-politico-philosophical. In such a scene, what is a philosopher? He who pronounces the law on the subject of the law, the true on the subject of the relations between the state, theology, medicine, law, all as such, and philosophy as such. The Kantian question par excellence is the question *quid juris*, even if it does not always appear as such, *stricto sensu*, in its literalness (as it does, for example, and at least by analogy, at the opening of the Deduction of the Pure Concepts of Understanding). It poses itself to every knowledge, every practice, and even to every determination of the pure concept of right, even before the General Division of Right (pp. 29–34) into right as systematic science or the moral faculty of constraining the other to a duty ("that is, as a legal principle concerning the other [*titulum*]"), then of the first into natural right and positive (statutory) right, and of the second into innate right (freedom, the only originary right, from which all others, in particular equality, derive) and acquired right.

Juridicism consists here in the limitless extension of the (nonstrict) form of the question *quid juris*,[44] even where it is up to the philosophical to pronounce the law on the subject of the law, to determine the essence of right and the pure concept of right, to interpret foundation as justification. Philosophy is the guardian of this tribunal of reason that, after the juridical history of reason in the first Preface to the *Critique of Pure Reason* (1781), institutes or convocates, in fact "invites" to "institute [*einzusetzen*]" or, more precisely (for these folds shelter all the difficulties), calls, names as the institution that responds to an invitation (*Aufforderung*) made to reason to "undertake anew [*aufs Neue zu übernehmen*]" "the most difficult of all its tasks . . . self-knowledge." The invitation *seems* to precede the institution of the tribunal of reason, which would, in short, be but a repetition of it.

But in fact this invitation is itself already a form of repetition, since it invites us to "undertake anew" an old task. It is "an invitation made to reason to undertake anew the most difficult of all its tasks, namely, that of self-knowledge, and to institute a tribunal which will guarantee reason its lawful claims [*der sie bei ihren gerechten Ansprüchen sichere*], and dismiss all groundless pretensions [*grundlose Anmaßungen*], not by despotic decrees, but in accordance with its own eternal and unalterable laws. This tribunal is no other than the *Critique of Pure Reason*."[45] As Nancy puts it so well concerning the "*faux pas* of judgment":

> The *Critique* thus comes to occupy the place of the foundation of the law; it is in principle charged with pronouncing the law of law, and thus with freeing *jus* from relying on cases in its *dictio*.
>
> Yet *precisely this founding operation indicates itself as the juridical act par excellence*: we are here before the tribunal itself, at the heart of *critique* as such. For this reason, the jurisdiction of all jurisdiction, just as much as it extricates itself from all juridical status (just as much as it sets itself up as *privilege*), *with the same gesture* digs in itself the infinite rift in which it cannot but constantly fall anew upon its own case. In other words, because philosophy thinks itself—*pronounces itself*—according to the law, it unavoidably thinks (unless it thereby stops thinking *itself*) ineluctably as itself structured (or affected) by the *lapsus judicii*, by the slipping and the fall that are an intrinsic part of the lack of substance in which jurisdiction takes place.[46]

The critique of pure reason (the project and the work that carry this title, whose title or rights are guaranteed by the entire juridical history of reason) is no doubt an institution, since it has the status of a nonnatural and nonoriginary event, but an institution that *responds* (to an invitation) and that *repeats* "anew" an "undertaking [*Unternehmung*]" much older than itself. The institution takes place in iteration, but the new, let's call it "modern," trait is the "tribunal" form of this reinstitution of an old task. No doubt, this modernity also inscribes itself in the element of a Latinity or Romanism of philosophy.[47] But before Kant, how did one end up constituting reason itself as tribunal? A tribunal whose power or violence (*Gewalt*, Benjamin would say[48]) stems from being guaranteed by no law other than its own, the law by which, incessantly preceding itself, it is at once before the law and before there was law, like the man from the country and the guardian of the law in Kafka's narrative. Such a tribunal is all powerful "by rights" and "in principle," potentially all powerful, since it does not claim to judge this or that, "books" or "systems," but rather, Kant specifies, "the faculty of reason in general." In other words, its own power, the foundation of its absolute self-legitimation: "I do not mean by this a critique of books and systems, but of the faculty of reason in general, in respect of all knowledge after which it may strive *independently of all experience*. It will therefore decide as to the possibility or impossibility of metaphysics in general, and determine its sources, its extent, and its limits—all in accordance with principles."[49]

The absolute autonomy of the tribunal of reason, that is, of a rational institution that is, by right and as regards pronouncing the truth of right, dependent only upon itself, has its reflection or academic psyche in the faculty of philosophy: inferior to the other faculties (law, medicine, theology) in the hierarchy ruled by power, it remains absolutely independent of the power of the state as regards pronouncing the truth in judgments. I question the structure of this privilege in "Mochlos."[50]

There is the tribunal of reason—which would be Critique itself. And then there is the discourse on the tribunal of reason, which would be the *Critique*, the work that carries that title, signed by a certain Kant whose *Critique of Pure Reason* presents the critique of pure reason. Is presentation adequate to what it is supposed to present? Kant inscribes this question in a judiciary space. Philosophical reading is a *trial*. The author is both judge and judged. He therefore recuses himself and leaves the reader to judge in the final analysis, even if he still claims to help him a bit by leaving him the only judge. The addressee (that is, the reader's reason) is the court of final appeal. "Reader, already you judge / There our difficulties," Ponge will say in *Fable*. Kant:

Whether I have succeeded in what I have undertaken must be left altogether to the reader's judgment [*dem Urteile des Lesers*]; the author's task is solely to adduce grounds [*Gründe vorzulegen*], not to decide [*urteilen*] as to the effect which they should have upon those who are sitting in judgment [*seinen Richtern*]. But the author, in order that he may not himself, innocently, be the cause of any weakening of his arguments [*Ursache*], may be permitted to draw attention to certain passages, which, although merely incidental, may yet occasion some mistrust.[51]

Let's back up a moment. Who, exactly, invited reason to "undertake anew" the old task and to institute a tribunal, that is, Critique? I have intentionally left this question hanging. In the final analysis, of course, reason itself *invites itself* thus. But what is its occasional and specific figure here? What is the grammatical subject of the sentence that begins: "it is an invitation made to reason to undertake anew the most difficult of all its tasks . . . "? It is an "indifference [*Gleichgültigkeit*]," the affected indifference of those who pretend they are no longer interested in these metaphysical stakes and claim to disguise themselves, to pass unperceived, or to throw us off the track by "transforming the language of the schools into a popular tone [*durch die Veränderung der Schulsprache in einem populären Ton*]." We have a lot to learn about this situation still today, and about Kant's double diagnosis. On the one hand, by adopting this popular tone in philosophy, by affecting to avoid jargon and metaphysics, these "indifferentists [*Indifferentisten*]" inevitably [*unvermeidlich*] return to the metaphysics from which they claim to distance themselves in order to speak directly to the people. On the other hand, this symptom must be taken seriously and give the philosopher cause to think. Whether those who are "indifferent" know it or not, their symptom expresses a "mature judgment of the age." This symptom or "judgment" invites reason to undertake anew the task that is no other than that of Critique. It invites or calls for refounding such an institution:

It is idle to feign *indifference* to such enquiries, the object of which can never be *indifferent* to our human nature. Indeed these pretended *indifferentists*, however they may try to disguise themselves by substituting a popular tone for the language of the schools, inevitably fall back, in so far as they think at all, into those very metaphysical assertions which they profess so greatly to despise. None the less this *indifference*, showing itself in the midst of flourishing [*mitten in dem Flor*] sciences, and affecting precisely those sciences, the knowledge of which, if attainable, we should least of all care to dispense with, is a phenomenon that calls for attention and reflection. It is obviously the effect not of levity but of the mature judgment [*Urteilskraft*] of the age, which refuses to be put off any longer with illusory knowledge. It is a call to reason to undertake anew the most difficult of all its tasks, that of self-knowledge, and to institute a tribunal. (8–9)

This status as tribunal, a court of final appeal, ensures the philosophico-pedagogical or philosophico-institutional tradition its formidable power. It ensures it in the entire post-Kantian history: not only in all neo-Kantianisms and in the phenomenological repetition of the transcendental motif but also throughout the critiques of Kant, the reversals of him, of a Hegeliano-Marxist and even Nietzschean type, in the project of fundamental ontology in *Being and Time*, and so forth. This power is paradoxical. That it is the other side or the alibi of a powerless abdication and that it is so essentially linked to a modern concept of the university is the interpretive hypothesis that orients, and is put to the test in, numerous essays in this book, just as it has often guided me in the "institutional" initiatives in which I have taken part over the last fifteen years.

What is this power(lessness), this all-powerful loss of power? Why and in what way is it ensured by the authority of the question *quid juris* across forms of discourse, writing, exposition, norms of evaluation and legitimation, *transcendental* (critical and strictly Kantian or phenomenological and Husserlian) or *ontological* (the absolute logic of the speculative or materialist dialectic—up to its most recent theoreticist or scientistic forms—and fundamental ontology) models of philosophical argumentation or the counter-models that reverse the question *quid juris*? The unity or unicity of this (in)capacity can be analyzed from at least three angles.

1. *Hyperjuridicism*. Despite appearances, the question *quid juris* is not posed by a judge who, in effect, summons every kind of knowledge and practice in order to evaluate, legitimate, or disqualify them, in short, to pronounce the law about them. No, the philosopher, as such, accords himself the privilege and gives himself the unique right to judge the judge, to posit-recognize-evaluate the very principles of judgment in its constitution and conditions of possibility. It is not a question of personal *hubris*, but of the very status of philosophy. A philosopher speaks and acts thus, whether he is a philosopher by profession or not, whether or not he occupies a statutory position in this regard. This is the case, occasionally, of no matter whom or, very often, of the representative of a nonphilosophical discipline, a historian or a jurist, a sociologist or a mathematician, a logician, a philol-

ogist, a grammarian, a psychoanalyst, a literary theorist. This philosopher who puts forward, explicitly or implicitly, in the broad or strict sense, the question *quid juris* does not content himself with examining a judgment or pronouncing the law at work in an established field. He prepares himself to pronounce the law (on the subject) of the law. We will verify this in its pure literalness later by reading *The Conflict of the Faculties*, notably concerning the relations between the faculty of law and the faculty of philosophy: there is a moment when the truth about the law is no longer the competence of the jurist but of the philosopher. The right to say the truth (in theoretico-constative statements) about the law and the judgments of jurists must be accorded to the faculty of philosophy as such without any limit by the power of the state (in this case a monarchical power, but the point is secondary here). Stripped of certain particular characteristics (the relationship between a certain state of philosophy, in a particular place and time, and a certain state, a certain state of the Prussian monarchy, etc.), the schema of this demand remains intact in its nervure throughout the structures, discourses, and concepts of the philosophical *universitas* after Kant. According to this schema, philosophy is not only a mode or moment of right, or a particular legitimacy authorizing particular legitimacies, one power of legitimation among others: it is the discourse of the law, the absolute source of all legitimation, the right of right as such and the justice of justice as such, in the reflexive forms of self-representation.

Such a power seems to remain formal, confining its effective powerlessness to the speculative self-representation of a few professors, books with a limited printing, effects of the library, whose light reaches the public space only extenuated through a series of filters and translations. That changes nothing in the structure of this self-representation. Its connection to the historical and political fabric is more complex. Even if this (in)capacity corresponded to the pent-up phantasm of a few experts closeted with their students in a seminar [*séminaire*], an institute, a college, or libraries, what it represents is paradoxically represented elsewhere and differently only by its statutory representatives: everywhere in the socio-historical structure that made this philosophical discourse possible. Since they still correspond to places of the onto-encyclopedia that are organized according to this schema, the ("socio-historical") words and the concepts "society" and "history" still designate things in language that are controlled by the structure we are analyzing. Their relevance is therefore limited in advance. A philosopher as such cannot analyze this structure that constructs him, but by definition no more so can a historian, sociologist, jurist, and so forth, *as such.*

2. *Hyperbole.* I have said that the excess of the question *quid juris* is re-layed. In the form of juridical hegemony, it revives philosophical hyper-boles of a pre-Kantian form: for example, the transcendence of *epekeina tes ousias*, which goes beyond beings (beingness), thus beyond all the re-gions of beings and knowledge, all disciplines, in Plato and Plotinus. Both Heidegger and Levinas, each in his own way, explicitly take on that tradi-tion. Plato speaks of this subject in *The Republic* as *hyperbole.* This excess carries beyond the encyclopedia, that is, beyond the *cycle* of the pedagogy covering the complete circle of knowledge and all the regions of beings (or, in Kant and Husserl, of objectivity: of beings determined as object). Hyperbole is destined at the same time to ensure the entirety of universal knowledge; it overhangs and masters *symbolically* the entirety of what is (in the form of knowledge, theoretical *praxis,* and even an enlightened ethics or politics, that is, ones claiming to be justified by knowledge).

Hyperbole is therefore also a *symbol*—a symbolic order, we could say in another sense—insofar as it brings together and constitutes, configures and maintains, what it exceeds. It makes appear by authorizing *itself.* The subject of this self-authorization institutes itself in this hyper-symbolic. It does not preexist the privilege by which its magistrality or mastery insti-tutes itself without having to appear before anyone whatsoever or account to some preexisting tribunal, only to state in a performative, "I am, I will have been he who I am or will have been." From the moment one autho-rizes *oneself* to pose the question *quid juris* to anyone whatsoever, to any knowledge whatsoever, to any action whatsoever, one can make appear, as before a tribunal that calls [*fait venir*] or summons [*prévenir*] (the de-fendant [*prévenu*] as well as the witness), the totality that pre-cedes [*pré-venue*], or is presupposed, presummoned, of the encyclopedic field as the field of *paideia, skholē,* culture, training, *Bildung, universitas.* The Univer-sity is a possibility, no doubt the major and essential possibility, of this ap-pearing. By right. It is the space of modern society as University, the gen-eral appearing before the truth of the law, of a teachable law, of a law that teaches as encyclopedia. It is totalizable. It is put into perspective from the *telos* of totalization, even if this totalization remains problematic, impos-sible, or forbidden, even if we have to distinguish between a totality (which is inaccessible to experience) and an infinite idea (the "Cartesian" idea of the infinite, on the basis of which Levinas explicitly delimits and critiques totality, the infinite Idea in the Kantian sense, which still plays a decisive role in the transcendental teleology of Husserlian phenomenology), even if the question of the meaning of being is torn from the question of the totality of beings for Heidegger. Even if he demonstrates the impossibility of totalization, even if he denounces the evil of totality or totalitarianism, even if he calls for the question beyond the whole, he is a philosopher who, in the tradition of the *quid juris*, says (something about) the totality of beings, about the *symbolic and hyperbolic, the hyper-symbolic* relation that connects the whole to what lies beyond it and permits one precisely to speak about it, authorizes discourse about it. The philosopher authorizes himself to speak about the whole: and thus about everything.

Such is his mission, such his power proper, what he bequeaths or delegates to himself in addressing it to himself, beyond every other instance. To say of this self-authorization that it defines the autonomous power of the University as philosophy and philosophical concept of philosophy does not mean that this discourse would be offered or implied only in the University, even less in chairs of philosophy. It corresponds to the essence of the dominant discourse in industrial modernity of the Occidental type. That, on the one hand, it deconstructs itself in every respect and according to different modes (the possibility of the hypersymbolic deposes what it posits, destructs by constructing), that, on the other hand, those who can articulate it in its magistral and philosophical form in academic institutions are endowed with so little "real power" changes nothing of the figure and essence of this power. The "truth" of this university discourse pronouncing the law of law is found elsewhere in other forms. We must correct our perception of it and recognize the university site outside the walls of the institution itself: in the allegory or metonymy of the University; in the social body that gives itself this power and this representation.

3. *Learned Ignorance.* A certain nonknowledge is intimately associated with the hypersymbolic excess of this power of critical questioning that summons every field of knowledge to appear and for that reason must remain formal. To translate this necessity into a malicious caricature, one could say that the philosopher authorizes himself to know about everything on the basis of an "I don't want to know." No effective content of positive knowledge in any region of the encyclopedia derives from philosophy. A paradoxical situation whose most concrete effects we sometimes experience. The philosopher gives himself the right (even if he does not always take it, in fact) to incompetence in all the domains of the encyclope-

dia, all the departments of the University. He does this while demanding the right to pronounce the law about the totality of these knowledges and about the essence of knowledge in general, about the meaning of each region of beingness or objectivity. This postulation is common, despite all their differences, to Kant and Husserl, to Hegel and Heidegger (the Heidegger of *Being and Time*, at any rate). Certain philosophers sometimes have a particular knowledge, of course, at least in certain disciplines, and, moreover, always to different degrees. Philosophical training of course necessarily implies a certain education (a scientific one, especially outside of France; in the "humanities"—arts, literature, and the human sciences—especially in France). This poses all kinds of interesting and serious problems but changes nothing of the essential structure of the philosophical position and of the generality of the mechanism. An essential and mandatory incompetence, a structural nonknowledge, constructs the concept of philosophy as metaphysics or the science of science. That does not exclude an impressive scientific competence in certain cases (Kant, Hegel, or others). But this competence is always "historical" in the sense Kant understands it in *The Conflict of the Faculties*: it concerns what one learns from others in the form of results; it is a knowledge that has already been produced and accredited elsewhere, that one can only display or must relate flawlessly. But by rights, precisely, the content of historical and positive knowledge is not required, as shocking as this might appear. It remains external to the philosophical act as such. This exteriority (which poses the enormous problems of the norms of philosophical training) potentializes the power *and* the powerlessness of the philosopher, in his posture armed with a *quid juris*, the powerless power of the modern University as an essentially philosophical place, its vital force and deconstructible precarity, its continuous, interminable, terminable death. Most of the texts collected in this book[52] associate the old theme of our modernity (the suspended death sentence of philosophy) with the historical situation of this privilege.

9. Objectivity, Freedom, Truth, Responsibility

We do not find this dramaturgy only in philosophical institutions, in their glory and agony. It is deployed in the other departments of knowledge in that they must interiorize philosophy's conceptual posture.

Is there a university discipline capable, as such, of knowing such a dramaturgy, of taking it into view, of staging it, of making it the subject of a show, a theme or an objective analysis? Of *judging it* [en connaître] in the double sense of knowledge and competent jurisdiction? The answer to this question is undecidable (as a yes or no) and that is why (1) the question has no critical status, and (2) the schema of what we have just described could not be completely summed up by the thematic visibility or objectivity a stage can offer. It is a question of a paradoxical tropology whose places are never fully exposed. No synopsis, no intuition, no discourse simply *faces* this thing. The knowledge that concerns it (the history or social science of intellectuals, culture, school and university institutions, here, more precisely, the philosophical institution) must at once struggle with this "Kantian" tradition and submit to its axiomatics. The "pragmatic" gesture of this knowledge is necessarily ambiguous, ambivalent, devious. It must at once criticize and overvalue its "object," reinstitute it by deconstituting its genealogy. My own discourse here cannot totally escape the law of that space, even if it at least attempts to let another glimmer filter through or, more precisely, to let itself be infiltrated by a glimmer that already comes from elsewhere and passes through so many cracks.

Work in the disciplines I just named (history or the social sciences) is always necessary, salutary, sometimes very new. I will take from it, as a rough guide and merely to initiate a possible discussion, but one example, the closest and to my mind the most interesting. For the reasons I just indicated, I will give it the name of its institutionalized discipline, although this title is also the name of the problem that interests me here. I want to talk about the "sociology" inaugurated or oriented by Pierre Bourdieu.[53] In what he writes, as in what certain researchers close to him write, references to Kant and the Kantian tradition receive an obvious privilege. One could multiply the signs of this, beginning with *Distinction: A Social Critique of the Judgment of Taste* (*La Distinction: Critique sociale du jugement*). Beyond the general title of the book, which plays upon citing a Kantian title by displacing it and turning it against itself, not without drawing from it, emphasizing it along the way, a stylistic effect and the ambiguous benefit of legitimacy, even beyond the "Postscript" ("Towards a 'Vulgar' Critique of 'Pure' Critiques"—"Eléments pour une critique 'vulgaire' des critiques 'pures'"), the whole book is *also* a sort of explication with Kant. Leaving aside everything necessary and new about this explication, I must confine myself here to a single trait, the interpretation of truth as "objectivity." Whatever all the critiques of Kant, the distance taken with regard to a tradition he inspires and to the social determinations that are displayed, by dissimulating themselves, in it, the very necessity of these operations, their axiomatics, I would even say the philosophical position that maintains the procedures of so-called "objectification," must habilitate or rehabilitate, re-institute the project of Kantian critique, reassume what it begins by assuming. The value of scientific statement, its truth, is in effect determined as "objectivity." Objectivity is interpreted as the "ethical," that is, lucid and *free*[54] relation to what must therefore have the form, place, status, identity, and the visible, reliable, available, and calculable stability of the *object*.

To constitute this objectivity, in the double sense of the attitude of the sociologist and the character, the being-objective, of his objects, what the subjects (for example, philosophers, Kant's heirs or readers) by definition cannot have objectified of their practice, their socio-institutional affiliation, their desire for symbolic power, etc., must be "objectified," constituted as objects. The "objectification of the cultural game"[55] is an imperative of which we are constantly reminded. The unavoidable consequence of the same imperative is clearly and rigorously drawn by Bourdieu himself at the end of *Distinction* (511–512). It is the program or regulating idea of a "complete objectification" also covering "the place" and operations of objectification, that is, here, sociology itself:

> Objectification is only complete when it objectifies the site of objectification, the unseen standpoint, the blind spot of all theories—the intellectual field and its conflicts of interest, in which sometimes, by a necessary accident, an interest in truth is engendered—and also the subtle contributions that it makes to the maintenance of the symbolic order, even through the purely symbolic intention of subversion which is assigned to it in the division of the labour of domination. (511)

We ought to limit ourselves here to what is most schematic. The consideration of the "necessary accident" no longer derives from the principle of reason in its dominant (objectivist and calculating) interpretation. It often marks the gap between deconstruction (the deconstruction, at least, that interests me), on the one hand, and philosophy and the sciences, on the other. Let's remember what we noted along the way about the lot reserved for "hybrid" concepts, "exceptions" and chance (*tukhē, alea*, fortune, etc.).

Two types of hypothesis can be envisaged here. In the hypothesis of a "complete objectification" (including all of objective or objectified sociology, its genealogy, its ethical and scientific axioms, its subjects, interests, institutions, its logico-rhetorical models, its strategy of working toward the

"subversion" but also the "preservation of the symbolic order" while objectifying—as much as possible—such a contradiction, etc.), a "complete objectification," that is, an objectification that has been achieved and is no
longer maintained as a regulating idea, such a consideration should recon-
stitute the metalanguage of an absolute knowledge that would place "sociology" in the place of the great logic and would ensure it absolute, *that is,
philosophical,* hegemony over the multiplicity of the other regions of knowledge, of which sociology would no longer simply be a part. It should find
(as I believe every time I subscribe to its most radical projects) another
name for itself. I do not believe Bourdieu considers this objectification *effectively* possible, even if he appears perfectly justified in doing everything
he can to approach it. And the task is infinite. But (a second type of hypothesis), if the task is infinite, it is not only because there will always be
more to do and because what is spread out as far as the eye can see is the
content of what is to be objectified, in particular concerning objectification
itself (a place and interests, the "habitus" of objectifying "subjects," heritage, all kinds of affiliation, style, methods—language! etc. See the first
hypothesis). The "objectifiable" is not objectifiable, because it always exceeds the scene of visibility. But beyond all the analyses, which cannot but
remain incomplete, the task is infinite for a reason *of another order,* which,
in a certain way, folds or interrupts the homogeneous unfolding of an endless progress—and finishes the infinite. The "necessary accident" that sometimes "engenders" the "interest in truth" can also induce a *supplement of
objectification* that no longer belongs to the order of objectivity, no more,
therefore, than it belongs to that of subjectivity, and leaves room for the
question of the "truth" of objectivity, of the genealogy of the value of objectivity, of the history of the interpretation of the truth as objectivity (a
history that eludes historians as it does all "objectifying" knowledge by definition). And thus leaves room for a new type of question about this very
determination of the infinite task that retains an essential relation with the
process of knowledge as process of objectification.[56]

Put differently, a different question: what if the truth of objectivity no
longer took the form of the object? Of the completeness of objectivity?
And what if the determination of the truth as objectivity called for a history or genealogy that would no longer respond only, simply, before the
tribunal of objective truth and the forms of reason that take it as their rule?
This does not mean abdicating all responsibility—quite the opposite. Nor

renouncing objectivity. What if "the interest in truth," leading one to question the authority of objectivity (not only in a speculative style but in the institutions and "social practices" founded on it), *cor-responded* to a freedom or *answered* for a freer freedom, differently free, than the freedom that reflects objectivity? On what conditions can one then speak of freedom and truth? On what conditions can one answer for them? Despite appearances, these questions are not abstract. Step by step, they traverse everything: history, politics (the idea of democracy), right and morals, science, philosophy, and thinking. It is indeed a question of *knowledge* again, but first of all of knowing how, *without renouncing the classical norms of objectivity and responsibility, without threatening the critical ideal of science and philosophy, and therefore without renouncing knowledge*, one can still pursue this demand for responsibility. How far? Endlessly, to be sure, for the consciousness of a *limited responsibility* is a *"clean conscience"*; but, first of all, to the point of interrogating these classical norms and the authority of this ideal, which amounts to exercising one's right to a sort of "right to respond," at least in the form of "questioning in return" what links responsibility to the response. Then, to the point of asking oneself what founds or rather *engages* the value of critical interrogation that cannot be separated from responsibility. And of knowing how to think the place this knowledge comes from—what one can and must do with it.

July–August 1990

Where a Teaching Body Begins
and How It Ends

(There will be more than one sign of this: these notes were not intended, as the saying goes, for publication.

Nothing, however, ought to keep them sealed. What could be more public, at its origin, and more presentable than a teaching? What could be more exposed than its staging or putting into question, as is the case here? That is why, the first reason, I accepted the proposal to reproduce these notes without the slightest modification.

There must have been other reasons, since I hesitated for a long time. What, in fact, could the fragment (chopped off more or less arbitrarily, as if by a mechanical knife) of a single class mean, the first class, moreover, more than others marked by the inadequacies, approximations, and programmatic generality pronounced before an audience more anonymous and undefined than ever? Why this class rather than another? And why my continuous discourse rather than others, rather than the critical exchanges that followed? Unable to answer these questions, I finally decided that the struggle in which Greph (Groupe de Recherches sur l'Enseignement Philosophique) is involved today[1] made them secondary: Since the proposed class essentially relates to Greph, why not seize (from the sidelines) the opportunity to make better known what is at stake in, and the objectives of, its work?

Another, more serious, objection: Was my participation in this volume compatible with the very intention one can read, at least in part and indirectly, in these notes? Should I be of service to (or make use of) one of the numerous undertakings (here in the immediate form of publishing) that multiply the skirmishes (but without questioning—it hardly matters—all the intentions of all their agents) against the very thing from which they draw their existence and

67

whose alibis they maintain? More precisely, do not collecting names, selecting figures, and displaying titles reveal one of the phenomena of authority (an already solid counter-institution, even if its unity, considered from other angles, must leave one baffled and invite the most circumspect of investigations) necessarily produced by the apparatus that, on the contrary, is to be dislocated? The connections between this apparatus and that of publishing are becoming more and more obvious. They form precisely one of the objects of the work, one of the targets rather, of Greph, which ought to link its activity with that of a research and information group about the publishing machine. Manifest (undisguised), the intention of what you read right here is to call for such activities, on the spot.

But I am simplifying a great deal. I have to be brief. The laws of this field are tricky. We have to begin to challenge them. In short, considering the greatest possible number of givens at my disposal, because the objectives of Greph seem to me to impose this, I prefer in the end to run the risk of posing here (this time from an internal border) spiraling questions that concern the places, scenes, and forces that still permit them to present themselves.

The fragment of this first class opened a sort of counter-seminar of the Centre de Recherches sur l'Enseignement Philosophique (Research Center on the Teaching of Philosophy). Established at the Ecole Normale Supérieure two years ago, this center is by right distinct from Greph, with which, of course, there is no lack of opportunities for exchange.

On the program, for the 1974–75 year, were the following questions:

—What is a teaching body—of philosophy?

—What do "defense" and "philosophy" mean today in the slogan "the defense of philosophy"?

—Ideology and the French ideologues (the analysis of the concept of ideology and of the politico-pedagogical projects of the French Ideologues at the time of the Revolution).)

Here, for example, is not an indifferent place.

One must not forget that. One must (try, first of all, just to see, a discourse without "one must," and not just without an obvious "one must," one that is visible as such, but without a hidden "one must"; I propose to bring these to light in so-called theoretical, indeed trans-ethical discourses, even when they do not claim to be discourses of teaching; at bottom, in the latter, the teaching discourses, the "one must"—the lesson given continuously, from the moment the floor is taken—is perhaps, naively or not, only more declared, which can, in certain conditions, disarm it more quickly), one must therefore avoid naturalizing this place.

Naturalizing always, very nearly at any rate, amounts to neutralizing.

By naturalizing, by affecting to consider as natural what is not and has never been natural, one neutralizes. One neutralizes what? One conceals, rather, in an effect of neutrality, the active intervention of a force and a machinery.

By passing off as natural (and therefore beyond question and transformation) the structures of a pedagogical institution, its forms, norms, visible or invisible constraints, settings, the entire apparatus that we would have called, last year, *parergonal,* and that, appearing to surround it, determines that institution right to the center of its content, and no doubt from the center, one carefully conceals the forces and interests that, without the slightest neutrality, dominate and master—impose themselves upon—the process of teaching from within a heterogeneous and divided agonistic field wracked with constant struggle.

Every institution (I again make use of a word that will have to be subjected to a certain critical reworking), every relation to the institution, then, calls for and, at any rate, implies in advance taking sides in this field: account being taken, effectively taken, of the effective field, taking a position, taking a side.

There is no neutral or natural place in teaching.

Here, for example, is not an indifferent place.

Although in principle a theoretical analysis is not sufficient to do so, becoming effectively "pertinent" only to put on stage and at risk the person who ventures one in practice, to the point of displacing the very place from which he analyzes, although it is therefore insufficient and interminable as such, a consistent (historical, psychoanalytic, politico-economic, etc., and still somehow philosophical) analysis would impose itself to define this here-and-now.

At first glance it appears to be a theater or cinema, a reception hall that has been transformed (for security reasons and for lack of space in the so-called classrooms that were formerly reserved for the small number of students chosen for the Ecole Normale Supérieure). Here, in the Ecole Normale Supérieure, in the place where I, this teaching body that I call mine and that occupies a very specific function in what is called the French philosophical teaching body today, I teach. I say now that I am teaching.

And where for the first time, at least in this direct form, I am getting ready to speak about the teaching of philosophy.

That is to say, where, after approximately fifteen years of experience called "teaching" and twenty-three years as a civil servant, I am only beginning to question, exhibit, and critique systematically. (I am beginning, rather, to begin in this fashion. I am beginning by beginning to do so systematically and effectively: it is the systematic character that is important if one does not want to remain content with verbal alibis, skirmishes, or scrapes that do not affect the system in place. No fairly alert philosopher will ever have neglected these; on the contrary, they make up part of the predominant system, its very code, its relation to itself, its self-critical reproduction—self-critical reproduction forming perhaps the driving force of the tradition and of philosophical conservation, its incessant sublation, along with the art of the question with which it will be discussed below. It is the *systematic* character that is important, as well as its *effectiveness*, which can never come down to the initiative of a single person. And that is why, for the first time, I am here linking my discourse to the group work engaged in under the name Greph.) I am beginning, then, this late, to question, exhibit, and critique systematically—in view of a transformation—the borders of that within which I have given more than one talk.

When I say "this late," this is not (principally, at least) to make a scene or put on a show of self-critique, *mea culpa*, or histrionic guilty conscience. I could justify at length why I abstain from such a gesture. Let us say, to cut things very short, that I have never had a taste for that and I even take it to be a question of taste. When I say "this late," it is rather to begin the analysis *both* of a belatedness that, as we know, is not mine alone, and that therefore cannot be explained only by subjective or individual inadequacies, *and* of a possibility that is not opened by chance today or by the decision of a single person. The belatedness and one's awareness of it, in diverse forms, and the beginning of (theoretical and practical, as the saying goes) work on the teaching of philosophy, all that responds to a certain number of necessities. All that can indeed be analyzed.

But even though what is at issue here, in the last resort, is neither individual mistakes nor merits, neither dogmatic slumber nor personal vigilance, let's not take that as a pretext for dissolving into anonymous neutrality what is, once again, neither neutral nor anonymous.

I have often insisted, as you know, that the Ecole Normale should be neither at the center nor even the origin of the works of Greph. Of course. But we must not omit the in no way fortuitous fact that Greph will at least have appeared to have begun to localize itself here. That constitutes a possibility, a resource to be exploited. It must be analyzed and put to work in all its historico-political scope. But this possibility also introduces its limits. We could cross them only on the (necessary though insufficient) condition of taking account, critically and scientifically, of this barely contestable fact. Without delay or further ado, we will have to keep a rigorous account (a theoretical and practical account, it must be said) of the role that this strange institution still plays and will above all have played in the cultural and philosophical machinery of this country. And whatever the outcome, this role will have been—any denial on this subject would be vain or suspect—very important.

Moreover, to submit that any contribution to the work of Greph will be merely partial or particular, and that I in no way commit or direct that group, should not amount to forgetting or leaving out of analysis (discounting) the fact that, after having announced that I would do so for a long time, I at least appeared to take the initiative, in a seminar I conducted, in forming Greph, and, first of all, in its "Avant-Projet," which is submitted to your discussion.

That is not fortuitous. I do not mention it in order to brand or take over a new institution or counter-institution, but on the contrary to turn over, give back, turn in, submit a very particular effect of my function in this process.

As for what I will call, to be brief, my place or my point of view, it had long been obvious that the work in which I was involved—let's name it algebraically, at the risk of new misunderstandings, the (affirmative) deconstruction of phallogocentrism as philosophy—did not belong simply to the forms of the philosophical institution. This work, by definition, did not limit itself to theoretical, or even cultural or ideological, content. It did not proceed according to the established norms of theoretical activity. In more

than one of its traits and in strategically defined moments, it had to have recourse to a "style" unacceptable to a university reading body (the "allergic"
reactions to it were not long in coming), unacceptable even in places said
to be outside the university. As we know, it is not always in the university
that the "university style" dominates. It sometimes sticks to those who have
left the university, and even people who have never been there. You can see
this from the sidelines. This work, then, tackled the ontological or transcendental subordination of the signifying body in relation to the ideality
of the transcendental signified *and* to the logic of the sign; it tackled the
transcendental authority of the signified as well as the signifier, and therefore that which constitutes the very essence of the philosophical. For a long
time, therefore, it has been necessary (coherent and programmed) that deconstruction not limit itself to the conceptual content of philosophical pedagogy, but that it challenge the philosophical scene, all its institutional
norms and forms, as well as everything that makes them possible.

If it had remained at a simple semantic or conceptual deconstitution,
which it never did except in the eyes of those who profited from their inability to understand it, deconstruction would have formed but a—new—
modality of the internal self-critique of philosophy. It would have risked
reproducing philosophical properness, philosophy's self-relation, the economy of traditional putting into question.

However, in the work that awaits us, we must be suspicious of all forms
of reproduction, all the powerful and subtle resources of reproduction:
among them, if one can still say so, that of a concept of reproduction that
cannot ("simply") be used here without being "expanded" (Marx), that
cannot be expanded without recognizing the contradiction at work in it,
and always heterogeneously, that cannot be analyzed in its essential contradiction without posing, in all its magnitude, the problem of contradiction (or dialectics) as philosopheme. Could an effective deconstruction, in
the "final instance," proceed with such a philosopheme (with something
like a "Marxist philosophy")?

Inversely, if deconstruction had disregarded the principle of the *internal*
destructuration of phallogocentric onto-theology, it would have reproduced, in a politicist, sociologist, historicist, economistic, etc., precipita-
tion, the classic logic of its surroundings. And it would have let itself be
guided, more or less directly, by traditional metaphysical schemes. That, it
seems to me, is what threatens or limits, in essence, the rare and therefore
very precious French works on the teaching of philosophy, whatever the

differences or oppositions linking them. But this reservation—I will try to argue it later by examining it more closely—does not lead me, far from it, to underestimate the importance that books by Nizan or Canivez, Sève or Châtelet, for example, can have in paving the way for such analysis.

Deconstruction—or at least what I have proposed under this name, which indeed is as good as another, but no better—has therefore in principle always concerned the apparatus and function of teaching in general, the apparatus and function of philosophy in particular and par excellence. Without reducing its specificity, I will say that what is underway now is but a stage to be crossed in a systematic journey.

A stage, no doubt. But it encounters a naked (or nearly naked, as befits the gymnastic context) and formidable difficulty, a historical and political test whose principial schema I would now like to point out.

On the one hand: the deconstruction of phallogocentrism as the deconstruction of the onto-theological principle, of metaphysics, of the question "What is?," of the subordination of all the fields of questioning to the onto-encyclopedic instance, and so forth, such a deconstruction tackles the root of the *universitas* [university; totality]: the root of philosophy as teaching, the ultimate unity of the philosophical, of the philosophical discipline or the philosophical university as the basis of every university. The university is philosophy. A university is always the construction of a philosophy. Now it is difficult (but not impossible, I will try to show) to conceive a program of philosophical teaching (as such) and a philosophical institution (as such) that consistently pursue, or indeed survive, a rigorous deconstruction.

But on the other hand: to conclude from a *project* of deconstruction that we are facing the pure and simple, the *immediate* disappearance of philosophy and its teaching, their "death," as one might say with the inanity of those who have not discovered how frequently the dead return—this would be to abandon, once more, the field of struggle to very specific forces. In ways we will have to study, these forces have an interest in installing a properly metaphysical dogmatics—more alive than ever, in the service of forces that have from time immemorial been connected to phallogocentric hegemony—in places that have apparently been deserted by philosophy and that are therefore occupied, preoccupied, by empiricism, technocracy, moralism, or religion (indeed, all of them at the same time). In other words, still remaining within the algebra of this preliminary positioning, to abandon the field under the pretext that one can no longer defend the old machine (a machine that one has even contributed to dismantling) would therefore be to miss the whole point of the deconstructive strategy.

That would mean confining it to a group of *theoretical*—immediate, discursive, and finite—operations.

Even if, as a theoretical and discursive operation privileging the philosophical form of discourses, deconstruction had already attained sufficient preliminary results (which, as should be all too obvious, is far from being certain), this philosophical discourse is itself determined (in fact) by an enormous (social, economic, impulsive, fantasmatic, etc.) organization, by a powerful system of multiple forces and antagonisms. This system is an "object" of deconstruction, but deconstruction is also, in the necessarily determinate forms it must take, *an effect* of it. (See what I say in *Positions* about the word "effect.")[2]

Always incomplete in this sense, and so as not to reduce itself to a modern episode of philosophical reproduction, deconstruction cannot join in a liquidation of philosophy (perhaps triumphant and verbose, or else shamefaced and ever-active), whose political consequences were diagnosed long ago. Nor can it cling to a given "defense-of-philosophy," to a reactionary rearguard struggle to preserve a decomposing body that would only facilitate things for the enterprises of liquidation.

Consequently, fighting as always on two fronts, on two stages, and in two registers, a rigorous and efficient deconstruction should at once develop the (practical) critique of the philosophical institution as it stands *and* undertake a positive, or rather affirmative, audacious, extensive and intensive transformation of a "philosophical" teaching. No longer a new *university design*, in the eschato-teleological style of what was done under this name in the eighteenth and nineteenth centuries, but a completely other type of proposal, deriving from another logic and taking into account a maximum of new data of every kind, which I will not begin to enumerate today. Some of it will come to light soon. These offensive proposals would both start from the theoretical and practical state of deconstruction and also assume very concrete forms, the most efficient ones possible in France, in 1975. I will be sure to take my chances or responsibilities as concerns these proposals. And I will signal as of now that—the name of René Haby[3] being the most glaring sign of this context—I will not enter into alliance with those who intend to "defend-philosophy" as it is practiced today in its French institution, nor will I subscribe to any form whatsoever of combat "for-philosophy"; what interests me is a fundamental transformation in the *general* situation in which these problems are posed.

If I have put forward these first remarks on the possible connection between the works of Greph and an undertaking of deconstruction, this is not only for the reasons just laid out. It is also so as not to neutralize or naturalize the position I occupy in it, so as no longer even to pretend to discount that place, except perhaps on a few occasions, as might sometimes have seemed useful. I would like to reconstruct the logic of that position.

This logic will perhaps introduce us to the question of the teaching body.

Within national education, my professional function links me first and foremost to the Ecole Normale Supérieure, where I occupy, under the title of maître-assistant of the history of philosophy, the position defined since the nineteenth century as that of agrégé-répétiteur. I stop at the word *répétiteur* for a moment to open the question of the teaching body to what forces it into repetition.

A repeater, the agrégé-répétiteur should produce nothing, at least if to produce means to innovate, to transform, to bring about the new. He is destined to repeat and make others repeat, to reproduce and make others reproduce: forms, norms, and a content. He must assist students in the reading and comprehension of texts, help them interpret and understand what is expected of them, what they must respond to at the different stages of testing and selection, from the point of view of the contents or logico-rhetorical organization of their exercises (*explications de texte*, essays, or *leçons*). With his students he must therefore make himself the representative of a system of reproduction. (The system is no doubt complex, traversed by a multiplicity of antagonisms, and relayed by relatively independent micro-systems. It always leaves, because of its movement, a sort of point of derivation [*prise de dérivation*], which its representatives can, under certain conditions, exploit and turn against the system; but this system is at every moment hierarchized and tends constantly to reproduce this hierarchy.) Or rather, he must make himself the expert who, passing for knowing better the demand to which he first had to submit, explains it, translates it, repeats and re-presents it, therefore, to the young candidates. This demand is necessarily that of what dominates in the system. (For the moment let's call it, for the sake of convenience, power, it being understood that it is not simply a question of what is generally supposed under this word, especially not simply of government or the current majority.) The system is represented by the relatively autonomous power of the teaching body, itself appointing the juries of its competitive examinations or theses, its commissions or advisory committees. The repeater passes for an expert in the interpretation of this demand. He must not formulate any other without submitting it through this or that channel for the approval of said power, which can let it pass—or may not, or may choose not to, or may be unable to, or may not wish to be able to do so. In any case, the demand of the dominant power is what the expert agrees, contractually, to represent to the candidates; he helps them satisfy this demand, all of which takes place under a general demand, which includes, of course, the candidates' demand.

Because this field remains a multiplicity of always overdetermined antagonisms in its operation, the drive belt traverses all sorts of resistances, counter-forces, and breakaway or contraband impulses. The most obvious effect of this is a series of dissociations in the practice of the repeaters and candidates: one applies rules in which one no longer believes or no longer believes completely, rules that are even criticized elsewhere, often violently. The candidate asks the repeater to initiate him into a discourse whose form and content appear outdated to one or both of them—outdated for reasons that are very specific and well known, by certain people, or for reasons that belong to a kind of foreign language (living or dead), this being a more or less serious matter depending on the case. In the best of cases, the repeater and the candidate exchange complicit winks and recipes at the same time: "What do I have to say? What can't I say? How should or shouldn't I speak?," and so forth, it being understood that we agree no longer to subscribe to the demand made of us, to the philosophy or the ideology (to put it this way, for the sake of convenience) implied in the demand, no more than we acknowledge the competence of those designated by those in power to judge us, according to modalities and goals that are open to criticism. Let's not limit this situation to "exercises" and explicit preparation for exams or competitive examinations: it is the situation of every discourse offered in the university, from the most conformist to the most contestatory ones, at the Ecole Normale or elsewhere. At the same time, the repeater and the candidate are divided, dissociated, or doubled. The candidate knows that he most often must present a discourse that complies to that demand, but in whose form and content he does not believe. The repeater puts on his official overalls to correct essays and "repeat" lessons, to give technical advice in the name of a jury and canons that in his eyes have been discredited. Like the candidates, he judges severely, for example, a given report by a given jury, and if they happen to send protests to the general inspectors or presidents of the juries, they know from experience that they will simply go unanswered.

In his "seminar," since for several years now the repeaters have been allowed to conduct a seminar in addition and next to the repetition exercises properly speaking, the repeater reproduces the division: he tries to help the "candidates," all the while introducing, like a long stream of contraband, premises that no longer belong to the space of the general agrégation,[4] that even undermine it more or less underhandedly. Such dissociation is so well accepted and interiorized on both sides that I myself have been able to abstain almost totally, in the course of the exercises, and partially, in the course of seminars, from implicating work that I pursue elsewhere and that can be consulted in publications. I act as though this work did not exist, and only those who read me can reconstruct the network that, although concealed, of course unites my teaching and my published texts. Everything in the seminar must, in principle, begin at a fictive zero point of my relation to the audience: as though we were all "complete beginners" the whole time. We will have to return to these two values (repetition and "complete beginners") to seek in them a general law of philosophical exchange, a general permanent law whose phenomena will have been no less differentiated, specific, and irreducible throughout history. This dissociating fiction is indeed accepted, but for a few ruses and detours, by both sides; I have heard it spoken by two students of the Ecole, long ago and of late, whom I cite not for their anecdotal but for their symptomatic value. While he was a student, one of them told me, "I have decided not to read you in order to work unbiased and to simplify our relations." And in fact he seems to have read me after the agrégation, has even cited me in certain of his publications (which are remarkable, by the way), which, he told me, would have caused him trouble with this or that commission before which he still found himself in the position of a candidate. The other, once his education was finished and he was appointed to a position as assistant in a Parisian university, recently told me that he preferred one of my publications to another and asked if I shared his feeling; since I showed some reticence and was unable to grade my own exercises, he concluded in the form of an apology: "You know, I am saying this about them most of all to show you that I now read you." Now, that is to say, now that I am no longer a candidate for the agrégation, now that the space of repetition in which you, repeater, had to reflect a code and a program before me, so that I could reflect them in turn, no longer risks (he believed) becoming distorted.

By program I do not mean only the program that, every spring, rather arbitrarily (at any rate, according to motivations that are never explained and about which no one can demand any justification) picks out an individual subject (for example, the president of a jury), himself selected by a ministerial decision from the teaching body of which he is a member. Neither the teaching body nor, *a fortiori*, the body of candidates can take any initiative for this private selection; and the mystery of the ministerial decision is reproduced in the mystery of co-optation. The place of this mystery, at any rate, can be clearly located: it is one of the points where a nonphilosophical and nonpedagogic power intervenes to determine who (and what) will determine, in a decisive and absolutely authoritarian fashion, the program and the filtering and coding mechanisms of all teaching. Given the centralist and military structure of French National Education, one can see what troop movements are set loose in the university and in publishing (there the connecting mechanisms are a bit more complex, but quite close) by the program planner's slightest quiver. From the moment it inherits such power from the ministry, without any consultation with the teaching body as such, the jury or more generally the control mechanism can put on a show of liberty or liberalism. (Even if it is elected, it is most often only partially so, and it in fact takes into account the results of competitive examinations assessed by an appointed jury.) It is, in fact, subject, whether directly or not, to ideological or political constraint, the real program of power. And therefore, it necessarily *tends* to reproduce that program in essence, reproducing the conditions in which it is exercised and warding off everything that comes to remove that order.

Under the name of program, then, I target not only the program that appears to fall from the sky every year, but a powerful machine with complex works. It is made up of networks of tradition or repetition, which no doubt function according to a particular historical or ideological configuration, and which have perpetuated themselves since the beginnings of sophistry and philosophy. And not only as a sort of fundamental and continuous structure that would support singular phenomena or episodes. In fact, this profound machine, this fundamental program, is reinvested, reinformed, and reemployed in its totality by each specific configuration.

One of the difficulties in analyzing it stems from the fact that deconstruction must not, cannot only, choose between long or barely mobile networks and short and quickly outdated ones, but must display the strange logic by which, in philosophy at least, the multiple powers of the oldest machine can always be reinvested and exploited in a new situation. That is a difficulty, but it is also what makes a *quasi-systematic* deconstruction possible by protecting it against any empiricist light-headedness. These powers are not only logical, rhetorical, and didactic schemas. Nor are they even essentially philosophemes. They are also sociocultural or institutional operators, scenes or trajectories of energy, clashes of force that use all sorts of representatives. Consequently, when I say, in such a trivial formula, that power controls the teaching apparatus, it is not to place power outside the pedagogic scene. (Power is constituted inside pedagogy as an effect of this scene itself, no matter what the political or ideological nature of the power in place around it.) Nor is it to make us think or dream of a teaching without power, free from teaching's own power effects or liberated from all power outside of or higher than itself. That would be an idealist or liberalist representation, with which a teaching body blind to power—the power it is subject to, the power at its disposal in the place where it denounces power—effectively reinforces itself.

This power is rather tricky: ridding itself of its own power is not the easiest thing for a teaching body to do, and the fact that doing so does not completely depend on an "initiative" or "gesture," an "action" (for example, a political one, in the coded sense of the word), is perhaps inherent to the structure of the teaching body I want to decompose here.

Wherever teaching takes place, therefore—and in the philosophical par excellence—there are, within that field, *powers*, representing forces in conflict, dominant or dominated forces, conflicts and contradictions (what I call *effects of différance*). That is why work like that we are undertaking (this is a banality whose experience shows us that we must incessantly be reminded of it) implies a political commitment on the part of all those who participate in it, whatever the complexity of the relays, alliances, and strategic detours. (Our "Avant-Projet"[5] is full of such detours, but it still made some "liberals" flee.)

There could therefore never be *one* teaching body or *one* body of teaching (teaching/taught: we will broaden the syntax of this word, of the corpus taught to the body of disciples): one homogeneous, self-identical body suspending within it the oppositions (for example, the politics) that take place outside it, and sometimes defending PHILOSOPHY IN GENERAL against the aggression of the nonphilosophical from the outside. If there is a struggle regarding philosophy, then, it is bound to have its place inside as well as outside the philosophical "institution." And if something threatened were to be defended, that also would take place inside and outside, the forces of the outside always having their allies or representatives on the inside. And reciprocally. It could well be that the traditional "defenders" of philosophy, those who never have the slightest suspicion regarding the "institution," are the most active agents of its decomposition at the very moment they become indignant when faced with those who cry for the death-of-philosophy. No possibility is ever excluded from the combinatories of "objective alliances" and every step is always a trap.

Defense, body, repetition. The defense of philosophical teaching, the teaching body (exposed, we will see, like a nonbody simulacrum reducing the body taught to a nonbody, or inversely, which amounts to the same thing, a body reducing a body to nothing but a body or a nonbody, etc.), repetition: that is what would have to be brought together in order to keep them together and in sight in their "system" if the task here were to think the whole together and keep it in sight, that is, if one still had to teach.

What is needed? (See *supra.*) (What does an aphorism need to become teaching? And what if the aphorism, like ellipsis, the fragment, the "I say almost nothing and take it back immediately," potentializing the mastery of the whole discourse being held back, placing an embargo on all the continuities and supplements to come, were sometimes the most violent didactic authority?)

One of the reasons for which I insist upon the function of the repeater is that if the word now appears to be reserved for the Ecole Normale, with the backward or old-fashioned air becoming to every self-respecting nobility, the function remains active everywhere today. It is one of the most revealing and essential functions of the philosophical institution. I will read, on this subject, a long paragraph from Canivez's thesis, "Jules Lagneau, professeur et philosophe. Essai sur la condition du professeur de philosophie jusqu'à la fin du XIXe siècle,"[6] one of the two or three works in France that, to my knowledge, take up certain historical problems of the philosophical institution directly. Indispensable material is dealt with there, that is also to say, read, selected, and evaluated according to the system of a philosophy, of a very specific ethic and ideology. We will study these here and will attempt to identify them not only in this or that declared profession of faith, but in the more hidden, subtle, and apparently secondary operations that produce—or contribute powerfully to—the thetic effect of every discourse; the latter, moreover, is a principal thesis for this doctorat d'Etat, which militates for a sort of liberal spiritualism, one that is eclectic in its liberalism, even if it sometimes condemns Cousin's eclecticism. But eclecticism does not exist, of course, at least never as an opening that allows everything to pass through. As its name indicates, it always puts into practice, whether openly or not, choice, filtering, selectivity, election, elitism, and exclusion. The passage I am speaking of describes *the teaching of philosophy in the eighteenth century*, in France: "It must not be forgotten that instruction was accompanied by an education that was religious in inspiration. Pedagogical practice always lags behind mores, no doubt because teaching is more retrospective than prospective" (82).

I interrupt my reading a moment for a first aside.

If "pedagogical practice always lags behind mores," a proposition that perhaps neglects a certain heterogeneity in their relations, but which does not appear, globally, very questionable, then the outdated structure of teaching can always be questioned as repetition. That does not make less necessary any other specific analysis but rather concerns a structural invariant in teaching. It originates in the semiotic structure of teaching, the *practically* semiotic interpretation of the pedagogical relation: Teaching delivers signs. The teaching body produces (shows and puts forward) signs or, more precisely, signifiers supposing the knowledge of a prior signified. In relation to this knowledge, the signifier is structurally second. Every university puts language in this position of belatedness or derivation in relation to meaning or truth. That the signifier—or rather the signifier of signifiers—is now placed in the transcendental position in relation to the system changes nothing: the teaching structure of a language and the semiotic belatedness of a didactics are reproduced insofar as they are given a second wind. Knowledge and power stay on the level of principles. The teaching body, as *organon* of repetition, is as old as the sign and has the history of the sign. It lives from belief (what, then, is belief in this case and on the basis of this situation?) in the transcendental signified. It comes back to life, more and better than ever, with the authority of the signifier of signifiers, that of the transcendental phallus, for example. Which amounts to remembering that a critical history and practical transformation of "philosophy" (one can say here, of the institution of the institution) will have, among their tasks, the practical (that is, effectively decomposing) analysis of the concept of teaching as a process of signifying [*signifiance*].

I return from this aside to Canivez: "Pedagogical practice always lags behind mores, no doubt because teaching is more retrospective than prospective. In an increasingly secularized society, the collèges maintained a tradition in which Catholicism appeared to be an untouchable truth. Such a pedagogy suits a monarchy of divine right, as Vial writes."[7]

I interrupt the citation again. Canivez's remark, and *a fortiori* the Diderot text that will follow, indeed show that the historical and political field could at no time be homogeneous. An irreducible multiplicity of conflicts between dominated/dominating forces immediately wracks the whole field, but also every discourse. Canivez (like Cousin) takes the side of secularism. He also notes the contradiction between a society that was becoming secularized and the pedagogical practice that survived in it for a long time. At this very time Diderot joined with others in a combat that is not yet finished; he also recalled the political motive concealed beneath the religious one or mixed up with it:

> Rollin, the famous Rollin, has no other goal than to make priests or monks, poets or orators: that's what it's really about. . . . It's about giving the sovereign zealous or faithful subjects; giving the empire useful citizens; society educated, honest, and even amiable individuals; the family good husbands and fathers; the republic arts and a few men of great taste; and religion edifying, enlightened, and peaceful ministers. That is no small goal.[8]

At the time Diderot wrote this, the body of teachers of philosophy was far from being, seamlessly and homogeneously, the servile representation of a politico-religious power itself wracked by contradictions. Already in the seventeenth century, in the archives of the proceedings of the University of Paris, one finds accusations against the independence of certain teachers, for example, against those who intended to teach in French (a very important stake that we will have to consider again). In 1737, Canivez recalls, teachers were ordered to dictate their courses. That, by the way, is a rule that is brought back more easily than it is established. Dictating was synonymous with teaching. "A regent could say he had 'dictated' for ten years in a certain collège." The "dictation" of the course repeated a fixed and controlled content, but it was not confused with "repetition" in the narrow sense that we will specify in a moment. Upon arriving in a collège, the teacher had to submit his teaching program to the hierarchy. Such a "prolusion" sometimes took the form of the "inaugural lessons" with which we are still familiar. He also often had to submit all of his course notebooks. Whence the advantage of a more controllable dictation.

> They passed imperceptibly from the reading and study of a text and its commentary to the dictated course and contact with the text became more distant. A course was first the summary of Aristotle's or a scholastic's doctrine, accompanied by a synopsis of his commentary, then became a copying out of the average opinions concerning the content of the philosophical subjects handled by the tradition. Not until the nineteenth century did the programs set questions to be learned, no longer authors to be studied.

We will see what in fact happens in the nineteenth century in this respect. But we should not imagine that the passage to questions radically transforms the pedagogical scene or that the suppression of "dictation" puts an end to all dictation. The program of questions (to be "learned," Canivez says: "question" means "subject" or "theme"), the list of authors, and other efficient mechanisms that we will try to analyze are there to make dictation more subtle, to make it more clandestine and more mysterious in its operation, origin, and powers.

> From the old point of view, that notebooks might have been personal work in any way other than their organization would never have crossed the minds of teachers and their superiors. They were concerned about the errors, awkwardnesses, and novelties the notebooks contained, arising from what was in the air at that time, more than about any attempt to be original. The teacher was the faithful transmitter of a tradition and not a laborer in a philosophy in the making. Often the regents handed down notebooks that had already served their predecessors or that they had composed in their first years of service, neglecting the recent contributions of science.[9]

The person Canivez calls "a laborer in a philosophy in the making," in the margin or outside of the dictating institution of philosophy, is already involved in a precise, pointed criticism of teaching power. This is the case of Condillac. He precedes and inspires most of the critical and pedagogical projects of the Ideologues under the Revolution and after it. We will have to examine all their equivocations. But the end of his course on modern history, by condemning without appeal the philosophical university, already places him in opposition to the institution of scientific academies and expresses regret that the universities do not follow their progress:

> Teaching methods are still suffering from the centuries when they were shaped by ignorance. For the universities are far from having followed the progress of the academies. While the new philosophy is beginning to be introduced in the universities, it is having a lot of trouble getting established, and even then it is allowed to enter only on the condition that it put on the rags of scholasticism. Institutions that were made for the advancement of the sciences can only be applauded. But they would no doubt not have been formed if the universities had been capable of fulfilling this goal. The vices of university studies therefore seem to have been known; however, remedies were not brought about. It is not enough to make good institutions: the bad ones must be destroyed or reformed according to the program of the good ones, even according to a better one, if possible.[10]

The intrainstitutional contradiction is such that the defense of the (university) teaching body ("defense" and "body" are Condillac's words; I will emphasize them) is not made against "the-powers-that-be," against a certain force then provisionally in power and already dislocated on the inside, but against another institution being formed or in progress, a counter-erection representing another force with which "the-powers-that-be" must reckon and negotiate, that is, the academies.

Moreover, the abbé Condillac, preceptor of the prince of Parma, whom he addresses here, condemns this university penetrated by the contraband of the "new philosophy"; he condemns it as *body*, and a body that *defends* itself, a body whose *members* are subjugated to the unity of the body. And he sees a worsening of this phenomenon of the dogmatic body in schools run by religious orders.

> I do not claim that the manner of teaching is as vice-ridden as in the thirteenth century. The scholastics removed some of its flaws, but unwittingly, and as though despite themselves. Caught up in their routine, they are attached to what they conserve; and with the same passion that they were attached to what they abandoned. They fought in the effort to lose nothing: they will fight to *defend* what they have not lost. They do not notice the ground they have been forced to abandon: they do not foresee that they will be forced to abandon more of it. And someone who stubbornly *defends* the remainder of the abuses that survive in the schools would have *defended* things he condemns today just as stubbornly, had he come two centuries earlier.
> The universities are old, and they have all the flaws of age: that is, they are

little made to correct themselves. Can one presume that the professors will give up what they believe they know in order to learn what they are ignorant of? Will they admit that their lessons teach nothing, or teach only things of no use? No. But like schoolchildren, they will continue to go to school to carry out a task. It is enough for them that it gives them something to live on, just as it is enough for their students that this eats up their childhood and youth. The esteem enjoyed by the academies is a thorn in their side. What is more, the members of the academies, who are free and independent, are not obliged to follow blindly the maxims and prejudices of their *body*. If the old are attached to old opinions, the young are ambitious to think better; and it is always they who make the revolutions most beneficial for the progress of the sciences in the academies. The universities have lost much of their esteem; emulation is being lost every day. A good professor is disgusted when he sees himself get mixed up with pedants disdained by the public and when, seeing what he would have to do to distinguish himself, he finds that it would be imprudent to attempt to do so. He would not dare to change entirely the whole scheme of studies, and if he wants to hazard only a few light changes, he is obliged to take the greatest precautions. If the universities have these flaws, what will be the case in schools run by religious orders, that is, by *bodies* that have a way of thinking to which all the members are obliged to submit? (235–36; my emphasis)

I have not cited this long text to play with its currentness, nor merely to note all the lines of cleavage that always, and always in a specific fashion, divide a field of incessant struggle concerning the philosophical institution. But to anticipate a little, Condillac opposes one institution to another, another institutional place (the academies), and he does so in the name of a philosophy that will massively inspire the pedagogico-philosophical projects of both the Revolution and the post-Revolution. (We will see the properly revolutionary episode reduced to almost nothing.) It will therefore be a matter of a central, visible, or dissimulated stake, the entire politico-pedagogical history from the nineteenth century to the present. We will begin to analyze it shortly. Seemingly revolutionary or progressivist in regard to a certain teaching body, Condillac's discourse already represents *another teaching body being formed*, an (ideological) ideology poised to become dominant, as the saying goes, itself destined to ambiguous reversals, to a whole complex and differentiated history, playing at once the role of the breaks and the motor for philosophical critique. In its most formal characteristics, this schema is also current.

To retain but one sign of this ambiguity today, let us not forget that this critique, while supporting the progress of modern academies, belongs to the pedagogical relation of a preceptor to a prince. And, a more lasting characteristic, it reproduces the ideal of self-pedagogy for a virgin body, an ideal that supports a powerful pedagogical tradition and finds its ideal form precisely in the teaching of philosophy: the figure of a young *man* who, at a very specific age, fully grown and yet still a virgin, teaches himself, naturally, philosophy. The body of the master (instructor, intercessor, preceptor, male midwife, repeater) is there only long enough to efface itself. Always withdrawing, the body of a mediator simulating his disappearance in the prince's self-relation, or for the benefit of another essential corpus, which will be at issue later: "It's up to you, my lord, henceforth to instruct yourself all alone. I have already prepared you for this and even accustomed you to it. Now is the time that will decide what you are to be one day. For the best education is not the one we have our preceptors to thank for; it is the one we give ourselves. You perhaps think you have finished; but it is I, my lord, who have finished; and you who are about to begin again" (237).

The repeater effaces himself, repeats his erasure, remarks it by pretending to leave the prince student—who must in turn begin again, spontaneously reengender the cycle of *paideia,* or rather let it engender itself principially as auto-encyclopedia.

Behind "repetition" in the narrow sense, the repetition that Canivez, for example, considers, there is always a scene of repetition analogous to the one I have tried to point out with this reference to Condillac. Canivez regrets that repetition and the repeater are increasingly lacking in current teaching. In the course of an apparently descriptive and neutral historical analysis, he adds, as though in passing, a personal assessment that, together with so many other remarks of this kind, constitutes the ethico-politico-pedagogical system of his thesis.

> To the fundamental exercise that is the course was added, first of all, repetition. Solitary study was avoided. The teacher, the repeater, or a good student, the décurion [or prefect], took up the course with the listener, corrected his mistakes, explained the difficult passages to him. It was a time of personal exchange between them and was particularly fruitful when his virtue was safeguarded and he did not turn to learning by rote or to a disciplinary interrogation. It is one of the exercises that is most lacking in current teaching.

After examining an essay from the university of Douai (1750), he writes, in the well-known style of such reports, "The papers of our high school graduates are not better; they are merely vaguer and not as well constructed."[11]

The repeater or repetition in the narrow sense only represents and determines a general repetition that includes the whole system. The course, that "fundamental exercise," is already a repetition, the dictation of a text that is given or received. It is always already repeated by a teacher before young people of a particular age (the question of age, which seems to me to capture what, to be brief, we call the psychoanalytic and political determinations of the teaching of philosophy, will constantly serve as my guiding thread in the course of the next meetings), by a male teacher, it goes without saying, who is preferably single. The more or less constraining rule of ecclesiastic celibacy, another sign of the sexual scene that will be of interest to us, was maintained, despite the secularization of culture; and you know what Napoleon's views were in this respect:

> There will be no fixed political State if there is no teaching body with fixed principles. . . . A teaching body would exist if all the headmasters, censors, and teachers in the Empire had one or several leaders, as the Jesuits had a superior and provincials. . . . Were it considered important that civil servants and lycée teachers not be married, this could be achieved easily and quickly. . . . All disadvantages could be prevented by making a law of celibacy for all members of the teaching body, except for teachers in special schools and lycées and inspectors. In these places marriage presents no disadvantage. But the directors and teachers in the collèges could not get married without giving up their positions. . . . While not bound by vows, the teaching body would be no less religious. (*Instructions à Fourcroy*)

We find this general repetition (represented by the tutor or the more advanced body of a former student) again in the spirit that defines the function that keeps me occupied here, in this place that is not indifferent. The agrégé-répétiteur was first, and still remains in certain respects, a student staying at the Ecole after the agrégation to help the other students prepare for the exams and competitions by making them repeat, with exercises, advice, a kind of assistance; he assists both the teachers and the students. In this sense, entirely absorbed in his function as mediator within the general repetition, he is also the teacher par excellence. As in the Jesuit schools, the agrégé-répétiteur is in principle a good student who has proved himself and who remains, on the condition that he is single, a boarder at the Ecole for several years, three or four at most, while beginning to prepare his own habilitation (his thesis), to reach the higher body of teaching. That was, very strictly, the definition of the agrégé-répétiteur when I myself was a student in this building. This definition is not completely outdated. A complication affected it a bit, however, when about fifteen years ago the compromise between two antagonistic necessities in France created the body of the maîtres-assistants: civil servants guaranteed (on certain conditions) stability in higher education but without the title or power of professor. Promoted fairly regularly to the rank of maîtres-assistants, agrégés-répétiteurs tend to settle at the Ecole. They are allowed to offer courses and hold seminars on the condition that they still assume the responsibilities of the agrégé-répétiteur. They no longer necessarily live at the Ecole and marry more frequently, which, together with other transformations, changes the nature of their relation to the students.

There is nothing fortuitous—this is the point I wanted to make with this remark—in the fact that the critique of the university institution is most often (all this has only a statistical, tendential, typical value) the initiative of maîtres-assistants, that is, subjects who, blocked or subordinated by the machinery, simply no longer have any interest in conserving it, unlike the highest-ranking teachers, nor the insecurity of dreading it or fear of massive reprisals. In that they are distinct from the assistants, who are dependent and in the position of job applicants, since they can always lose their position. The schema is at least analogous in secondary education (a higher and lower body of permanent teachers, and a body of temporary teachers). The maître-assistant translates a contradiction and a breach in the system. It is always in places of this kind that a front has the greatest chances of establishing itself. And in the analysis that Greph should incessantly pursue regarding its own possibility or necessity, as well as its limits, it will have to consider, among other things, these laws and these types. I only want to point that out.

Here is therefore not a neutral and indifferent place.

In addition to what I have just recalled, this place transforms and dislocates itself. That the majority of you do not belong to the Ecole Normale Supérieure and even, if I am not mistaken, claim to be relatively little attached to it (let's content ourselves with this euphemism) is a first sign of that, one visible here, then, in a cinema or theater hall barely transformed into a seminar room. Here in the Ecole Normale Supérieure, which transforms itself by resisting its own transformation, here in the place where I,

this teaching body that I call mine, a very specific *topos* in the body supposed to teach philosophy in France today, I teach.

In a sort of contraband between the agrégation and Greph.

I say that I am only going to make proposals, which will always be submitted to discussion, that I am going to pose questions, for example, the
question that, apparently via my own initiative, I have put on the program today, that is: "What is a teaching body?"

Of course, anyone can interrupt me, pose their "own" questions, displace or cancel mine. I even ask that they do so, with a barely feigned sin-
cerity. But everything seems organized, does it not, so that I keep the initiative that I have taken or that I had given to me, that I could only take
by submitting to a certain number of complex and systematic normative
demands of a teaching body authorized, by the government, to confer
the title, right, and means of this initiative. In reality the contract to
which I am referring is still more complicated, but it also demands that I
be brief.

When I say I pose questions, I pretend to say nothing that would be a
thesis. I pretend to pose or posit something that at bottom would not pose
or posit itself.[12] Since the question is not, it is believed, a thesis, it would
not pose, impose, or suppose anything. This alleged neutrality, the non-
thetic appearance of a question that is posed without even seeming to *pose
itself*, is what constructs the teaching body.

Of course, even in the barest, most formal, most questioning form itself
(What is? Who? What? : we will identify in them, next time, the recourse
of recourses for institutional erection and counter-erection) there is no
question that is not constrained by a program, informed by a system of
forces, and invested with a battery of determining, selecting, sifting forms.
The question is always *posed* (determined) by someone who, at a given
moment, in a language, a place, etc., represents a program and a strategy
(which is by definition inaccessible to individual and conscious, repre-
sentable control).

Every time the teaching of philosophy is "threatened" in this country,
its traditional "defenders" warn, in order to convince or dissuade, while
reassuring: careful, it is the possibility of a pure questioning, a free, neutral, objective, etc., questioning, that you are going to put into question.

An argument neither forceful nor relevant, which, it should come as no surprise, has never reassured, convinced, or dissuaded anyone.

So, here I am the teaching body.
I—but who?—represent a teaching body, here, in my place, which is not indifferent.

In what way is this a glorious body?

My body is glorious. It gathers all the light. First of all, that of the spotlight above me. Then it is radiant and attracts all eyes. But it is also glorious in that it is no longer simply a body. It is sublimated in the representation of at least one other body, the teaching body of which it should be at once a part and the whole, a member letting the gathering together of the body be seen; a body that in turn produces itself by erasing itself as the barely visible, entirely transparent, representation of both the philosophical and the sociopolitical corpus, the contract between these bodies never being brought to the foreground.

Benefit is derived, always, from this glorious erasure, from the glory of this erasure. It remains to be known by what, by whom, in view of what. Accounting for it is always more difficult than one believes, given the erratic character of a certain remainder. The same goes for all the supplementary benefits derived from the very articulation of these calculations, for example, here, today, by he who says: "I—but who?—represent a teaching body."

His body becomes teaching when, the place of convergence and fascination, it becomes more than a center.

More than a center: a center, a body in the center of a space, is exposed on all sides. On the one hand, it bares its back, lets itself be seen by what it does not see. On the other hand, the excentricity of the teaching body, in traditional topology, permits at once the synoptic surveillance that with its glance covers the field of the body taught—every part of which is indistinguishable and always surrounded—and the withdrawal, the reserve, of the body that does not surrender, offering itself from only one side to the glance that it nonetheless mobilizes with its entire surface. That is well known. Let's not insist. The body becomes teaching and exercises what we will call, even if it means complicating things later, its mastery and magistrality only by playing upon a stratified erasure: in front of (or behind) the global teaching body, in front of (or behind) the corpus taught (here in the sense of philosophical corpus), in front of (or behind) the sociopolitical body.

And we do not *first* understand what a body is in order *then* to know what is at stake in these erasures, submissions, and neutralizations whose effect is to master it: what a philosopher would still call the being or essence of the so-called body "proper" (the answer to the question "What is a body?") will perhaps come into its own (that is, something other) on the basis of this economy of erasure.

This capturing by erasure, this fascinating neutralization, always takes the form of a cadaverization of my body. My body only fascinates while playing dead, the moment when, playing dead, it is erected in the rigidity of the cadaver: stiff but without strength proper. Having no life of its own but only a delegation of life.

I do not name this scene of cadaverizing seduction the simulacrum of *erasure* out of a vague equivalence between the negativity of death and that of a removal of writing. Erasure, here, is indeed, on the one hand, the erosion of a text, a surface, and its textual marks. This erosion is indeed the effect of a suppression *and* a repression, of a reactive bustle. The philosophical as such always takes place there. On the other hand, and at the same time, erasure makes disappear, by sublime annihilation, the particular characteristics of a *facies* and of everything in the face that cannot be reduced to the vocable and audible.

All the rhetorics of this cadaverizing erasure, then, are body-to-body relations.

The bodily effects upon which I am playing—but you understand perfectly well that when *I* say *I*, you already no longer know who is speaking and to whom *I*, an *I*, refers, whether or not it has the signature of a teacher, since I also claim to describe in terms of essence the operation of the anonymous body in transit, teaching—these effects pretend to suppose or make one believe that my body has nothing to do with it: It would exist, would be *here*, only to represent, signify, teach, deliver the signs of at least two other bodies. Which . . .

Appendix

The Groupe de Recherches sur l'Enseignement Philosophique—Greph —was formed during a first general assembly on January 15, 1975. Preparatory meetings had taken place since the preceding year. During the meeting of April 16, 1974, a group of about thirty teachers and students unanimously adopted the "Avant-Projet" below. This document, deliberately open to the broadest possible consensus, accompanied the invitation to the first constituent assembly, an invitation addressed to as many instructors in secondary or higher education and students (in philosophical or nonphilosophical disciplines, in Paris and the provinces) as possible.

Avant-Projet:
For the Founding of a Research Group
on the Teaching of Philosophy

Preliminary work has made clear that it is now possible and necessary to organize a set of research investigations into what relates philosophy to its teaching. This research, which should have both a critical and a practical bearing, would attempt initially to respond to certain questions. We define these questions here, under the rubric of a rough anticipation, with reference to common notions, which are to be discussed. Greph would be, first of all and at least, a place that would make possible the coherent, lasting, and relevant organization of such a discussion.

1. What is the connection between philosophy and teaching in general?

What is teaching in general? What is teaching for philosophy? What is it to teach philosophy? In what way would teaching (a category to be analyzed in the context of the pedagogical, the didactic, the doctrinal, the disciplinary, etc.) be essential to the philosophical operation? How has this essential indissociability of the didactico-philosophical been constituted and differentiated? Is it possible, and under what conditions, to propose a general, critical, and transformative history of its indissociability?

These questions are of great theoretical generality. They obviously demand elaboration. Such would be, precisely, the first work of Greph.

In opening up these questions, it should be possible—let's say, only *for example* and in a very vaguely indicative way—to study:

(a) models of didactic operations legible, with their rhetoric, logic, psychagogy, etc., within *written* discourses (from Plato's dialogues, for example, through Descartes's *Meditations,* Spinoza's *Ethics,* Hegel's *Encyclopedia* or *Lessons,* etc., up to all the so-called philosophical works of modernity, as well as

(b) *pedagogical practices* administered according to rules in fixed places, in public or private *establishments* since the Sophists: for example, the *quaestio* and *disputatio* of the Scholastics, etc., up to the courses and other pedagogical activities instituted today in the colleges, lycées, grade schools, universities, etc. What are the forms and norms of these practices? What effects are sought and obtained from them? Things to be studied here would be, for example: the "dialogue," maieutics, the master/disciple relationship, the question, the quiz, the test, the examination, the competitive exam, the inspection, publication, the frame and programs of discourse, the dissertation, the presentation, the *leçon,* the thesis, the procedures of verification and control, repetition, etc.

These different types of problematics should be articulated together as rigorously as possible.

2. How is the didactico-philosophical inscribed in the so-called instinctual, historical, political, social, and economic fields?

How does it *inscribe itself there,* that is, how does it operate and represent—(to) itself—its inscription, and how is it *inscribed* in its very representation? What are the "general logic" and specific modes of this inscription? Of its normalizing normativity and of its normalized normativity? For example, at the same time as they prescribe a pedagogy indissociable from a philosophy, the academy, the lycée, the Sorbonne, preceptorates of every kind, universities, or royal, imperial, or republican schools of modern times also prescribe, in specific and differentiated ways, a moral and political system that forms at once both the object and the actualized structure of pedagogy. What about this pedagogical effect? How is one to de-limit it, theoretically and practically?

Once again, these indicative questions remain too general. They are above all formulated, by design, according to current representations and therefore must be specified, differentiated, criticized, and transformed. They could in fact lead one to believe that essentially, indeed uniquely, it is a matter of constructing a sort of "critical theory of philosophical doctrinality or disciplinarity," of reproducing the traditional debate that philosophy has regularly opened about its "crisis." This "reproduction" will itself be one of the objects of our work. In fact, Greph should above all participate in the transformative analytics of a "present" situation, questioning and analyzing itself in this analytics and displacing itself from the position of what, in this "situation," makes it possible and necessary. The previous questions should therefore be constantly reworked via these practical motivations. Also, without ever excluding the importance of these problems outside of France, we would first of all insist strongly on the conditions of the teaching of philosophy "here-and-now," in today's France. And in its concrete urgency, in the more or less dissimulated violence of its contradictions, the "here-and-now" would no longer simply be a philosophical object. This is not a restriction of the program, but the condition of Greph's work on its own field of practice and in relation to the following questions:

1. What are the past and present historical conditions of this teaching system?

What about its power? What forces give it this power? What forces limit it? What about its legislation, its juridical and traditional code? Its external and internal norms? Its social and political field? Its relation to other (historical, literary, aesthetic, religious, or scientific, for example) kinds of teaching? To other institutionalized discursive practices (psychoanalysis in general and so-called training analysis in particular—for example, etc.)? From these different points of view, what is the specificity of the didactico-philo-sophical operation? Can laws be produced, analyzed, and tested on objects such as (these are still only empirically accumulated indications), for example: the role of the Ideologues or of a Victor Cousin? Of their philosophy or their political interventions in the French university? The constitution of the philosophy class, the evolution of the figure of the philosophy professor since the nineteenth century, in the lycées, in the khâgne,[13] in the écoles normales, in the university, the Collège de France; the place of the disciple, the student, the candidate; the history and functioning of:

(a) the examinations and competition programs, the form of their tests (the authors present and those excluded, the organization of subjects, themes, and problems, etc.);

(b) the juries, the *inspection générale*, advisory committees, etc.;

(c) the forms and norms for assessment and sanction (grading, ranking, comments, reports on competitions, examinations, and theses, etc.);

(d) so-called research organisms (CNRS, Fondation Thiers, etc.);[14]

(e) research tools (libraries, selected texts, manuals on the history of philosophy or on philosophy in general, their relations with the field of commercial publishing, on the one hand, and with the authorities responsible for public instruction or national education, on the other);

(f) the places of work (the topological structure of the class, the seminar, the lecture hall, etc.);

(g) the recruiting of teachers and their professional hierarchy (the social background and political stances of pupils, students, and teachers, etc.).

2. What are the stakes of the struggles within and around philosophical education, today, in France?

The analysis of this conflictual field implies an interpretation of philosophy in general *and*, consequently, taking stands. It *therefore* calls for action.

Greph could be, at least at first, the well-defined and organized place where

(a) these stands would be declared and debated from the position of *real* informative and critical work;

(b) these actions would be undertaken and explained according to
modalities to be determined by those who would participate in
the research.

Divergences or conflicts will necessarily appear within Greph. The rule
it apparently must impose upon itself at the outset would therefore be the
following:

That positions taken and possible disagreements be able to be formulated freely, and that decisions be made according to modalities decided on
by the majority of those who actually participate in its work. This contract
would be a minimal condition of existence. *At least to the extent* that the
objective of this work can be located only in the philosophical and univer-
sitary space, it must be admitted that the group's practice still derives—*at
least to this extent*—from philosophical critique. To this extent it therefore
excludes dogmatisms and confusionisms, obscurantism and conservatism
in their two complicit and complementary forms: academic chatter and
antiuniversity verbiage. To this extent, to be sure, but only to this extent,
Greph proceeds from a certain inside of the philosophical university in order to de-limit it. It neither can nor wants to deny this, seeing in it, on the
contrary, a condition of efficacy and relevance.

How would Greph organize its work? Here are some initial proposals;
they are also submitted for discussion and transformation.

As of the beginning of the 1974–75 academic year, and regularly thereafter, general debates will take place to prepare, then to discuss and develop, work to come or work under way. Specialized groups, more or less
numerous at the outset, will be formed. That in no way excludes the individual participation of isolated researchers.

As of now, Greph asks all those, in particular instructors and students
of philosophy, who would like to participate in this research (or simply to
be kept informed of it), to come forward and define their projects, proposals, or counterproposals.

An administrative office will undertake to coordinate the group's work
and provide information. It would be desirable, in particular, that Greph
maintain regular and organized relations with all those, whether individuals or groups, who, in the lycées, the écoles normales, or the universities, in
professional, union, or political organizations, feel that these projects interest them.

All of Greph's work and interventions will be circulated: at first, at least, among all the participants and all those who ask for them. Then, at least partially and according to modalities to be provided for, by way of publication (whether collective or individual, signed or not).

For this reason, it is desirable that, whatever the object (formally elaborated research, global or fragmentary documentation, bibliographic or factual information, questions, critiques, diverse proposals), communications within Greph take, whenever possible, a written (preferably typed) and easily reproducible form. As of now (until the election, at the beginning of the university year, of a secretaryship) they can be addressed to the provisional administrative office of Greph, c/o J. Derrida, 45, rue d'Ulm, 75005 Paris.

(This Avant-Projet was approved unanimously at the preparatory meeting of 16 April 1974.)

(During its first General Assembly, Greph defined its modes of operation (statutes). Here are some excerpts:

Modes of Operation of Greph
(Statutes)

Greph, formed on January 15, 1975, takes as its goal to organize a body of research on the connections that exist between philosophy and its teaching. In order to clear up any ambiguity, we specify that:

—We do not think that reflection on the teaching of philosophy is separable from the analysis of the historical and political conditions and functions of the teaching system in general.

—Since there is no theoretical research that does not have practical and political implications, Greph will equally be a place where stands taken regarding the university will be debated and actions undertaken on the basis of real informative and critical work.

—At least to the extent that the objective of our work can be located only within the university institution, it must be admitted that the group's practice still derives from philosophical critique and that Greph is formed from a certain inside of the philosophical university. But this point of departure and immediate locating cannot and must not limit the theoretical and practical field of Greph.

Divergences or conflicts will necessarily appear. Greph seems to have to impose upon itself as a rule that positions and disagreements be able to be

formulated clearly and that decisions be made according to modalities decided on by the majority of its members.

We propose as the basis of belonging to Greph an acknowledgment of
the minimal orientations thus defined and of the structure of operation
proposed below.

From a practical point of view, anyone who identifies himself by filling
out a written request for a subscription to the internal bulletin of Greph
and who receives confirmation of this request will be recognized as a member of Greph.[15]

....

From this date on, Greph will form work and action groups, in Paris and
in the provinces. It will define positions and engage in coordinated conflicts. All the available information on this subject is gathered in an internal bulletin addressed to whomever requests it from the administrative office. Until the month of October 1975, the date on which new statutes[16]
will be proposed in view of a larger and more effective decentralization (the
creation of autonomous and united groups wherever possible; the definition of a new phase of work and of a new phase of conflict, and so forth),
requests for information or memberships, as well as all correspondence,
should be addressed to the provisional address of the administrative office:
45, rue d'Ulm, 75005 Paris.)

The Crisis in the Teaching of Philosophy

The invitation with which you have honored me was accompanied by a proposal. This proposal defined a possible title for a potential paper. Happy to accept this invitation, and for more than one reason, convinced also of the opportuneness of such a proposal, I immediately kept this title and I begin by recalling it: *the crisis in the teaching of philosophy.*

Proposing a title does not merely amount to supposing that I myself am somehow entitled or particularly justified to speak of said "crisis," and to do so in a pertinent manner, which may already appear uncertain or problematic. Let's leave that doubt aside. Proposing such a title involves another presupposition. It implies—by rights—the legitimacy of a *topos.* What is one to understand here by *topos?*

It is, on the one hand, something about which one can and must speak. The crisis in the teaching of philosophy is a subject of discourse or reflection. It is for us a commonplace of analysis, deliberation, theoretical elaboration, even political practice. But it is also, on the other hand, *the* crisis in the teaching of philosophy, something that *takes place,* whose event and location can be determined. (That is at least what the title by rights presupposes, is it not?) We could name *the* crisis, identify it in its (historical, geographical, political, etc.) site, in its essential site, to be sure, and, situating it, we could, in principle, know or precomprehend what we are referring to when we say *the* crisis in *the* teaching of philosophy, using these definite articles to mark the thing's generality and specific precision at the same time

Now, an entire network of contextual traits permits *us,* I think, first of all to say "us" and to agree on an understanding of this statement ("The

Crisis in the Teaching of Philosophy"), which, in fact, is not a statement because it says nothing about said crisis; it has only the structure of a title, which presupposes merely that it makes sense to speak about *that*, said crisis, no matter what we say about it. These contextual traits would be enough for us to relate this title not to *the* crisis in general in the teaching of philosophy *in general*, but to a singular, situated phenomenon that takes place and has its place in a historical or geopolitical area that, at least to a certain point, we share. Hence the relative generality of the title. But we would all be disappointed and convinced we missed the mark if we did not relate our discourse as closely as possible to what takes place *right here*, today. The definite articles (*the* crisis in *the* teaching of philosophy) operate in *this* context, which we are supposed to share, all of us who, by virtue of a contract or consensus itself supposed or produced by our *convention* (in the English sense of the word), gather here to hold an international seminar on *Philosophy and the Development of the Sciences in Africa*. Naturally, the limits of a context are always difficult, indeed impossible, to define, more than ever in a case like this. First of all because things like a crisis, teaching, philosophy, the sciences—and even Africa!—pose problems of the limit, borders, and autonomy, which perhaps make the crisis itself; and then because the effective context of this seminar will be defined, to an extent that is difficult to evaluate, by what will be said here, and by the manner in which the participants will treat their own contract.

I do not multiply these remarks on the structure of reference, the value of contextuality or contract, the definite article in a title, and so forth, to lose you in linguistic or logico-grammatical generalities or to divert into stylistic effects a certain urgency, however we determine it: historically, politically, scientifically, philosophically. On the contrary, I proceed thus to attempt to determine this urgency and to submit to your discussion a few hypotheses on its nature.

To identify more strictly, in its singularity, the urgency that brings us here, I will propose, first, to expose two *alibis*.

Both take the form of a generality, which is not bad in itself, but also of a generality that is empty and destined to avoid the here-and-now that situates us.

First alibi, first generality, first triviality as well: philosophy, some would say, is not only a universal project with no historical, linguistic, and national borders. It is also a project structured continuously by *its own crisis*. Philosophy would always have been the experience of its own crisis; it would always have been lived by questioning itself about its own resources, its own possibility, in the *critical* instance of judging or deciding [*krinein*] on its own meaning, like its survival, and of evaluating itself, of posing itself the question of its rights and legitimacy. From that moment, the movement of self-critique, if it can be put this way, would belong to what is most proper in the philosophical as such. Philosophy would repeat itself and would reproduce its own tradition as the teaching of its own crisis and as the *paideia* of self-critique in general. This *paideia* always goes hand in hand, and there is nothing fortuitous about this, with what I will call, without taking it lightly, an *imperialist* self-confidence of philosophy. Philosophy is an ontology and its *paideia* an encyclopedia. It has the right to define and situate all the *regions* of beings or objectivity. It has no particular object proper because it legislates on objectivity in general. It *dominates*, in a precisely *critical* fashion, all the so-called regional sciences, assigning them their limits and legitimacy. Dominating the field of the so-called regional disciplines and sciences, cultivating it and marking its property lines, the philosophical onto-encyclopedia is at home everywhere, and its self-critical movement is merely the reproduction of its own authority.

This schema is well known. Excuse me for recalling it here. To be introduced to philosophy, to teach philosophy, is often to authenticate this schema. Without disqualifying it as such, without even having the means or the time to discuss it here, I will designate it as an alibi. Why an alibi?

Because we have ceased to live simply in the place where such a crisis was destined to reproduce itself. We have not simply left it—and that is why the schema of this repetition did not, all of a sudden, cease to require us—but we have *exceeded* it in a way; rather, we are exceeded insofar as we would have identified ourselves in this place. For what we today, making use of an old language, call the "crisis of philosophy" already takes part in a completely different historical necessity: where what comes into "crisis" is this very perpetuation of the philosophical as self-critical freedom *and* (they are *the same thing*) as onto-encyclopedic project bound to the *universitas*, as self-repetition through the language of *krinein*, through the possibility of decision, according to a logic of the decidable, in other words, of opposition, whether dialectical or not, whether an idealist or materialist dialectics. The era of deconstruction—and in making use of this word for the sake of economy I name neither a method (even if critical, for deconstruction is not simply a critique), a technique, nor even a *discourse*, whether philosophical, metaphilosophical, or scientific—would be the era in which, throughout all the instances classically identified as the historical, political, economic, psychological, logical, linguistic, and so forth, the authority of philosophy, its at once self-critical and onto-encyclopedic authority, would come to vacillate. And thus, with it, the very concept of "crisis" insofar as it belongs to a logic of opposition and decidability. A crisis of crisis, if you will, but you can see that the two occurrences of the word are merely homonyms here: "crisis" does not have the same meaning twice. When the crisis of crisis concerns the mode of production and reproduction of *the* philosophical as such, of self-critique and the onto-encyclopedic itself, it is naturally also a matter of teaching, of the element in the tradition that in the Occident is called *paideia, skholē, universitas,* and so forth, notions that I do not assimilate to one another and to which I will return in a moment.

I have described here in very abstract terms a situation whose effects besiege us in the most noticeable, everyday way. These effects sometimes appear terrible and implacable, sometimes also terribly liberating and stiflingly new.

Now, there is no doubt nothing fortuitous about the paradoxical synchrony that brings us together here. At a time when, in a no doubt very diverse, very unequal, and unequally thematized fashion, the different European philosophical traditions are being worked over by these deconstructive shakings—which are not the end or the death of philosophy—at this very moment, on this continent that, as the saying goes, *is called* [s'appelle] Africa, peoples, nations, *and* states have to define *practically* (that is, not only according to a conceptual operation of definition but in the concrete and detailed implementation of cultural institutions and pedagogical politics) a new relation to the philosophical. These peoples, nations, and States—these are not necessarily the same thing, and this noncoincidence, as you know, poses formidable problems—must define this new relation after movements of diverse types of decolonization, even in the very process of a decolonization that is under way. What would follow here if the concept of decolonization and, above all, of colonization could have a radical meaning? That this new relation to the philosophical, in order to be neither colonized nor neo-colonized, should not import either the self-repetition of Occidental philosophy or even its crisis or its "models" of crisis, not even its values of property and reappropriation, which have sometimes imposed their strategic necessity on liberation and decolonization movements. The very idea of importation or the opposed motif of nonimportation belongs to the same logic. Hence the extraordinary—

theoretical and practico-political—difficulty: how to do something more and other than overturn and (thus) reappropriate? This—more than critical—difficulty is common to the movements of both deconstruction and decolonization. For I believe—in a word, but without demagogic facileness or conventional deference toward my hosts, but rather as the sort of uprooted African I am, born in Algiers in an environment about which it will always be difficult to say whether it was colonizing or colonized—that between the effectiveness of the deconstructive era and the effectiveness of decolonizations historical concatenation is necessary, irreducible, and thoroughly significant. To say that it is historical is still to qualify this concatenation by drawing on one of the conceptual resources (here, a certain concept of history) that are no longer self-evident. If, like philosophy and the deconstruction of the philosophical, decolonization is interminable, it is because it cannot be effective either as a simple mode of reappropriation or as a simple mode of opposition or overturning. Pushed to its extreme limit, and it is there that it is interminable, it should not import, interiorize, or retain in itself either that which connects the philosophical to another nation, another culture, another State, that is, to their model no less than to their reality (supposing that these dissociations even make sense), or even, consequently, to the model or reality of their crisis, that is, the style of their deconstruction. For there is no *one* deconstruction. There are only singular movements, more or less idiomatic styles, strategies, effects of deconstruction that are heterogeneous from one place to another, from one (historical, national, cultural, linguistic, even "individual") situation to another. This heterogeneity is irreducible and taking account of it is essential to every deconstruction. Here I will very quickly venture a proposal in order to submit it to your discussion.

One of the European aspects of the crisis—if there is one—derives from national differences. That is no doubt a permanent and structural characteristic of Philosophy, of the crisis of Philosophy and of Philosophy[1] as a crisis and unity that is posited only in its critical precariousness. It is also true in Europe, as you know, that national differences do not match up rigorously with linguistic differences, no more so than with state differences. But to this multiplicity, whose interlacing I cannot attempt to disentangle here, correspond philosophical differences that are not limited only to questions of style, method, or even problematic field in the conventional and supposedly external sense of these terms. These differences—for example, between so-called continental and Anglo-Saxon philosophies—are sometimes so serious that the minimal conditions for communication and co-operation are lacking. The minimal contract of a common code is no longer ensured, and when I speak of a code I do not mean only the strictly linguistic element of these rules of exchange. Within a single linguistic area, for example, the anglophone world of Britain or America, the same interference or opacity can prevent philosophical communication and even make one doubt the unity of *the* philosophical, of the concept or project supposed behind the word *philosophy*, which then constantly risks being but a homonymic lure. These two examples (the so-called continental European and Anglo-Saxon idioms) imposed themselves upon me because they intersect, through all sorts of other overdeterminations, with what people would like to identify as the *properly African* givens of our problem, of a problem or problematicity that affects not only this or that content (the teaching of philosophy, philosophy and the development of the sciences, etc.) but also the rigor and unity of the "properly African." Whatever the processes of decolonization, cultural, national, or state constitution or reconstitution, whatever the linguistic strategies and politics of the different countries in Africa in this regard, we will have to consider what comes to pass, what passes or does not pass between these two so-called European areas or politico-philosophical forces. They have been and remain in many respects dominant. However, if the very unity of the philosophical appears this precarious and enigmatic across its differences, national or other, how is this crisis overdetermined in non-European cultural and political areas, ones still marked, however, in one mode or another, by these types of European philosophy? This domination does not necessarily have the easily identifiable form of politico-economic hegemony, whether colonial or neo-colonial. Mastery can, of course, still be exercised through (a) *philosophical language*, in the broadest sense of this word, when the other forms of domination, the most spectacular and coded ones, beat a retreat. Since I assume this essential question of language will not be absent from this seminar, I would like to define, without—for lack of time—premises and proof, what I think can be proposed for your examination and debated during the discussion as the principle of a politics of language in this area. We will no doubt have to avoid a linguisticism or logocentrism that would claim to solve all problems by voluntary decisions concerning *langage, langue*, or discourse. Nonetheless, the position that, making language a transparent medium or extrinsic accident, makes the linguistic secondary is also, paradoxically, a logocentrist position. I will state this principle summarily: *there is no choice*, and the choice that does not exist is not between one language and another, one group of languages and another (with everything a language entails). Every monolingualism and monologism restores mastery or magistrality. It is by *treating* each language *differently*, by *grafting* languages onto one another, by *playing* on the multiplicity of languages and on the multiplicity of codes within every linguistic corpus that we can struggle at once against *colonization* in general, against the colonizing principle in general (and you know that it exerts itself well beyond the zones said to be subjected to colonization), against the domination of language or domination by language. The underlying hypothesis of this statement is that the *unity* of language is always a vested and manipulated simulacrum. There are always language*s* in language and the structural rigor of the system of language is at once a positivist dogma of linguistics and a phenomenon that can be found nowhere. I have attempted to show this elsewhere. All of this is not without political consequences; better, it is a political theme, through and through.

It also traverses the space that relates philosophy to the sciences. On this subject, too, I will have to limit myself to the rough statement of a proposition. This proposition concerns a kind of double bind, a contradictory double postulate, two incompatible and simultaneous demands. Let us begin with the fact that, if every philosophical language retains in itself an irreducible connection to a so-called natural (or mother) language, with scientific language tending, on the contrary, toward a growing formalization, then this polarity organizes and dynamizes a kind of strange front. The growing autonomization of the sciences and of the techno-scientific, the indissociably techno-scientific powers tends, through formalization and, above all, axiomatic self-jurisdiction, to avoid the reappropriation of epistemological instances by all sciences, etc., the authority of the philosophical as the science of sciences, general ontology or absolute logic, onto-encyclopedia. In this way, the sciences at the same time enable a more effective resistance to the monologic political power that is exerted through philosophy and that its national or continental forces can exert. This power is not only exerted through the entire "ideology" (I use this word out of convenience, conscious that it still belongs to what is to be deconstructed here) of a kind of philosophical centralism, of a court of final appeal, and of onto-encyclopedic hegemony; it is also exerted, indissociably, from what connects this hegemonic project to a language or family of European natural languages. To this extent, every formalizing movement (and they always already exist in philosophical language itself, just as there is always still linguistic "naturalness" in scientific languages) develops means to resist onto-encyclopedic hegemony, that is also to say, let us not forget, to resist the state structure and even the concept of the State, which we could show is indissociable, in its history and architecture, from this philosophical hegemony.

But inversely—and this is why I spoke of a double bind and a strange front—the development of the sciences can entail risks against which philosophical critique, in its classic form or in a form more appropriate for detecting the dogmatic philosophemes implicated by so-called scientific discourse, can still be indispensably effective. The development of the sciences *in itself* does not, of course, produce these risks, but what is this self, this *in-itself*? As for the physico-mathematical sciences, techno-economic investment allows itself less and less to be dissociated from the scientific process "itself." What we call the *politics of science* is in this respect no longer a secondary discipline, and there is no development of the sciences that does not immediately put it in play, whether we are conscious of this or not. It is there that a critical vigilance finds a way to exert itself, and it implements instruments of analysis, forms of questioning, problematic schemas that derive from philosophical critique and that assume an expert knowledge of the history of philosophy, as history and combinatory of conceptual possibilities. A State that does not intend to let its scientific policy be held hostage by forces that it is fighting against and that can make gains on the terrain of dogmatism or prescientific obscurantism must train philosophers and extend the field of philosophical analysis in its education programs. This philosophical critique sometimes turns its vigilance against the State itself, whether in the form of state rationality as such or specific and particular forces that have for a time appropriated the power of the State. Hence the trickiness of the problem, of the theoretical problem, and of the strategic problem. It is always difficult to know where the State is.

What I just said about the physico-mathematical sciences holds *a fortiori* for the so-called human sciences, taken one by one or as a group. They offer a privileged ground for ideological investments of the most ingenuous kind, ones that at the same time are the most massively manipulable by (politico-economic or other) forces or interests. The precritical, the prephilosophical, indeed, the prescientific or preepistemological lies in wait for the human sciences as for an easy and precious prey. What here takes the form of *knottiness*, and what gives the knot the structure, once again, of a double bind is that the precritical that holds back or delays the so-called human sciences is often of a philosophical nature: often residues of old philosophemes that are not recognized as such come, more or less coherently, to predetermine the discourse of said sciences. And, of course, the place of the State—which can also be the place of the specific forces it represents at a given moment—is all the more difficult to pinpoint when it is necessary to develop at once the sciences *and* their critical instruments, philosophy *and* the instruments of a philosophical deconstruction.

To respond to the urgency of such a demand, we must no doubt deny ourselves a second *alibi*. It relates, precisely, to the question of the State. And it also takes, at first sight, the form of ahistorical generality. Philosophy has always been, in essence, linked to its teaching, or at least to a *paideia* that at a given moment in history was able to become "*teaching*," in the strict sense that links educative practice to a certain concept or institution of the sign. In any case, philosophy has never been conceived or experienced without this dialectico-pedagogical relation that we today call "teaching." It follows, for the reasons I evoked a moment ago, that the permanent, founding, instituting crisis of philosophy will always have been simultaneously a crisis of the pedagogical. But if we want to situate what takes place *for us, today,* we must no doubt return from the fluctuating generality of this schema to a *stricter* historico-geographical, political, and, in general, epochal determination. Let's put it this way: in *Europe,* the structures of the teaching of philosophy are now being nationalized directly or indirectly. I cannot undertake here the analysis of this process, which dates back to the first half of the nineteenth century. I am simply remarking that it is not by chance that it is contemporary with great colonial enterprises of a new type and that, as far as the French example is concerned, the colonial imposition of pedagogical models set up, at least to some extent (the pedagogy of the Missions that stemmed from prerevolutionary and prestate models is another matter), the state structures being established in France.

Consequently, the specificity of the crises in the teaching of philosophy will always be closely related to this phenomenon of nationalization, either in European States, whatever their nature, or in African States, whether the structures of their nationalization (notably, as concerns school and university mechanisms) remain analogous to European models, deviate from them, or are opposed to them. How the process of nationalization comes to regulate the relations between philosophy and its teaching, between the teaching of philosophy and the teaching of the sciences, of the so-called human sciences and the others, between its "politics-of-science" and its "politics-of-philosophy," and so forth, is a consequence of the question whose necessity, it seems to me, cannot be reduced by asking ourselves about the crisis in the teaching of philosophy. To this degree of great generality, this question seems to me just as valid for "Europe" as for "Africa," proper names I put between quotation marks for the moment for the reasons I mentioned a moment ago. No more so than the unity of (European or African) philosophy do I believe we can trust today the unity of the "properly European" or "properly African" in general. The crisis of the crisis lies there. And if the critique of "ethnophilosophy" seems to me just as legitimate for Europe as for Africa (and truthfully speaking, it reflects a project of reappropriation, as well as a value of the *proper* shared by every philosophy as such), I believe that the radicalization of this critique is necessary. It therefore cannot leave intact any criterion of essential unification or identification, especially not the geographical.

If, therefore, said crisis in the teaching of philosophy always has a profound relation with the paths of nationalization, its forms will vary from one state entity to another, even if this entity is a recent, unstable, or provisional formation.

Clearly, then, I will not speak to you about the crisis in the teaching of philosophy *in Africa itself,* first of all because I would have nothing to tell you about it. Considering the generalities I have just mentioned, I doubt that the "crisis" in Africa has a unity, even unity as a crisis, unless it is linked to the crisis of African unity, which is something else again. Moreover, I have neither the means nor the pretense to teach you anything at all about the diversity of African situations. And finally, the scene of a European or even a Euro-African coming to diagnose a crisis of African teaching before African philosophers, researchers, and teachers seems unbearably laughable.

I will therefore speak to you about something of a completely different sort. If I bring you only a *limited* testimony of my experience of said crisis in France, it will certainly not be to proceed to export a "model" of crisis or of response to a "critical" situation. I will nonetheless select, in this brief presentation, a few characteristics of the French situation whose analysis and discussion, it seems to me, because of a certain network of analogies that I will form by hypothesis, will broaden out to a certain extent beyond France.

Let's consider, first, the spectacular sign of a crisis by nature older and more structural. It is a matter, precisely, of an intervention by the State in its own education apparatus. What has since been called the Haby Reform[2] put in place, beginning in 1975, a whole group of measures meant to lead relatively quickly—the process is already under way—to the quasi-disappearance of philosophical teaching and research in France. I cannot analyze the procedures and expectations of this reform in detail. In many ways, it did nothing but accentuate an already-old politics, and its principal role, as far as philosophy is concerned, was to reduce the teaching of philosophy massively in the lycées, in the class, the Terminale, that was one of the specificities of the French model of secondary education. The explicit and implicit motivations for this reform are numerous and would merit a long analysis. I will limit myself to the following points:

1. The techno-economic necessity—at a certain stage of development and at a certain phase of the market in industrial society—of rerouting a great many students of disciplines considered in France to be "literary" and not scientific. When I say "necessity," I translate the interested *interpretation* of certain technocrats or managers of the system in question and not an objective necessity. The unprofitability of philosophy in this industrial society—its immediate unprofitability—which it would share with all the "humanities," notably history, had for years already justified an active, indeed violent and frenzied orientation of students selected as the "best" toward scientific disciplines in the lycées. Although this "techno-scientist" politics responds to a demand of the capitalist market and sometimes even to a demand formulated expressly by the representatives of French employers, we can reasonably suppose that it would be maintained, essentially, by a management by the so-called "left" of the same techno-industrial society, at least if we take into account the real state of philosophy and the philosophy of education in the traditional parties of the left. Nothing in their programs indicates anything other than secondary reforms in this regard. The fundamental idea of education remains the same. That is why, when Greph—about which I will say a few words in a moment—organized a struggle against the Haby Reform, it was not only by taking positions that were untraditional as regards parties of the left and the unions (even if, here or there, it entered into alliance with them in this or that phase of the struggle), it was also with the conviction that this struggle should continue in what was then the perspective of and hope for the left's coming to power. We knew that then the struggle would be different, perhaps

easier, on new ground, at any rate. But we did not delude ourselves: we would have to continue to fight to avoid the same interpretation, imposed by the constraints of the market, both domestic and global, to avoid falling in line with the education systems of other industrial countries (notably European ones, in the framework of the so-called unity of Europe), to avoid, then, the same interpretation and the same politics imposing themselves under the authority of the "left." These moderate fears were, as we have known for a few months now, still optimistic.[3]

2. Another motivation (this one not admitted) of the Haby Reform: the destruction of the "philosophy class" should stop masses of high school students from exercising philosophical and political critique. Historical critique as well: since the nineteenth century, every time the philosophy class has been threatened in France, the teaching of history has equally been a target, for analogous political reasons. The philosophy class was the only place in which one had the chance to take up theoretical modernity—elements of Marxism and psychoanalysis, for example. Never before, never after, for those who did not specialize in these directions—and who therefore risked being all the fewer in doing so, since they were not introduced to them before their university studies. Moreover, after '68 all the signs of a repressive surveillance against the Terminale, certain of its students, and certain of its teachers were multiplied.

3. When philosophical education was stifled from the lycée on, an ideology and, in the end, implicit but very particular philosophical contents that had insinuated themselves, necessarily, through other teachings were allowed to take hold without critique. These other teachings are above all (not uniquely, but above all) "literary" teachings (language and literature, French and foreign), but also, and this is the point I want to emphasize, the teaching of what are called the "human sciences"—notably the economic and social sciences—which people were simultaneously trying to develop in the lycées. In principle, there is nothing to reproach in such teachings, on the condition that they be given in a critical fashion, that they not be, directly or indirectly, ideological and/or techno-economic imperatives. Everything in the effective and concrete conditions of these teachings, however, leaves one to fear that these so-called human, economic, and social "sciences" are the object of uncritical discourses, ones crammed with very particular ideological contents. And thus also a certain implicit philosophy,

for the front here does not form between philosophy and nonphilosophy, but between specific philosophical practices and contents. The Haby Reform does not represent an antiphilosophy, but rather certain forces linked to a certain philosophical configuration, which, in a historico-political situation, have an interest in favoring this or that institutional structure.

Although it was not formed in response to the project of the Haby Reform, although its "Avant-Projet" (a few passages of which I will be able to read in the course of the discussion) predates that reform, Greph has spread considerably throughout France and has made better known its positions, its program of research and action, in the context of the urgency created by the government plan. Rather than lay out the entire argument that Greph has attempted to advance for several years, it seems to me preferable to define the singular position it took faced with the Haby Reform, precisely at a time when the "crisis" appeared the most urgent and spectacular. For my part, this position seems relatively revealing regarding our whole problematic. Greph opposed simultaneously the forces represented by the government's position—and thus the politics whose aim was the disappearance of the teaching of philosophy—and the forces that seemed to want to defend, in a conservative fashion, the status quo and the Terminale class as it was. In fact, these two apparently antagonistic positions would lead, given the real state of teaching in these Terminales and the general politics of education, to the same consequence: the progressive asphyxia of all teaching of philosophy. The particularity of Greph consisted in demanding not only that philosophy continue to be taught, and not as an option, in the Terminale, but that it be given the right accorded to every other discipline, that is, a progressive and "long" teaching from the "youngest" classes on. That naturally supposed a general reelaboration of its contents, methods, interdisciplinary relations, and so forth. This reelaboration concerns the groups that have been formed within Greph and that bring together lycée and university instructors and students. Naturally, Greph is not only a group for theoretical research. It is also a movement that intends to intervene in the institution, according to specific political modes that are not those of either political parties or unions (our independence in this regard is precious and absolute, even if some of us belong to political and union organizations), nor those of a professional and corporate organization. I could, if you wish, give you more specifics on the texts and arguments concerning what we first called the "progressivity" of this teaching of philosophy. The target of what was at that time, and remains, our slogan is the politico-sexual deadbolt that reserved the access to the teaching of philosophy for seventeen- or eighteen-year-old men, most often belonging to a certain social class and coming to philosophy once the other teachings (notably those of the "humanities" and of the so-called "human" sciences) had played their role of ideological impregnation. Therefore, rather than taking up again our entire argument on this subject (and, one can quickly see, it concerns the whole philosophical tradition and its teaching, since what is at stake in *age* is a kind of general sign), rather than telling you about the struggles and experimentations underway around this slogan, it seems preferable to me here to insist upon the reasons why we very quickly abandoned the word "progressivity" and have replaced it with "extension." It appears to me preferable to insist upon that because it concerns precisely the role of the State in this crisis, no matter which forces claim to serve this State or upon which it claims it relies, even if they are "progressivist" or "left-wing" forces. What is at issue here?

Very quickly, and within Greph itself, a certain equivocation came to light, one linked to the word, if not the thing, called the "progressivity" of the teaching of philosophy. We wondered if spreading the teaching of philosophy over a number of years would not risk leading to its dispersion and empiricist disarticulation; or reiterating traditional teaching by weakening it, by making it more accessible to ideological misappropriations or to its dissolution in nonphilosophical disciplines; or spreading the philosophical *imperium*, indeed, in this or that political situation, the hegemony of this or that philosophy surreptitiously become the official philosophy, the philosophy of the State, given as a dogma throughout students' schooling. In this case, the slogan of progressivity would reproduce and even worsen a situation that we wanted, on the contrary, to transform from top to bottom. To this objection, which we took seriously and which in fact had immediately been considered within Greph, our response was principally the following. No doubt, the value of progressivity derives from the most traditional pedagogy. We should neither greet it as something new nor, above all, "fetishize" it. But in a specific phase of the struggle, it was strategically opportune to demand for the teaching of philosophy the respect of traditional norms that made it legitimate for other disciplines to benefit from a long and "progressive" teaching. Once a legitimate and "natural" extension was acquired, other debates could be developed more easily about the contents and forms of the teachings, their articulations, and the communications between them and with the outside of the academy. Greph's proposals concerning progressivity were all directed at this profound transformation. And I would like to cite here a declaration in which I then expressed, I believe, an essential preoccupation of Greph, and which I submit to your discussion because it seems to me to have a relatively general scope beyond the narrowly French context in which it was formulated:

> Of course if, under the pretext of progressivity, an apprenticeship or even a training (whose ends remain suspect) were reestablished, if the schools were to issue a "training" oriented like a progress toward the harmonious fulfillment of some telos, whatever it be, we would, we will, certainly have to fight against such a reappropriation, whose risk (or security) will always reappear. Other fronts will emerge. But once philosophy is no longer the lot of one class, the broadening of the field will make the work, the critical exchanges, the debates, and the confrontations more effective. This much at least is already certain: to refuse the extension of the teaching of philosophy under the pretext that the motif of "progressivity" does not resolve all the problems and can be reappropriated by what is called the opposing camp is to give credence to a mystifying argument, whether or not it is advanced in good faith. Mystifying and without future, it has been shown.
>
> We must, on the contrary, work from now on to create the conditions for an extension and transformation of so-called philosophical teaching. We must open debates, fashion experiments, join with the greatest number of instructors and students, not only in the "discipline" of philosophy, and not only in school. The process is underway. We have more than one symptom of it. And the ground for struggles to come is already laid out in it.[4]

Since this time, Greph has multiplied its activities and work groups, extended the scope of its first slogans, in particular with regard to what we now call the necessary "delocalization" of the teaching body: mobility, dehierarchization, the circulation of teachers in accordance with new "training" methods. We will be able, if you wish, to return to this during the discussion. What I would simply like to situate, or at least name, if not analyze, before concluding, are the *kinds* of difficulty Greph encounters in its theoretical work and militant activity. Perhaps this typology is not, in its generality, limited to the French scene. The law of this typology is the necessity and sometimes the impossibility of fighting on two fronts, while demultiplying the scope and rhythms of this struggle.

1. On the one hand, we believe we must maintain the *unity* of the discipline of philosophy against all the seductive tropisms of the human sciences (psychoanalysis, sociology, political economics, ethnology, linguistics, lit-

erary semiotics, and so forth), and through this unity maintain the critical force of philosophy and philosophical epistemologies. Instructors in growing numbers would have a tendency to give way to these tropisms and thus to limit the training of students, their training in critical vigilance faced with all the ideological contents, dogmatisms, or precritical philosophemes that constantly lie in wait for the discourse of the social sciences.

But on the other hand, we do not want to accept what is reactive, indeed sometimes obscurantist, in this slogan ("the unity and specificity of the discipline"). It is often put forward by the most legitimate, or, at any rate, the most official, representatives of the institution. We are therefore fighting to maintain concern for the specificity of philosophy, up to a certain point, in the face of a pseudo-scientific, and in fact feebly philosophical dispersion, but also, at the same time, to extend the field of scientificity in teaching, even if it might appear to threaten what certain philosophers represent as the untouchable unity of their discipline. This contradiction or law of the double bind, whose fate I name dryly here, can, as you know, have very concrete effects in our practice. To treat it thoroughly, one would obviously have to deploy a long and powerful discourse on the scientific and the philosophical, on a "crisis" that no doubt exceeds what Husserl wanted to evoke under the title of *The Crisis of European Sciences* or *The Crisis of European Humanity and Philosophy*.[5]

2. In its relations to the State, to everything the State attempts to program in the teaching of philosophy and its relations to scientific teachings and practices, to all the modes of training and reproduction by which the State finalizes the education system, Greph attempts to be as independent, the master of its critiques, its problematic, its grounds for action, as it is in relation to the dominant code of the political, to political parties, union organizations, and corporative associations. Far from being a factor of depoliticization, this (relative) freedom and distance without detachment should allow us to repoliticize things, to transform the dominant political code, and to open to politicization zones of questioning that eluded it for reasons that are always interested and interesting. We do not seek, in the first place, to take up this freedom in relation to a State in general, to the State in itself, but, as precisely as possible, in relation to the specific forces that, dominating the powers of the State at a given moment, dictate—for example—its politics of science and philosophy.

Moreover, inversely, our relation to the State is neither simple nor homogeneous. A certain state rationality seems to us to have been granted to the unity of the philosophical. We do not want to abandon that purely and simply, but to represent the most powerful means of struggling against the class forces or interests (for example) that would profit from empiricism or political anarchism. To be sure. Nonetheless, in its most complete form, state-philosophical rationality (whether we think it in a right- or left-wing Hegelian, Marxist or non-Marxist, etc., fashion) must also remain within reach of (theoretical) questioning or (practical) putting into question.

3. We try not to conceal all the contradictions traversing the reflection and practice of Greph and we believe they are significant. In their most formalized generality, they perhaps all amount to the necessity of renouncing neither a *deconstruction* (of the philosophical, of what links the philosophical to the State, teaching, the sciences, etc.), nor a philosophical *critique* in the most rigorous and effective form in its tradition, today, here, now. Renouncing neither deconstruction nor critique, Greph is split, differentiated, divided according to place, individuals, urgencies, situations. In a way, it has no status [*statut*], no place, and no fixed form. It has indeed had provisional statutes [*statuts*], but the history of these statutes shows nicely that it never could and never wanted to give itself *one* status [*statut*]. It is for the moment, as far as the contradiction I just named is concerned, a rather vague place in which, over the last four years, a minimal consensus for a relatively common practice and, above all, for as vigilant and liberal a debate as possible has been renewed.

As vigilant and liberal a debate as possible was also the promise of this conference. And that is what encouraged me to bring you—like a greeting—this testimony and to speak to you about this place or from this place called Greph. About which I forgot to specify that, as French as it appears, and as confined as it is for the moment within France's borders, ever since its "Avant-Projet" it has indicated that it did not intend to "exclude the scope of these problems outside of France."[6] In fact, more than one work group has tried to consider non-French or non-European problematics and situations, sometimes by working with fellow members of Greph who are not French. They are quite numerous in Europe, North and South America, and especially in Africa, where analogous problems are experienced, which is in no way fortuitous for francophone Africa.

I could try to extend and argue this very limited testimony, if you wish, during our discussions. But I wanted above all to insist on this fact: what I have related or analyzed contained no message. What I have related was not a report on the *state* of philosophy, the teaching of philosophy and of the sciences, addressed to you by a foreign correspondent, not even a report on the rapport between the State and Philosophy. Rather, quite a long preamble (excuse me) to the questions I would like to ask *you*, as well as to the discussion in which I hope to take part. A rather slow way, mine, of preparing to listen to you.

The Age of Hegel

"And if I may be permitted to evoke my own experience . . . I remember having learned, in my twelfth year—destined as I was to enter the theological seminary of my country—Wolff's definitions of the so-called *idea clara* and that, in my fourteenth year, I had assimilated all the figures and rules of syllogism. And I still know them."[1]

And he still knows them.

Hegel in his twelfth year. You can see the scene from here.

And he still knows them. And he remembers, with a suppressed smile, no doubt with a twinkle in his eye (it would be wrong of you to overlook Hegel's sense of humor), that he remembers old Wolff's *idea clara* and all the syllogistic formalities; in short, the whole machine. With the implication: I'm getting off the point; I'm being ironic: I would never say anything like this in my *Greater Logic*. But, perhaps I would, after all, since if there is as much modesty as coyness in my irony, this irony does indeed serve my argument; the seriousness of the concept is not absent for a single moment.

All the same. Hegel in his twelfth year. That doesn't happen every day.

In 1822 he is fifty-two years old. He has all his "major works" behind him, in particular the *Encyclopedia*, and the still very recent *Philosophy of Right* of Berlin,[2] without which the scene you think you are witnessing would be (in its essentials, as he would say) indecipherable.

At the age of fifty-two, he speaks of his twelfth year. He was already a philosopher. But just as everyone is, right? That is, not yet a philosopher since, in view of the corpus of the complete works of his maturity, this *already* will have been a *not yet*.

If we don't think through the conceptual, dialectical, speculative structure of this *already-not-yet*, we will not have understood anything (in its essentials, as he would say) about the *age* (for example, that of Hegel). Or about any age whatsoever, but especially and par excellence that *of* philosophy or *for* philosophy.

All the same, what a scene, this *Ecce homo* in the ministerial mail. It must have packed enough power, however trivial it might seem. For, at the end of the same century, another *Ecce homo*, sufficiently contemporary with Hegel to enter into an endless argument with him, adopts him as its more or less principal adversary.

Under the cover of the *already-not-yet*, autobiographical confiding enlists the anecdote in a demonstration, treating the issue of (the) age as a figure in the phenomenology of spirit, as a moment in the logic. He has opened up the family album to just the right place for the minister, to whom he would—we should add—have spoken a great deal about his private life. To just the right page, but so that no single illustration is detachable from the interminable, continuous philosophical discourse that opens the album and that permeates every image. The scene becomes difficult to envision as soon as we imagine the subtext: "You see, Your Excellency, That's-me-in-my-twelfth-year-between-eleven-and-thirteen-years-that's-me-in-the-photograph-there-in-my-first-connection-with-philosophy-I-read-much-I-was-very-gifted-I-knew-all-that-already-I-was-very-gifted-but-basically-just-like-everyone-else-don't-you-think-besides-it-wasn't-yet-really-philosophy-just-old-Wolff-the-syllogistic-formulas-and-then-an-exercise-of-memory-already-me (that is, Hegel) but-not-yet-Hegel (that is, me), etc."

It seems at first a comic sidelight, a pleasurable bonus, for this false confidence to have been addressed to a Minister. It is part of a report, a "special report," commissioned by the Ministry, by a State bureaucracy in the process of organizing the nationalization of the structures of philosophical education by withdrawing it, based upon a historical compromise, from clerical jurisdiction. We shall have to return to this techno-bureaucratic region of Hegelian reminiscence. It is indispensable if we are to understand the philosopher-civil-servants of today, who no longer address their letters to the prince, the king, the queen, or the empress, but whose reports now and then make their way more or less directly to the upper echelon civil servants formed by the ENA[3] (who, like Hegel's interlocutors, are often more cunning, *ostensibly* more open to "contemporary philosophy" than are the powers-that-be within the University). It is indispensable if we are to understand that the philosopher-civil-servants of today belong to what I call the age of Hegel.

In the *Philosophy of Right* Hegel did not simply propose a theoretical deduction of the modern State and of its bureaucracy. He did not simply comprehend, in his fashion, the role of the training of civil servants and of pedagogical structures when placed in the service of the State. He did not take a merely theoretical interest in the transmission, through instruction, of a philosophy whose rationality was supposed to culminate most universally and most powerfully in the concept of the State, with all the wrinkles, stakes, and convolutions of such a "paradox." Very quickly and very "practically," he found himself implicated, advancing or foundering, more or less speedily, in the techno-bureaucratic space of a highly determined State. And he gave an account of this determination.

But we're getting ahead of ourselves. Let's keep this confidence to ourselves. It is private, since it has to do with a childhood memory confided in a letter by a singular philosopher who remembers, and who remembers his memory—what he learned by heart and still remembers. And yet, this confidence is so little private that it is addressed to the offices of a Ministry, to the technocracy of a State, and to its service, in order to help it put into practice a concept of the State that informs the entire letter.

The Correspondence Between Hegel and Cousin

Twenty-two years later, in France, in a context that, although different in many respects, remains analogous and contiguous, Cousin, too, will confide something to the file. His age will be touched upon. (He was not so precocious: "Without being a particularly slow learner, I studied philosophy at the age of nineteen.") This took place in the House of Peers [Chambre des Pairs], in the famous discourse *La Défense de l'université et de la philosophie* (*The Defense of the University and of Philosophy*).[4] The Peers wanted to abolish the teaching of philosophy in the collèges and professed concern about the effects on young minds of contact with philosophy. The gist of Cousin's reply: On the contrary, since philosophy teaches natural certitudes (for example, the existence of God, the freedom or immortality of the soul), in principle, it is never too early to begin. In other words, as long as the contents of instruction comfort, as it were, the predominant forces, it is best to begin as early as possible. And the contradictory unity that reconciles the predominant force with itself and constitutes the basis of historical compromise is a contract to be worked out between the secular State and religion. Cousin exclaims: "They will object: Are fifteen- and sixteen-year-olds to hear lectures on metaphysics? I reply, yes, of course." Let's put aside for the time being the definition of the young philosopher as a *hearer* and the issue of aural education. Let's focus on the fact that the teaching of *metaphysics* causes the objection of age to be raised, at least apparently so, and insofar as a distinction can be drawn here between metaphysics and dogmatic theology. It remains to be seen how the content of metaphysics is determined. Cousin, who declares himself in favor of its being taught, would seem more audacious than Hegel, who, at the moment he proposes to extend and improve the *preparation* for the study of philosophy offered in the lycées, excludes metaphysics from such a propadeutic. He calls attention to the "higher reasons" that work "to exclude *metaphysics proper from the Gymnasium.*" But once we have analyzed this difference between Hegel and Cousin, we find it to be a mere detail within a fundamental analogy. Cousin's adversaries have nothing against allowing such disciplines as psychology and logic to be taught in the lycée on the same footing as the humanities. But metaphysics—that name given to philosophy "proper"— is more worrisome. Rightly or wrongly, metaphysics seems more slippery [*retorse*], less malleable, "ideologically" less flexible. Which, generally speaking, is neither right nor wrong, but would demand a different analysis of the philosophical stubbornness [*retors*] in this regard. Perhaps this scheme still operates in an *analogous* way today: it is well accepted that young "listeners" should receive instruction in the "human sciences" often related, even annexed, to philosophy, but not in philosophy "proper."

So we have Cousin—who once confided to Hegel that he did not seek a political career but was a truly persecuted liberal (let's not simplify, let's never forget, no more than in Hegel's case), and yet became a *Pair de France*, State Counselor, Director of the Ecole Normale Supérieure, Rector of the University, Minister of Public Education—the very same Cousin addresses his Peers:

> You exclaim, we have fifteen- and sixteen-year-olds hearing metaphysics! And I reply, "Of course, the soul and God at the age of fifteen or sixteen. You seem, furthermore, to take some particular pleasure in the notion that the philosophers in our collèges are fifteen or sixteen years old. Without being a slow learner, I myself took my degree in philosophy at the age of nineteen, and none of my students was younger than eighteen. Don't you think that an eighteen- or nineteen-year-old who has mastered the humanities and rhetoric, as well as

the physical sciences and mathematics, should be capable of understanding a few simple and unambiguous deductions of *natural* truths? (123)

I emphasize *natural*: it is always by insisting upon the "natural," by naturalizing the content or the forms of instruction, that one "inculcates" precisely what one wishes to exempt from criticism. Greph must be particularly careful in this respect, since its tactics could expose it to this risk of naturalist mystification: by demanding that the age at which a young person begins the study of philosophy be lowered, and that the scope of instruction be extended, there is a risk of being understood (without intending it; but the adversary will do his best to further this impression) to be suggesting that once prejudices and "ideologies" have been erased, what will be revealed is the bare truth of an "infant" always already ready to philosophize and *naturally* capable of doing so. The modes of discourse currently held to be the most "subversive" are never entirely free of this naturalism. They always appeal to some sort of return to primitive desire, to the simple lifting of repression, to the unbinding of energy, or to the primary process. Cousin's version of naturalism is—here as elsewhere—immediately theological. The natural truths taught by metaphysics proceed from a divine writing that will have engraved in the soul of the student what the teacher of philosophy need only reveal through self-effacement, like an invisible writing that he allows to appear upon the body of the pupil. Are the discourses of Greph always free from this pattern? Does it not return, necessarily, in a more or less disguised form? Cousin:

> Do you believe that, at the age of eighteen or nineteen, when one has entirely completed one's humanities and rhetoric [premises that Greph has now denounced], when one is studying physics and mathematics, one is incapable of understanding the simple and solid proofs proceeding from the great natural truths! The more necessary these truths are for the moral life of man, the more God wanted them to be available to human reason. He has engraved them in the mind and in the soul with luminous characters, which a skilled teacher [*maître*] must endeavor to reveal rather than obscuring them beneath the hieroglyphs of ambitious science. (Ibid.)

Along stages that are always idiomatic, we are guided back to the most durable tradition of the philosophical concept of teaching: revelation, unveiling, the discovered truth of the "already-there" [*déjà là*] according to the mode of "not-yet" [*pas encore*], a Socrato-Platonic anamnesis sometimes taken up by a neo-Heideggerian philosophy of psychoanalysis. Through-

out these specific determinations may be found, time and again, the same
scheme, the same concept of truth, of the truth of truth linked to the same
pedagogical structure. But the interpretation of these specificities must not
succumb to this determination, as though one had no higher aim than to
uncover the same beneath all variations. One should never settle for this
but also never forget to take the power of the same into account. In the age
of Cousin (which is still ours as well), the question at issue is always, as it
was for Plato, one of a double metaphoric of inscription: a bad writing [*une
mauvaise écriture*], secondary, artificial, cryptic or hieroglyphic, voiceless,
intervenes to cover up good writing [*la bonne écriture*]; it overdetermines,
occults, complicates, perverts, makes a travesty of the natural inscription of
truth in the soul. By effacing himself, the teacher [*maître*] must also promote the unlearning of bad writing. But if this motif retains a certain "Pla-
tonic" allure, the specificity of its "age" is signaled by a profound "Cartesian" reference. My use of its (traditional) philosophical name is a matter of
provisional simplification; ultimately, the specifics do not have a philosophical claim on us. Cousin himself sends us back to Descartes; what is at
stake is an appropriative interpretation of Cartesianism, an attempt both to
confirm that the teaching of philosophy in France must derive from the
Cartesian tradition (since *true* and *French* coincide, natural truth is also national; Descartes *is* France), and also to demonstrate that, contrary to the
allegations of certain adversaries of secular schools and State education,
Descartes is not dangerous: Cartesian doubt, as we all know, remains provisional and methodical; it is not a skeptical doubt. The Commission of
Peers concerned with the business of the law under debate had indeed subscribed to this statement, penned by the Duc de Broglie: "What is the philosophy that is and should be taught in France, not only because its origin
is French, but also because it is really the true and sound philosophy? Most
certainly that of Descartes" (120).

Let us put aside for now the issue of philosophical nationality, its implications, and its effect upon the history of the relative nationalization of
French education since the time of Cousin. We will return to it elsewhere,
so far as it concerns the case of France; here (and later) we will be concerned
with its bearing on the case of the Prussian State. Let's also put aside the
question of the asserted equation of a philosophy that is "really true" and
one that is "sound." For the moment, I wish simply to emphasize the determination of truth as certitude. This constitutes a common ground for
Hegel and Cousin in its philosophical phenomenon. And Cousin needs it,

as a decisive argument to impose his discourse upon the majority of Peers in this hard-fought struggle between two contradictory interests of the then-prevailing force. By insisting upon the value of certitude, we can begin to put the situation into some kind of systematic perspective that would take into account—in order to put it to the test, or take one's distance from it—the basic interpretation of the philosophical "age" as *epochality* (for example, a Heideggerian interpretation that would designate the Cartesian event as one of *certitude*, as a reassuring foundation of subjectivity that becomes the basis of all post-Cartesian metaphysics up to and including Hegel). This *epochal* interpretation, with all its machinery, could be connected (either as proof or as derivation) to the Hegelian, onto-teleological interpretation of the philosophical "age" as moment, form or figure, totality or *pars totalis*, in the history of reason. We could then pose the question whether, in this form or in ancillary ones, such a debate still looms over, perhaps even sheds light on, the problematic of the structures of teaching we have expounded—whether that which we first recognize in terms of its regional determinants (psycho-physiological, technical, political, ideological, and so forth) could be grasped from the perspective of such a debate, or whether it would, instead, force us to transform its premises.

A detour through France before returning to Berlin. We will travel the opposite route another time. Cousin was in the process of citing M. le Duc de Broglie: "This is how M. le Duc de Broglie puts it. If the philosophy taught in the schools of the University is the one that really should be taught there, if it is the sound, the true philosophy, then, it seems to me, all is for the best. How could such a philosophy constitute a dangerous teaching? Because, they say, Cartesian philosophy proceeds from doubt" (ibid.). Cousin goes on to demonstrate, without refinement but with due precision, that provisional doubt is destined to establish the existence of the soul and the existence of God. With confident oratorical skill and political rhetoric—the likes of which has not since been seen in our chambers—he assimilates Descartes with Fénelon and Bossuet. Appropriately so, because if this amalgamation appears unrefined to a historian of philosophy, it is the refinement of *that* historian that is "crude," whenever it blinds him to the nature of the very mechanisms that must be analyzed here. In regard to certain massive effects, in teaching and elsewhere, the difference between Descartes, Fénelon, and Bossuet may be negligible, and may be taken to be so when the situation demands; the texts will always allow it, and as for the alliance (or the alloy) that enables Descartes, Fénelon, and Bossuet to be melted into one, we can judge its reality by the massive effects it produces. And those produced by Cousin's impeccable rhetoric. Here is the "age" that stems from Descartes:

> How could such a philosophy constitute a dangerous teaching? They attribute it to the fact that Cartesian philosophy begins with doubt—provisional doubt to be sure—and proceeds in search, above all, of certainty; it is also because it proclaims the distinction between and the reciprocal independence of philosophy and theology. *These are excellent principles*, says Mr. Chairman [*M. le Rapporteur*]. If they are excellent, it follows that they are simultaneously true and useful; it is, therefore, good to teach them. Please note that I am not the one who introduced the issue of the value of the principles of Cartesian philosophy into a parliamentary debate. I had no intention of turning this assembly into an academy of philosophy. . . . Doubt, even provisional philosophical doubt, is not the true principle of Cartesian philosophy. Descartes' professed intention is to destroy the foundations of skepticism and to prove unshakably the existence of the soul and the existence of God. . . . The principles of Cartesian philosophy are those of Fénelon's *Treatise on the Existence of God* [*Traité de l'existence de Dieu*] and Bossuet's *Treatise on the Knowledge of God and the Self* [*Traité de la connaissance de Dieu et de soi-même*]. The second of these two works was compiled for a pupil [*auditeur*] who wasn't yet fifteen years old, and whom Bossuet was educating to be a man and then a king—and not a philosopher. He also taught the Dauphin logic; his notebooks contain matter enough to intimidate the readers of today. Did Bossuet stop there? No. His aim was to impart to his august, but very youthful pupil not the elementary psychology that mere understanding allots to us, but rather that sound and strong metaphysics that builds on reason and the soul to reach the knowledge of God. But, it will be said, "metaphysics for fifteen- and sixteen-year-olds?" (120–23)

With such a logic of certainty, based on *natural* and *native* grounds— here revealed in the language and history of a philosophy that is both *national* and yet sufficiently natural to be universal—Cousin should have gone back much further than the age of sixteen. Why didn't he? In order to account for this "contradiction" and hence for its "logic," what must be addressed is the problem of ideology, the Ideologues, and the relation between Ideology and the "unchangeable givens with which we must begin," namely, the existence, "in every civilized society," of "two classes of men").[5] For Cousin and Hegel, the question was how to *situate* the connection between, *on the one hand*, a certain problematic of the-age-for-the-teaching-of-philosophy as an allegedly natural state of development of the soul and body, and, *on the other hand,* a certain problematic of the-teaching-of-philosophy in the age of the State, at the moment when new social forces tended to divest the Church of the monopoly on education in order to confer this monopoly upon the State they are in the process of taking over [*arraisonner*]. The concept of the onto-encyclopedic *universitas* is inseparable from a certain concept of the State. In the course of the struggle for the monopoly of public education, Cousin never ceased to reiterate: "If the University is not the State, then [our adversary] is correct. . . . Unless I am mistaken, however, it has been proved that the University is the State, that is to say, public power brought to bear on the instruction of the young. (Objections from numerous ministers and of M. le Vicomte Dubouchage: "That is exactly what we would contest.")"[6]

Cousin had begun, logically enough, by recalling that education is an institution and arguing from the fact that "to teach is not a natural right": the State, he says, has not only the right to oversee teachers, it has the right to confer upon them the power of teaching; and public education as a whole constitutes an enormous social power that the State has the right and the duty not only to oversee, but also, to a certain extent, to direct from above. "The right to teach is neither a natural right of the individual nor a private enterprise; it is a public authority" (6). And in one of those agrégation-reports that Greph will one day have to reassemble into an (incomplete) corpus and then analyze, Cousin in 1850 admonishes: "A professor of philosophy is a functionary of the moral order, appointed by the State for the purpose of cultivating minds and souls by means of the most *reliable* [certains] aspects of the science of philosophy" (my emphasis).

Correspondence between Hegel and Cousin. Between 1822 and 1844, the birth of philosophy into the age of European civil service.

Hegel's discourse on the State presided at this birth, to the extent, at least, that a discourse can be said to preside. This discourse on the State is also, inextricably, an onto-encyclopedic system of the *universitas*. The power of this discursive machine and of the forces it serves no longer needs to be demonstrated. All the blows it has sustained—those inflicted by Marx, Nietzsche, Heidegger, and everything for which these names stand—all these blows, as violent and as *heterogeneous* as they seem, compared to each other as well as in their relations to the Hegelian program, continue to reverberate with it, to justify themselves in its terms, to negotiate within its space, and to risk being overcodified [*surcodé*]—even today—by the interchange into which it forces them. Even to the point, each time, of running the risk of merely reproducing it, with or without the "liberal" modifications we have observed in Hegel and Cousin.

Hegel's Heritage and the Future of His Establishment

Am I reading all this in the image of the child Hegel, in his confidential snapshot ("if I am permitted to evoke my own experience . . . in my twelfth year")? Do we see the scene? No, not yet. This image, which we would be wrong to pounce upon, has been, to a certain point, staged by Hegel. He has it on the end of a string, and the Hegelian manipulation of the performance [*représentation*] always takes place inside a bag full of negatives, among which more than one trick is hidden.

All the same, what a scene. Hegel didn't always eschew autobiographical confidences. In those of his philosophical works that we call "major" (But where are we to situate that letter? How are we to classify it in the hierarchy? Must we indeed accept the very principle of this hierarchy?), it happens from time to time that he tells his story,[7] that he whispers private things into the reader's ear. About Antigone, for example, and the calm he acquires from the awful carnage. These confidences are always required or precipitated by the philosophical necessity of demonstration. Here too, no doubt. But this time, it's the little Georg-Friedrich Wilhelm between the ages of eleven and thirteen.

A few years ago, in Strasbourg, I saw, or think I saw, a photo of Martin wearing short pants. Martin Heidegger. You don't necessarily have to have trembled before Thinking or Philosophy, or to have had masters or pastors who delighted in provoking fear and promoting the delight engendered by fear, to explode in laughter on seeing the short pants of this great man who was defrocked (he too a product, if we can say that, like Hegel, of an unforgettable "Theological Seminary"). There, it wasn't Martin himself who displayed the photograph. Rather, his brother, "the sole brother," as one of Heidegger's dedications reads. The brother played this trick on him with the naive, affectionate mischievousness of someone swelling with pride at having written a little book of family memories—"Heidegger" family memories—but who also has (perhaps) something of a (deadly) grudge against his brother in short pants. In short pants, at an age when one has not yet learned philosophy, much less thinking, there is no difference yet between two sole brothers.

Here, it's Hegel himself who holds up the snapshot (with one finger over the seam of the breeches) for the Minister: this is me between the ages of eleven and thirteen. And he does it in the ripeness of age, at a moment when the philosopher (fifty-two years old) and his philosophy begin to speak of their death, at nightfall. The next month (June 1822), addressing the same ministerial sponsor, with a slight hint of services rendered but consistently with systematic philosophical rigor, Hegel speaks of a "supplementary income," of his children, his death, his widow, and of the insurance he has taken out for the future. To Altenstein:

> Your Excellency was generous enough, on the occasion of my appointment to the University of this city, to nourish my hopes that the development of the projects that Your Excellency envisages for the institutions of learning would afford you the opportunity to open up a new field of activity for me and to augment my future resources. The realization of these benevolent promises is conceivable for me only in connection with Your Excellency's noble plans for the development of knowledge and the education of the young, and I regard the improvement of my own economic situation only as a subordinate element in this totality. Since, however, four and one-half years have passed since my appointment in Berlin, and since various domestic troubles have made my situation difficult, I have recalled Your Excellency's previous favorable statements on my behalf; and Your Excellency's benevolent wishes authorize me to express to you the wishes to which these circumstances have given rise. I did not fail to acknowledge my gratitude when, as a consequence of the duties assigned me at the Royal Examination Commission [to which our letter of 22 April alludes as a legitimizing experience], I received a supplement to my income. But this supplement is already almost entirely exhausted, owing to the fact that, as I approach old age, I am obliged to think of the future of my wife and children—all the more so, since I have devoted all my personal resources to my intellectual development, which I now place at the service of the royal government. My insurance premium for the General Fund for Widows, in order that my heirs may receive 330 thalers per year, in addition to my mandatory contributions to the University Widows' Fund, amounts to an annual expenditure of 170 thalers. I make this sacrifice year after year with two concerns imposing themselves on me: first, that if I do not die a professor of the Royal University, my contributions to the University Widows' Fund will be entirely lost; and second, that because of my insurance at the General Fund for Widows, my future widow and my children may not be able to count on the generous help of His Royal Majesty.[8]

The rest of this letter is worth reading, as is this correspondence as a whole, but note immediately (there could, of course, be only widows and no widowers at a university) the contradiction Hegel confronts with such anguish and which he begs the Minister to help him resolve. This insurance fund for widows at the University already represents a socialization that should give the families of civil servants all necessary security. But since the fate of professors is determined by royal power (Hegel is afraid of not dying a "professor of the Royal University"; he will do everything to die a professor of the Royal University), if Hegel were to lose his job before his death, he would have taken out this insurance for *nothing*: the University Widows' Fund would not pay (since he would not be a member of the University), nor would the King (since he had taken out insurance at the General Fund for Widows). It is acutely necessary to resolve this contradiction between the insufficiently developed rationality of civil society and a State that is still too determined in its particularity. As always, Hegel raises the contradiction to *catastrophic* proportions in view of the best resolution. In order to turn the situation around.

How to avoid taking out a policy at the University fund for nothing? So that, after all, there need never be a widow or children left unprovided for after the death of the Philosopher; which is to say that there need never be a widow or children of the University; for is a widow who can still count on the revenues (the return) of her husband really a widow? Or else, hasn't she always been one? And are children insured against the death of the father (capital or revenue) still children? Or rather, haven't they always been?

Hegel was reassured by Altenstein, the Minister, as early as the following month. By the State. But by a State still conferring special favors and acting by decree, it will be said.

Yes. Nevertheless, this State did help its philosopher, the apologist for its rationality. The philosopher who, at least, conferred the justification of universal form upon the particular forces represented by *this* State, or, rather, upon certain of its fractions. Would it have helped him otherwise? And, conversely, would Hegel have said just anything, would he have renounced the "internal" demands of the system (*Encyclopedia*, the *Logic*, and especially the *Philosophy of Right of Berlin*), of the system at the height of its development, simply for the love of Marie, Karl, or Immanuel Hegel? All that, moreover, for a widow and children about whom he already thinks posthumously and thus with the paradoxical disinterestedness of the dead? How could all these particular interests (family or civil society) be reconciled so neatly with the system of the interests of reason, with the history of the system and the system of history, without a hitch? That is the question.

This unity is not easy to conceive, but we can neither omit any of the pertinent terms, forces, desires, or interests, nor relegate any of them to secondary status. We will return to this.

In satisfying Hegel's demands the month following the letter about the Gymnasium, Altenstein knew whom he was supporting. On 25 June he sent Hegel a letter informing him of what he had procured (travel reimbursements, 300 thalers for the previous year, 300 thalers for the current year, etc.). In order to secure these "extraordinary allotments," he had had to speak to Chancellor Hardenberg in praise of Hegel's philosophy *and* politics, in praise not only of his political philosophy, but of his *political influence*—of his political influence in a difficult situation, in an atmosphere of considerable student unrest. Altenstein knows exactly what *he has to say*, even if what he actually thinks is more complex:

> Certainly I need not expand upon Hegel's merits as a man, a university professor, or a scholar. His scholarly merits are widely recognized. He is undoubtedly the most profound and most solid philosopher in Germany. But his value as a man and as a university professor is even *more important* [my emphasis]. His influence upon the young is infinitely salutary. With courage, seriousness, and competence, he has opposed the pernicious infiltration of a philosophy without depth, and he has dashed the presumptions of the young. His opinions render him worthy of the highest esteem and this fact—combined with his salutary influence—is recognized even by those who have nothing but disdain for anything that has to do with philosophy. (June 6, 1822)[9]

Hegel knows all this. Practically every thread in this skein where "private interests" and the interests of historical reason, special interests and the interests of the State, the interests of a particular state and the universal historical rationality of the State, are so effectively intertwined. He had just recently expounded this in the *Philosophy of Right*. And he knows, at that moment, how his *Philosophy of Right* "had thoroughly scandalized the demagogues."[10] When he thanks Altenstein, the terms of his gratitude serve to define the locus of the exchange and of the contract, the insurance of the one and the assurance of the other:

> As regards subsequent developments in my situation, I must refer myself most respectfully to the sage judgment of Your Excellency with the same spirit of absolute confidence in which I responded to Your Excellency's summons to enter the service of the Royal State. . . . In my work, for which freedom and serenity of mind are particularly necessary, I need not fear being troubled in the future

by extrinsic cares, now that Your Excellency's benevolent promises have relieved me of my worries, and now that manifold and unequivocal evidence has secured for me the reassuring conviction that possible misgivings regarding philosophy on the part of the high authorities of the State—misgivings readily occasioned by false tendencies within philosophy itself—have not only remained foreign to my public activity as a professor, but also that I myself have labored, not without commendation and success, to aid those young people studying here to think properly, and thus to render myself worthy of the confidence of Your Excellency and of the Royal Government. (Berlin, July 3, 1822; 276)

Having taken out all this insurance on the Heirs (of Hegel), on the State (of Prussia), on the University (of Berlin)—he does not forget Bavaria, where he plays the lottery. In July, after having congratulated Niethammer on the budget for public instruction adopted by the Bavarian State Legislature ("the other branches don't concern me"), after informing his correspondent of the disciplinary measures against "demagogic" instructors under consideration in Berlin (a week before dispatching the Letter about the Gymnasium), Hegel continues: "The brilliant state of the Bavarian budget reminds me that I am still in possession of Bavarian lottery tickets, of whose fate I have heard nothing. . . . I take the liberty of attaching a scrap of paper on which I have jotted down their numbers, and would ask your son—since he works in the Department of Finance—to make inquiries in this matter." He then alludes to the difficulty of receiving approval in matters of philosophy, theology, and Christianity: "It is in applying concepts and reason to matters concerning the State that one encounters the most difficulty [in gaining this approbation], but I myself have already made it very clear that I have no desire to ally myself further with our gang of libertarian apostles. But there is no sense in trying to please those who are on the other side, either" (282).

And indeed, if, because of his political behavior as well as his political philosophy, Hegel would seem to uphold the State against a "gang" of "demagogues," this support is conditional, complex, and an entire strategic reserve can make Hegel pass for an enemy in the eyes of those "who are on the other side." We have plenty of signs of this strategic reserve, of the recourse it might find in the system of the philosophy of right, of the concrete effects it had back then in the political arena. For obvious reasons, we will have to limit ourselves, in a moment, to those legible in the "Letter about the Gymnasium."[11]

Ecce homo, that's me between the ages of eleven and thirteen. The man who says this is not simply a mature man, already contemplating death, thinking about the University Widows' Fund, and of a post-Hegelian era (will he ever have thought of anything else?). It is Hegel the philosopher, who is not an adult like any other, one mature man among others. It is a philosopher who presents himself as the first adult philosopher, the first to think the beginning and end of philosophy, truly to think them through conceptually. It is the philosopher of a philosophy that thinks itself [*qui se pense*] as having left childhood behind, that claims to think, along with its own history, all the ages of philosophy, the whole time and teleology of its maturation. And that, therefore, has nothing but childhoods in its past, in particular, childhoods under representation, if representation is, *already without yet being*, "the thought that conceives." Hegel's childhood is thus more serious, more amusing, more singular, singularity itself: not impossible, nor inconceivable, but practically unimaginable. He did everything to render it unimaginable, until the day when—until that nightfall when, anxious about the future of the teaching of philosophy in the State, anxious as well about the future of his widow and his sons, he evokes, for argument's sake, his childhood; he remembers, he says he remembers, that which he already remembered between the ages of eleven and thirteen. For *already* it was but a matter of memory or understanding, not of speculative thought.

The scene seems all the more comical for its absolute lack of braggadocio. Were there even the faintest suspicion of this, it would have to be neutralized, legitimized, and thereby effaced with whatever good reasons we would then invoke. And indeed, the comical element is a result precisely of the *good reasons* with which Hegel can authorize himself to say such things in all modesty. First of all, it is true, he must have been very, very gifted. We have only to read his works—so well known and extremely profound, as Altenstein reminds the Chancellor. And then, we have the additional testimony about that brilliant schoolboy, who read so much and recopied long passages of the things he read. And again, if he offers himself as an example [*pour exemple*] but not as exemplary [*en exemple*]; if he plays with the example the way, elsewhere, he teaches the *Beispiel*,[12] it is in order to render apparent the essence of a possibility: every normally healthy child should be Hegel. At the moment when the old Hegel remembers the child Hegel, but also thinks him and conceives him in his truth, this child Hegel plays, as do all children, no doubt, but plays here the role of a figure or of a moment in the pedagogy of the mind. Moreover, the anecdote serves to support a thesis; it is intended to carry conviction and pave the way for political decisions. It justifies itself, thereby effacing its anecdotal singularity, by invoking an older common experience [*die allgemeine ältere Erfahrung*]. Common experience certifies that this instruction does not exceed the intellectual powers [*Fassungskraft*] of Gymnasium students. Finally, this capacity, to which the little, eleven-year-old Hegel bears witness, is *not yet* a philosophical capacity as such (that is, a speculative capacity) but, rather, memory, the recollection of certain lifeless contents, contents of the Understanding [*entendement*], contents that are forms (definitions, rules, and figures of syllogisms). And this not-yet propagates its effects throughout the letter, throughout the entire pedagogical machinery that Hegel proposes to the Minister. This *not-yet* of the *already*, as we shall see, forbids precisely that which it would seem to promote, namely, the teaching of philosophy in the Gymnasium.

When Hegel says that he still remembers the *idea clara* and syllogistics, we note a mixture of coyness (refinement and play, the put-on puerility of the great mathematician who feigns being astonished that he still remembers his multiplication tables), a certain affected tenderness for the remnants of the child in himself, most of all, a portion of irony in his challenge to pedagogic modernity, "a challenge directed at current prejudices against autonomous thought, productive activity." And what is more current (even today, for the age of Hegel will have lasted that long) than the monotonous pedagogic modernity that takes issue with mechanical memorization, mnemotechnics, in the name of *productive* spontaneity, of initiative, of independent, living self-discovery, etc.? But Hegel's irony is double: He knows that he has, elsewhere, objected to mnemotechnic formalism and learning "by heart." We cannot, therefore, suspect him of being simply and *generally a* partisan of such techniques. It is a question, precisely, of age, of the order and teleology of acquisition, of *progress*. And this progress, from age to age, is not only that of the schoolboy in the Prussian Gymnasium. We discover its stages and its sequence in the history of philosophy. The age of formalism and quantitative technique—the age of Leibniz, for example—is that of "incapable childhood" (*unvermögende Kindheit*), as the *Greater Logic* puts it. But the modernist theme of productive spontaneity remains just as abstract, and hence childish (for the child is more abstract than the adult, like a concept still undetermined), just as empty or incapable as are formalism and mechanical memory insofar as they have not been worked through, sublated. The entire "system" of speculative dialectics organizes this childhood anamnesis to suit the ministerial project—its conformism, respectful and sometimes inane; its irony; its coyness; its imperturbable thoroughness.

I've been somewhat precipitous in foregrounding this scene, removing it from the context of a report that frames it and exceeds it substantially. Why? In order to be a step ahead of impatient readers, in order to anticipate the adversaries of Greph, those for whom Greph is first and foremost a gathering of eccentrics (oh yes) who would teach philosophy at the cradle: some call us destructive and antiphilosophical, while others accuse us of excessive zeal and pan-philosophism at a time when, as everyone knows —for example, since Hegel—that philosophy is finished; which is to say that there is a de facto alliance between these two reactions. Nor will they hesitate to seize on this: now Greph claims to base an argument upon the fact that the great Hegel, between the ages of eleven and thirteen . . . etc. And they'll continue, no doubt: not satisfied simply with invoking the example of Hegel, Greph hopes to Hegelianize children, starting them on the *Greater Logic* or *The Philosophy of Right* in the seventh grade . . ., etc. We are already familiar with such stereotyped objections, with the code of this reaction, which, as always, begins with the fear of comprehending. Of comprehending that we are trying to get at something utterly different, as should already have become manifest and perhaps will become more so. For example, by reading this letter of Hegel's.

I do not want to say how this "minor" text of Hegel's *should be read*— "in itself," in its "proper context," within the scene into which Greph has opted to translate and reproduce it. I do not want to say what *should be made* of this text (a point I make for the sake of those who believe that to read is, immediately, to do; or for those who are equally certain that to read is not to do, not even to write; both are caught up in those oppositions—in the form of conceptual guardrails [*gardefous*]—whose practices, finality, and directions for use are familiar by now). I do not want to say *what is needed*, nor, of course, what is needed *according* to Greph. For in writing I am also addressing Greph, as, I presume, we all are here. From the outset, Greph has defined itself as a locus of work and debate, and not as a center for the broadcasting of slogans or doctrinaire messages. When we do reach agreement—in order to take a stance, to take political initiative, and to undertake appropriate actions—Greph will no doubt not shrink from "slogans," which it does not consider *simply* to be the opposite of the concept: there is something of the slogan in every concept, and vice versa. Certainly, there was an initial agreement about the conditions of such a debate, about the new objects (excluded until now) that must be brought to light; about the old objects that must be seen in a new light; about a certain number of forces that must be combated. And this consensus still exists. But so does the initial openness [*ouverture*] of the debate. It is in order to take part in such a debate—keeping in mind certain common assumptions—that I would like to develop certain hypotheses and advance certain propositions, using, as my point of departure, an applied reading that might, for the moment, interest no one but myself. What is to be done with this letter of Hegel's? Where is it to be situated? Where does it take place? Evaluation is inevitable: is it a "major" text or a "minor" one? Is it a "philosophical" text? What status, as they say, do we grant it? What title? One of the tasks of Greph could be a (not only formal, but effective and concrete) critique of all the existing hierarchies, of all the criteriology, implicit or explicit, that secures certain evaluations and classifications ("major" or "minor" texts). Further: a general reelaboration of the entire problematic of hierarchies. Without this reelaboration, no profound transformation will be possible. The force that dominates the process of classification and hierarchization allows us to read whatever it is interested in having us read (which it then labels major texts, or texts of "great import"), and it renders inaccessible whatever it is interested in underestimating, which in general it *cannot read* (describing such texts as minor or marginal). This holds true for the discourse of the educator and for all his evaluatory procedures (grading; juries for examinations, competitions, theses; so-called supervisory committees; etc.); it is the evaluative standard determining all discourse: from that of the critic and the upholder of tradition to that determining editorial policy, the commercialization of texts, etc. Once again, it is not simply a matter of texts in print or on blackboards, but rather of a general textuality without which there is no understanding and no action. Reread the "Avant-Projet" of Greph: every sentence demands that the censured or devalued be displayed, that the vast holdings of a more-or-less forbidden library be exhumed from the cellars. And that there be a lack of respect for prevailing evaluations: not simply in order to indulge certain perverse bibliophilic pleasures (on the other hand, why not?); nor even in order better to understand what links *philosophy* to *its* institution, to its institutional "underside" and "recesses" [*dessous et envers*]; but rather to transform the very conditions of our effective intervention in them. "Underside" and "recesses," because it is not a matter of discovering today, belatedly, what has been known all along: that there is such a thing as a philosophical institution. Indeed, "Philosophy" [*"la" philosophie*] has always had a dominant concept to take this into account, and *institution* is at bottom the name it has reserved for this task. "Underside" or "recesses," because we are not satisfied with what the institution reveals about itself: neither with what we can perceive empirically, nor with what we can conceive according to the law of the philosophical concept. "Underside" or "recesses" would no longer have a signification dominated by the philosophical opposition that continues to order discourse in terms of a concealed substance or essence of the institution, hidden beneath its accidents, circumstances, phenomena, or superstructures. "Underside" and "recesses" would designate, rather, that which, while still being situated within this venerable (conceptual *and* metaphoric) topos, might begin to extricate itself from this opposition and to constitute it in a new manner.

The critical reelaboration of this hierarchy and of this problematics of hierarchy must not be restricted to new "theorems" in the same language [*langage*]. It requires that we also write in a language [*langue*] and that we operate (practically) according to schemes that can no longer be determined by the old divisions.

This is why the *overturning* [renversement] of the authorized hierarchy is no longer enough. This is why it is no longer enough to canonize "minor" texts or to exclude, and thereby devalue, "major" texts. The *same* philosophical program can lead to evaluative or classificatory statements that seem contradictory: this text is a "minor" text (for example: circumstantial, "journalistic," empirico-anecdotal, feebly philosophical); or the *same* text is a "major" text (addressing a "great" philosophical theme, engaging the great problematic tradition, manifesting all the signs of a profound theoretical responsibility). But are these statements contradictory? If the *same* premises lead to evaluations that are apparently contradictory, what does this tell us about the system of reading and hierarchization at work? If this system of reading has an essential rapport with "Hegelian philosophy," with everything this philosophy seems to collect, complete, configure into its "age," then the "letter" in which we are interested can no longer be a mere example, a case in point evoked to illustrate this question.

Hegel's Letter on the Gymnasium has, quite obviously, been treated as a minor text. And not only in France. The letter does not belong to the "textbook" corpus of Hegel. It was not vouchsafed a place in the corre-

spondence. Even if we don't allege deliberate censorship or willful exclusion, how are we to believe this "omission" is fortuitous or insignificant?
But its necessity is the complicated product of factors that cannot be analyzed until we acknowledge the traditional marginalization [*minorisation*]
of texts of this kind and of the entire system in which this takes place, as
well as the complicated strategy involved in the relations between Hegel
and royal power. This extreme (philosophico-political) complexity makes
any attempt to situate this gesture in a particular, determinate context
both difficult and ambiguous. And this holds true in our case—that of
Greph today.

If this "special report" has more or less disappeared from the great circulation of "canonized" texts, can this be explained entirely by reasons re-
lating to its "form"? It is, first of all, a letter. Of course, there is a venerable tradition of philosophical letters. But of what does this tradition
consist and what does it preserve? Either "fictive" letters on topics that
tradition has sanctioned as great philosophical themes, or correspondence
between philosophers, at least one of whom must be considered "great,"
which treats subjects worthy of the great philosophical vein. Or perhaps
letters written by a "great philosopher" to some worldly dignitary: the
custodian of public power receives a philosophical message from a subject
who is a philosopher (even if he is a foreigner, he occupies the position of
the respectful subject of the King, Queen, Princess, or, we might say, the
Prince-in-General) on a subject already designated as philosophical. Or,
on a topic of grand political philosophy, which amounts to the same thing.
However, until the age of Hegel, questions pertaining to schooling or to
the university were not located in the domain of grand politics [*la grande
politique*]. The question of education is not yet the business of a State occupied with reclaiming power from the forces of feudalism. (The Altenstein episode is, in this respect, a transition of extreme historical complexity and considerable symptomatic value: although we cannot do so
here, one would have to analyze it as closely and minutely as possible in
order even to begin to "open up" this letter of Hegel's.) In the "great" tradition of philosophical letters, the great addressee is assumed to be a philosopher or a philosophical power; the great philosopher speaks to him in
the manner of an adult tutor. With the respect owed to a Prince by a subject, but with the authority of a subject who is a philosopher—educated,
mature—a sort of specialized technician. Double dissymmetry. But the
report (and rapport) is a double one and, at any rate, education is not

raised here as a political issue, nor is the teaching of philosophy seen as a problem of the State.

Besides these great philosophical letters, there are the private correspondences of the great philosophers: they are published because of their biographical-anecdotal interest and only insofar as they illuminate the lives of philosophers who have been granted admission to the Pantheon of Western Metaphysics. They are usually read as if they were novels or memoirs.

The tradition, as we have described it, cannot find a place for Hegel's "letter." It is not really a "letter," although it bears all the external characteristics of one. It is addressed less to a person than to a function. It is a report [*rapport*] commissioned by a Ministry: commissioned by a very particular Ministry and a very particular Minister in a situation that is very difficult to analyze, even today, in a situation whose political interpretation is immediately and necessarily relevant to the fundamental stakes of all the political struggles in Europe during the nineteenth and twentieth centuries. And in a situation in which Hegel's place cannot really be determined without the *simultaneous* and *structural* cognizance of an entire general textuality, consisting at *least* of: (1) his "great" philosophical works, the most obvious being the entire *Philosophy of Right*, which is to say, at least that which Jacques d'Hondt calls the "three" philosophies of right;[13] (2) his other writings, that is, *at least* all his letters, even the secret ones, those he kept out of the hands of the police in order to communicate with certain people the police were pursuing; (3) his actual practice in all the complexity that has always been more or less evident, but which, as we know better now, cannot be reduced (far from it) during the Berlin period to that of an official and respectful, indeed, obsequious State philosopher.

Interpreting the age of Hegel involves keeping in mind this boundless textuality, in an effort to determine the specific configuration that interests us here: the moment at which systematic philosophy—in the process of becoming philosophy of the State, of Reason as the State—begins to entail, more or less obviously, but essentially, indispensably, a pedagogical systematics governed by the necessity of entrusting the teaching of philosophy to state structures and civil servants. The business most certainly began before Hegel. The philosophical-pedagogic interventions of the French Ideologues at the time of the Revolution are signs of it, and we know the significance the French Revolution held for Hegel. But can we not date from the age of Hegel the most powerful discursive machine of this problematic? Is this not indicated by the fact that the Marxist, Nietzschean, and Nietzscheo-

Heideggerian problematics that now dominate all questions concerning the relations of education and the State must still come to grips with Hegelian, that is, post-Kantian discourse? They cannot do without it: *at least* in regard to this problem of education and the State, of the teaching of philosophy and the State, which, it seems to me, no philosophy prior to the "age of Hegel"—no political philosophy, no philosophy of education—treated with the kind of irreducible historical specificity that interests us. Such is, at least, the hypothesis I submit for discussion. If my hypothesis is admissible, then any treatment of this "Report" as a minor writing, any evasion or subordination of this *type* of text is, among other misunderstandings, tantamount to a failure to move beyond a prestatist problematics of education and of philosophical education. It involves a refusal to recognize the original, irreducible configuration in which our questions are asked. And consequently a refusal to identify its borders and its exterior, a refusal, therefore, to transform or transgress.

The Principles of the Right to Philosophy

What happens in this "Report"? Hegel is not simply the "great philosopher" consulted by the powers-that-be [*Le Pouvoir*]. He was summoned to Berlin by Altenstein, who offered him Fichte's chair. Altenstein, Minister of Public Instruction since 1817, incorporates the struggle (waged with suppleness, negotiation, and compromise) for the enforcement of mandatory schooling, recently adopted, for academic freedom, and for the defense of the universities against feudal powers. Engels will praise his liberalism. Along with Schulze, Director of Higher Education in his Ministry, a disciple and friend of Hegel's, a freemason and courageous liberal, Altenstein occupies a very sensitive, precarious, vulnerable place in the budding bureaucracy, struggling against the forces of feudalism: that of a compromise formation. To the extent that he is allied with Altenstein and Schulze, Hegel is caught between the "feudalists" and the "demagogues," giving signs of allegiance to the "right" when the situation or the relation of forces seems to require that he do so, secretly protecting his persecuted friends on the "left." By addressing his report to Altenstein, he is not simply acting as a "realistic" philosopher, compelled to reckon with the powers that be, with the contradictions inherent in these powers, and with his interlocutor, himself situated within these contradictions. It is not the powers-that-be that are compelled to reckon with the Hegelian system, and indeed, Hegel will say nothing in his pedagogical-philosophical propositions that is not in keeping with this system, a system that, admittedly, can fold and turn in on itself, often without breaking. The summons to Hegel is a maneuver performed by no more than a fraction of the forces in power. At any rate, the space for the intricate negotiation between the forces in power (however contradictory they may be and however determined may be a particular stasis of contradiction) and Hegel's philosophical strategy must be open, possible, already practicable. Without this, no compromise, no implicit contract would even have been sketched. This space, like the topic it derives from, can construe itself neither simply within Hegel's intra-philosophical *oeuvre*—even if something of the sort existed in a pure state—nor in what we could regard as the nonphilosophical realm exterior to it. Neither the "internal necessities of the system" alone nor the generally accepted opposition between "system" and "method" can account for the complexity of these contracts or compromises. They are neither simply *within* nor simply *external to* philosophy. (Engels: "That is how the revolutionary side of Hegelian doctrine is stifled by the expansion of its conservative side . . . therefore, the internal necessities of the system themselves *alone are sufficient* explanation of how a profoundly revolutionary mode of thought can lead to a very moderate political conclusion" (my emphasis). Is the distinction between "system" and "method" inherent in the systematic? Is it intra-philosophical? etc.)[14]

The essential foundation of the contract is the necessity of making teaching—particularly the teaching of philosophy—into a structure of the State. But of which State? The State itself, as conceived in *The Philosophy of Right*, should no longer be at the disposition of a prince or a particular force as a form of private property engaged in a contract.[15] But if the State is above civil society, the idea of the State is not a Utopia, and the Preface to the *Philosophy of Right* insists upon this in the famous paragraph about the philosophy that does not leap over its own time ("*Hic* Rhodus, *hic* Saltus," and then, "Hier ist die Rose, hier tanze," 43). This is not the place to reopen the debate about the deduction of the Prussian monarchy, and about Hegelian philosophy as an official philosophy or a philosophy of the State. The elements of this debate have always been too oversimplified for us to presume, here, briefly to reconstruct the entire problematic. The fact that Marx and Engels *themselves* judged it necessary to take violent exception to the simplifications that reduce Hegel to a mere State philosopher—this should be enough to put us on our guard against hasty conclusions. For the present, let us be content with locating the space of the strategic negotiations: *between* the Idea of the State as defined in the third part of *The Philosophy of Right* (reality as an act of substantial will, as a goal in itself, absolute, immobile, knowing what it wants in its universality) and personal subjectivity or particularity, whose most extreme forms the modern State has the power to perfect.

Within this space, Hegel seems to anticipate the ministerial request. Then, as now (the analogy would take us far, even though it must be followed with care), the Ministry wants to keep "the teaching of philosophy in the Gymnasium from losing itself in a babble of hollow formulas [*sich in ein hohles Formelwesen verliere*] or from transgressing the limits of schoolteaching." Then, as now, these two fears are related, if not confounded. What is the hollowness of formulas? What is babble? Who is to define it? From what point of view? According to what philosophy and what politics? Does not every new or subversive discourse always constitute itself through rhetorical effects that are necessarily identified as "gaps" in the prevailing discourse, with the inevitable phenomena of discursive degradation, mechanisms, mimetisms, etc.? The relation of the *Formelwesen* to the alleged plenitude of the completed discourse will be definable only in terms of a strictly determined philosophy. Here Hegel is no more able than anyone else discoursing on babble to avoid proposing a philosophy—in this case the dialectic of speculative idealism—as a general criteriology that distinguishes between empty and full language in education. And which also determines the limit between schoolteaching and that which lies outside. Nowhere in the letter is the question of this criteriology and these limits posed. Nor, furthermore, are either politics or what lies outside the school so much as mentioned. But it is in the answer to this unposed question that, as always, an educational system constructs or reforms itself.

Hegel—Hegel's philosophy—responds to the request, which we can here distinguish from the question: in order to avoid babble, he advises loading the mind with content, with a good content as is necessarily determined by the Hegelian system, and beginning there, beginning, indeed, with a content that has been recorded: with memory, with memory as its concept is dialectically determined within the system ("for in order to possess knowledge of any kind—even the highest sort—one must have memorized it [*im Gedächtnisse haben*]; regardless of whether this is to be a beginning *or* an end in itself." Whether this is to be a beginning *or* an end in itself, to be sure. But Hegel goes on to justify his pedagogical proposition:

it is preferable that this happen at the beginning, for "if one begins there, one has that much more freedom and inducement to think for oneself"; ibid.). For Hegel, memory was both a beginning and an end; he remembers (being eleven) and remembers that he began by remembering that which he first learned by heart. But at the same time, this homology of the system (the dialectical concept of *Gedächtnis*) and of the autobiographical experience that gave Hegel the inducement and the freedom to think, this homology is to be enriched again by its pedagogical version: by beginning with teaching the content of knowledge, before even thinking it, we are assured of a highly determined prephilosophical inculcation that paves the way for good philosophy [*la bonne philosophie*]. We know the schema, and Greph was quick to criticize certain of its current consequences.

To remain within the "limits of schoolteaching," this prephilosophical content will consist of the humanities (the Ancients, the great artistic and historical conceptions of individuals and peoples, their ethics and their religiosity), classical literature, the dogmatic content of religion—so many disciplines that will be studied in light of the content that is essential to the preparation for speculative philosophy. Time and again, content is privileged in this propaedeutic, and the material part stressed over the formal part. The treatment reserved for religion and its dogmatic content is remarkable enough. Indeed, it defines fairly accurately the lines of negotiation. There is, of course, as we know, a war between Hegel and religious authority. The two parties indulged in violent verbal exchanges. Hegel was accused and suspected of the worst. But at the same time, his interest is in wresting religious instruction from the religious powers; the philosophy of religion defines the conditions and the perspectives of this reappropriation. At stake is the raising of religion to the level of speculative thought, making apparent those aspects of religion that are *sublated* in philosophy, as in their truth. The pedagogical version of this movement is not a mere corollary of the philosophy of religion, without which the Letter would be incomprehensible. It is, rather, central to it. In 1810, he had written to Niethammer: "Protestantism has less to do with a particular confession than with a superior, more rational spirit of reflection and of culture; its spiritual foundations are not a sort of training adaptable to this or that utilitarian purpose." This objection to pedagogical training or utilitarianism, as expressed in the letter of 1822, whose trace one can follow in Nietzsche and Heidegger, is therefore indissociable from this Protestant philosophy-pedagogy. In 1816, Hegel writes again: "Protestantism is not entrusted to the hierarchical organization of a church, but is, rather, found only in a general intelligence and a general culture. . . . Our universities and our schools are our churches."[16] This implies that the teaching of religion, in its dogmatic and ecclesiastical contents, be carried out neither as a solely historical matter (*nur als eine historische Sache*), as a narrative [*récit*] of events, as a narration without a concept, nor, formally, as the abstractions of natural religion, the guarantees of abstract morality, or subjective fantasms. In other words, there is but one way to rescue the teaching of religion from the ecclesiastical authorities while, at the same time, upholding its *thought* content against the conscious or unconscious destructors (atheists, deists, Kantians) of religious truth: to teach religion as it is *thought* in a speculative manner in the *Phenomenology of Spirit*, the *Philosophy of Religion*, or the *Encyclopedia* ("the contents of philosophy and those of religion are the same").[17] But *teaching* it this way can only be carried out in a teaching of the State, of a State that conducts its rapport with the Church according to the *Principles of the Philosophy of Right*. There again, the Letter of 1822 is legible only if we read, concomitantly, chapter 270 of the *Philosophy of Right* about "philosophical knowledge which recognizes that the conflict between the State and the Church has nothing to do with the content of philosophy and that of religion, but rather, only with their form." The place of "dogmatic content" in education is defined in a footnote:

> Like knowledge and science, religion has as its principle its own form, which is different from that of the State, they [religion, science, and knowledge] enter into the State partly as means of educating [*Mitteln der Bildung*] and of forming attitudes, partly insofar as they are essentially ends-in-themselves, by virtue of their outward existence. In both respects, the principles of the State relate to them in terms of application. A comprehensive, concrete treatise on the State would also have to deal with such spheres—as well as with art and with mere natural relations—and to consider their relations to and position within the State.[18]

The last section of the same chapter situates the question of teaching at the center of the rapports between Church and State. The example of Protestantism plays a very important role here, although it is alluded to only parenthetically: it is the case in which there is no "particular content" that can remain exterior to the State, since "in Protestantism" there is no "clergy which would be the sole depository of Church doctrine, for [in Protestantism] there is no laity."

The same demonstration is possible for the other branches of knowledge that Hegel wishes to integrate into preparatory teaching (empirical psychology and the basics of logic). It would refer the pedagogical proposition to its own foundation in the Hegelian system of speculative dialectics, to the relations between understanding and reason, and to the critique or the sublation of Kantianism. In short, no *philosophy* except Hegel's can take on or justify such pedagogy—its structure, its progression, and its rhythm—and remain rigorously consistent. Is this to say that the basis of negotiation with the ministerial request was extraordinarily narrow? Does this not explain why the Altenstein-Hegel episode remained without issue [*sans lendemain*]?

Certain of the sharper features of this episode indeed remain without issue. But rather than constituting a philosophical, political, or pedagogical revolution, it developed (like Hegelian philosophy) and accumulated a past; and to a large extent it has survived. It was quite necessary, in this negotiation between political forces and a philosophical discourse, that an ideal and common line be drawn. In the most spectacular case, that of religion, it was necessary that the European State, in its new forms and in the service of new forces, reclaiming a certain power from feudalism and the Church, manage to remove teaching from the jurisdiction of the clergy, at the same time "preserving" religion and putting it in the right. Putting it in the right while refusing it a certain, particular, determinate power, thinking it philosophically in its truth (philosophy): this was the formula, Hegel's formula. Which is neither to allege that Hegel responded so admirably and in such detail (by art or chance) to a demand formulated *elsewhere*, in the empirical field of historical politics, nor vice versa. But a possibility had been opened to this common language, to all its secondary variations (for Hegel was not the only philosopher to propose his pedagogy, and the entire systematic range of these variations remains to be studied), to its *translatability*. This common possibility is legible *and* transformable neither simply *within* the philosophical system, if such a thing existed in a pure state, nor in a domain simply foreign to any sort of philosophy.

Taken in its greatest singularity, the Altenstein-Hegel endeavor was undoubtedly a failure, but the general structure that opened it and that Hegel tried to keep open is where we find ourselves today, and it does not cease to modify and insinuate itself. This is what I call the *age of Hegel*.

At the moment when he seems to respond to the highly specific demands of a particular faction of the then-prevailing forces, Hegel means to distinguish their national and bureaucratic *particularity*. For example, in order to free up the time necessary for the teaching of logic, he does not hesitate to propose encroaching upon the "so-called teaching of German and German literature" (thus taking a stand in a competition whose issues and stakes we know all too well—between philosophy, "French," and French "literature"); or, similarly, upon the juridical encyclopedia, distinct from the theory of right. What is behind this choice? In the eyes of Hegel, it is the precondition for the development of logic. For logic is what conditions "the *general* formation of the mind [allgemeine *Geistesbildung*]," "general culture." And it is general culture that should thrive in the Gymnasium instead of its being oriented toward "training" for civil service or "professional" studies.

We can no more attempt an *immediate* analogical transposition of this "liberal" motif than of any other, especially if we are in search of some kind of guarantee or slogan. First of all, because we must draw a scrupulous distinction between a reading in its own context, its historical and political context (Hegel's complex and mobile strategy vis-à-vis the different forces then struggling for the power of the State and its bureaucracy), and its seemingly intraphilosophical context, which is neither simply permeable nor hermetically sealed, and which, according to specific constraints whose principle of analysis has yet to be formulated, is ceaselessly in negotiation within the historico-political sphere. And then, because this "liberal" motif, like all the motifs we can identify in this letter, is structurally equivocal. By loosening the hold of the "civil services," of a particular State, of the forces of civil society that control it and command the "professional" market, Hegel extends the field of a "general culture," which, as we know, always remains highly determined in the contents it inculcates. Other forces of civil society manifest themselves here, and any analysis must be extremely vigilant in this regard. When we "repeat" Hegel's "liberal" utterance in the present situation (directed against premature specialization and the requirements of the capitalist market, against the call to order issued to the Inspectors General, who are supposed to "apply themselves in the service" of the Haby Reform, against the inquisition of the Rectors into everything pertaining to "academic freedom" or the autonomy of the universities, etc.), we should know that neither in Hegel's situation nor in our own can this utterance raise itself above the demands and commands of given forces in civil society, and that the relation between liberal discourse and the mobile, subtle, sometimes paradoxical dynamic of these forces must constantly be reevaluated. The Haby Reform invokes a wide range of "liberal" and neutralist themes, which are not sufficient—far from it—to neutralize its quite definite political and economic purpose. On the contrary, such themes contribute to it in very precise ways.

This equivocation is reproduced everywhere, in accordance with a structural necessity. Let us take the example of (the) age, since it is our primary interest here. Greph has devised a strategy in this regard: it involves extending the teaching of philosophy (revised in both "form" and "content") to classes far earlier than the Terminale. In order to legitimize this extension, we had to, indeed, must still, appeal to a logic currently accepted by the forces with which we are at odds and whose contradictions we hope to expose: Why not grant philosophy what is taken for granted in other disciplines, that is, the "progressivity" of education over a relatively long period? This provisional strategic argument, borrowed from the logic of the adversary, might cause us to rush to embrace Hegel and brandish this "Letter on the Gymnasium": Doesn't he say there that a child of eleven (for example, Hegel) is capable of access to very difficult philosophical content and forms? Doesn't the letter confirm that there is no natural age for philosophy and that, in any case, this age would not be adolescence? Does it not define a calculated "progressivity"—a "progressivity" organized teleologically, regulated according to a great systematic rationality?

Any and all services such argumentation might render are double-edged. They subordinate the broadening we seek to a "progressivity" considered natural: that is, naturally regulated by the Hegelian teleology of the rapports between nature and spirit, by the philosophical concept of (the) age that dominates both Reason in history and Hegel's pedagogy and theory of *Bildung*. All this forms that concept of (the) age, beginning with the age of the concept (the age of Hegel), that Greph would have to deconstruct even as it enlists it for strategic purposes. This is neither primarily nor exclusively a theoretical necessity, but rather the precondition of a political practice that seeks to be as coherent as possible in its successive steps, in the strategy of its alliances, and in its discourse.

Let us look more closely and more concretely at the trap this seductive Hegelian reference could become for Greph. It appears that Hegel prescribes a progress and a progression—both qualitative and quantitative—in the teaching of philosophy in the Gymnasium. In fact, and even if this were actually "progressive" in every sense of the word, in respect to the struggles of Hegel's time, today this gesture puts in place the very structure

against which we are struggling. One could say that it excludes all access to
the practice of philosophy before the University. Hegel proposes introducing in the Gymnasium a better *preparation* for the "proper essence of philosophy [*das eigentliche Wesen der Philosophie*]," that is, for its pure contents
in the "speculative form." But access to this content remains impossible or
forbidden in the Gymnasium: "But I need not add that the exposition of
philosophy is still to be excluded from instruction in the Gymnasium and
reserved for the University, since the high rescript of the Royal Ministry has
itself already presupposed this exclusion [*diese Ausschließung schon selbst vo-
rausgesetzt*]." This *presupposition* functions as do all presuppositions (*Vo-
raussetzungen*) in Hegelian discourse; furthermore, it situates the point of
contact between a state of political action (philosophy reserved for the University) and the logic of Hegelian discourse, here exempted from the need
to explain itself. The whole paragraph following the allusion to this ex-
emption makes its consequences explicit. Up to the point of the strict exclusion of the history of philosophy from the circle of secondary education.
Here is the beginning of the next paragraph: "With respect to the more defined circle of the fields of knowledge to which Gymnasium instruction is
to be restricted, I would like expressly to exclude the *history of philosophy*."
Now, such an exclusion is justified by the concept of the presupposition of
the Idea (projection or result of beginning at the end) as it organizes the entire Hegelian systematic, the entire onto-encyclopedia. And thereby the entire *Universitas*, which cannot be dissociated from it. The "ministerial" presupposition matches the Hegelian proposition, both in its principle and in
its end: "But without presupposing the speculative Idea, this history [of
philosophy] will often be no more than a simple narrative [*Erzählung*] of
superfluous opinions." In our analysis of this justification of the exclusion
of the history of philosophy from the curriculum of the Gymnasium, we
should not forget that today, in our own lycées, resorting to the history of
philosophy as such still meets with official disapproval, especially if it takes
the form of an exposé or a narrative. The "good reasons" invoked to justify
this attitude make sense only within the Hegelian concept of presupposition. It is not a matter here simply of disputing these reasons, but rather,
first of all, of recognizing precisely their presupposition, the presupposed
logic of presupposition. Finally, another exclusion, metaphysics: "A final
consideration has to do with the higher reasons for excluding *metaphysics as
such* from the Gymnasium" (Hegel's emphasis). This exclusion postpones
(until the University proper) access to thought—in its speculative form—

of something whose *content* is already present, Hegel insists, in secondary education. If metaphysics as such, in its speculative form, is excluded, we can, on the contrary, teach on the secondary level that which refers to will, freedom, law, and duty, everything that would be "all the more called for in that this teaching would be related to the religious teaching carried out at every level, for at least eight to twelve years." In other words, philosophy proper is excluded, but its content continues to be taught, albeit in an *improperly* philosophical form, in a nonphilosophical manner. Its content is inculcated through the teaching of other disciplines, notably prescriptive and normative teachings such as morals, political morals (the "just concepts of the nature of duty which bind the man and the citizen," for example), or religion. This schema, so familiar by now, is one of the principal targets of Greph.

Finally, everything in the letter concerning the extension (*Ausdehnung*) of content and progression by stages (*Stufenfolge*) in the acquisition of knowledge refers, on the one hand, to what was said about "religion and morals," and, on the other hand, to a psychology of (the) age (youth being more "docile" and "more teachable [*folgsamer und gelehriger*]"). And the naturalist determination of the different ages recovers, necessarily and according to a profound homology, the entire philosophical teleology of Hegelianism as we find it from the works on Judaism (the Jew is childish, *kindisch*—not even childlike, *kindlich*, as is the Christian—especially because the Jew appears more docile, more *submissive* to the heteronomy of his God) to the anthropology of the *Encyclopedia* and the definition of the "natural *course* of the ages of life," the "child," the "young man," the "mature man," the "old man."[19] The differences of age are the first (and hence the most natural) of the "physical and spiritual" differences of the "natural soul." But this naturality is always already the spirituality it has not yet become in the (teleological and encyclopedic) speculative circle that governs this entire discourse.

It has been impossible to read this letter as a "minor" text, alien to the "great" philosophical problematic, addressing itself to secondary problems and allowing itself to be determined immediately by matters external to philosophy, for example, by conjunctions of empirico-political forces. In order to decipher what the (pre-Hegelian) philosopher would have considered secondary, it has been necessary to invoke all the philosophemes of the "great" works, as well as the entire "internal" systematic. And this letter increasingly resembles, in every respect, the canonical corpus. Is this a reversal, and can we be satisfied with that? This passage from "minor" to "major" is tautological and reproduces the Hegelian gesture, the heterotautology of the speculative proposition. For Hegel, there is, with respect to the philosophical, no simple exteriority. What other philosophers (the ones I just called pre-Hegelian) would consider—on account of their formalism, empiricism, dialectical impotence—to be "everyday," "journalistic" empiricity, accidental contingency, or external particularity is no less alien to the system and to the development [*devenir*] of Reason than, according to Hegel, the morning "gazette" is heterogeneous, insignificant, or illegible from the point of view of the *Greater Logic*. There is a Hegelian hierarchization, but it is circular, and the minor is always carried, *sublated* beyond the opposition, beyond the limit of inside and outside in(to) the major. And inversely. The potency of this age without age derives from this great empirico-philosophical cycle. Hegel does not conceive of the school as the consequence or the image of the system, or even as its *pars totalis*: the system itself is an immense school, the thoroughgoing auto-encyclopedia of absolute spirit in absolute knowledge. And it is a school we never leave, hence a mandatory instruction, mandated by itself, since the necessity can no longer come from without. The letter—let us not forget this homology —follows closely on the establishment of obligatory schooling. Altenstein was one of its most active advocates. As under Charlemagne, schooling is broadened, and the attempt is made to reduce the Church to the service of the State.

The *Universitas* is that onto- and auto-encyclopedic circle of the State. Whatever the particular forces in "civil society" may be that dispose over the power of the State, every university as such (be it on the "right" or the "left") depends upon this model. Since this model (which, by definition, claims universality) is always in negotiated compromise with the forces of a particular State (Prussian, Napoleonic—I and II—republican-bourgeois, Nazi, fascist, social democratic, popular democratic, or socialist), the deconstruction of its concepts, instruments, and practices cannot proceed by attacking it *immediately* and attempting to do away with it without risking the *immediate* return of other forces that would welcome its disappearance. *Immediately* to cede and make way for the other of the *Universitas* might represent a welcome invitation to those very determinate and very determined forces, ready and waiting, close by, to take over the State and the University. Whence the necessity for a deconstruction not to abandon the terrain of the University at the very moment when it begins to come to grips with its most powerful foundations. Whence the necessity not to abandon the field to empiricism and thereby to whatever forces are at hand. Whence the political necessity of our alliances, a necessity that must be constantly re-evaluated. For Greph, as we know, this problem is neither remote nor abstract. If the current French State is afraid of philosophy, it is because extending its teaching contributes to the progress of *two* types of threatening forces: those wanting to change the State (those, let's say, belonging to an age of left-wing Hegelianism) and to wrest it from the control of those forces currently in power, and those that, on the other hand or simultaneously, allied or not with the former, *tend* toward the destruction of the State.[20] These two forces cannot be classified according to the prevailing divisions. They seem to me, for example, to cohabitate today within that theoretical and practical field commonly known as "Marxism."

Charlemagne died a second time, but things go on, and a Hegel can always be found to occupy his throne.

In 1822 (the year of our letter), the beneficiary of Hegel's insurance policy at the University Widows' Fund received another missive:

> You see, my dear wife, that I have arrived at the goal of my voyage, which is to say, at its most distant point. . . . We arrived at 10 P.M. at Aachen. The first thing I saw was the cathedral and I sat down on Charlemagne's throne. . . . Three hundred years after his death, Charlemagne was found *seated* upon this throne—by the Emperor Frederic, I believe . . . and his remains were interred. I sat on this throne—on which, as the sacristan assured me, thirty-two emperors have been crowned—just like any other person, and the entire satisfaction is simply to have been seated there.[21]

Translated by Susan Winnett

Appendix

To the Royal Ministry of Spiritual, Academic,
and Medical Affairs

G. W. F. Hegel

Berlin, April 16, 1822

In its gracious rescript of November 1 of the preceding year, in which I was given the task of reporting on the lessons held by Dr. von Henning, the Royal Ministry at the same time—in view of the widely held complaint that student youth generally arrive at the University without the preparation requisite to the study of philosophy—deigned most graciously to take into consideration what I, with the utmost respect, might proffer, and to charge me with expressing, in an advisory report, how an adequate preparation in this regard might be organized in the Gymnasium.[22]

In this regard, I would first take the liberty of remarking that a reorganization that aims at alleviating this deficiency in the Gymnasiums could itself have an effect only on those who have attended those institutions before entering the University. According to existing laws, however, University rectors are required to admit to the University even uneducated and ignorant youths, so long as they are in possession of a diploma attesting to their brilliant immaturity. The former arrangement in the Universities, whereby the Dean of the College to which the prospective student applied submitted the student to an examination—which, to be sure, had long since sunk to the level of a mere formality—still granted the Universities the possibility of and justification for excluding those who were completely uneducated and not yet mature. Although one could cite a provision from the statutes of our University (Chap. VIII, §6, art. 1, p. 43) that appears to contradict both practice and the aforementioned situation, its effect is superseded and annulled [*aufgehoben*] by a more precise provision to be found in the October 12, 1812, edict relative to the examination of Gymnasium students applying to the University, to which actual practice accordingly conforms. As a member of the Scientific Examination Commission, to which the Royal Ministry deigned to name me, I have had occasion to see that the ignorance of those obtaining a diploma to enter the University extends to all levels and that the preparation required by the more or less considerable number of such subjects would at times have to begin with the orthography of their native tongue. Since at the same time I am also a professor in this University, I cannot but be extremely alarmed for myself and my colleagues in the face of such utterly deficient knowledge and culture in college students, whom we are asked to teach and for whom we must bear responsibility if the aims and expenditures of the Government are not fulfilled: the aim that those leaving the University take with them not merely vocational training, but an educated and cultivated mind. No further elaboration is required to demonstrate that the honor and esteem of the University also do not benefit from the admission of such utterly immature young people.

In this context I would like respectfully to offer the Royal Ministry my own experience stemming from my membership in the Scientific Examination Commission. Namely—insofar as the examinations are designed *to inform* those persons, by ascertaining the extent of their knowledge, who are still thoroughly unprepared for the University, and *to advise* them to postpone entering the University until they have completed their deficient preparation—this aim appears rarely to be attained, since those examinees whose ignorance is thereby revealed learn nothing new; rather, being entirely aware that they know no Latin, no Greek, nothing of mathematics or of history, they have already made their decision to enter the University and hence seek nothing from the Commission but the acquisition of the certificate that allows them to register. They are all the less likely to take such a certificate as advice against entering the University, since, independently of its content, it gives them the possibility of being admitted to the University.

In order now to proceed to the object at hand designated by the Royal Ministry, that is, *preparation in the Gymnasium for speculative thinking and for the study of philosophy*, I find myself compelled to take as my point of departure the difference between a *more material* and a *more formal preparation*. Although the former may be more indirect and less accessible, I believe it should be considered to be the proper foundation of speculative thinking and hence should not be passed over in silence. However, since I would consider studies in the Gymnasium to be the material component of that preparation, I need only name these objects and mention their relation to the end in question.

The first object that I would like to take into account would be the study of the ancients, insofar as through such study the mind and the imagination [*Vorstellung*] of the young are introduced to the great historical and artistic visions [*Anschauungen*] of individuals and of peoples, their deeds and their destinies, as well as their virtues, basic moral principles, and religiosity. But the study of classical literature can only be truly fruitful for the spirit and its more profound activity when, in the higher grades of the Gymnasium, formal linguistic knowledge is seen more as a means, the matter of which, on the contrary, becomes the prime concern, whereas the more scholarly aspects of philology are reserved for the University and for those who want to dedicate themselves exclusively to philology.

The other material, however, does not contain the content of truth only for itself—a content that also constitutes the interest of philosophy, with its characteristic mode of knowledge—but also entails an immediate connection with the formal element of speculative thought. In this regard I would here make mention of the *dogmatic content of our religion*, inasmuch as it not only contains the truth in and for itself, but elevates it so far in the direction of speculative thinking that it simultaneously entails the contradiction of the understanding and the abandonment of rationalization [*Räsonnement*]. Whether or not such content, however, will have this exemplary relation in regard to speculative thinking depends on the manner in which religion is treated: if it is dealt with merely historically, and, instead of implanting a veritable and profound respect, the main emphasis is placed upon theistic generalities, moral doctrines, or even upon mere subjective feelings, a frame of mind opposed to speculative thought will be inculcated: the idiosyncrasies [*Eigendünkel*] of the understanding and of a certain willfulness are thereby elevated to prominence, which immediately either leads to a simple indifference toward philosophy or succumbs to sophistry.

I would view both of these, classical vision and religious truth—inasmuch as the latter would still constitute the older dogmatic doctrine of the church—as the substantial portion of the preparation for philosophical studies. If the intellect and spirit of the young have not been imbued with that vision and that truth, the University would be faced with the nearly impossible task of arousing the mind for substantial content and overcoming an already entrenched vanity, oriented toward ordinary interests that are all too easily gratified.

The proper essence of philosophy would have to be posed in terms of the process by which that solid, tempered content acquires speculative form. But I need not add that the exposition of philosophy is still to be excluded from instruction in the Gymnasium and to be reserved for the University, since the high edict of the Royal Ministry has itself already presupposed this exclusion.

Thus, what remains for Gymnasium instruction is the *intermediary link*, which is to be viewed as the transition from the belief in and representation of that tempered material to philosophical thinking. This intermediary link would have to be situated in the activity of engaging *in general representations* and, more proximately, in the *forms of thought* common to both philosophical thinking and to mere rationalization. Such activity would entail a closer relation to speculative thinking: in part, insofar as this thinking presupposes exercise in moving about in the medium of abstract thoughts, in and of themselves, without the sensible material that is still present in mathematical contents; in part, however, insofar as the forms of thought, the knowledge of which would be provided by instruction, are subsequently used by philosophy, while also constituting a principal component of the material upon which it works. Precisely this acquaintance and habituation in dealing with formal [*förmlichen*] thoughts, however, should be viewed as the more direct preparation for University studies of philosophy.

With respect to the more defined circle of the fields of knowledge to which, in this regard, Gymnasium instruction is to be restricted, I would expressly like to exclude the *history of philosophy*, although it frequently seems to offer itself as suitable for it. But without presupposing the speculative idea, it might well become nothing more than a narrative [*Erzählung*] of contingent and superfluous opinions; this easily leads to a disparaging and contemptible opinion of philosophy—and sometimes such an effect might even be viewed as the purpose behind the history of philosophy and those recommending it—which produces the impression [*Vorstellung*] that all efforts involved with this science have been futile and

that it would be an even more futile effort for student youth to give themselves over to it.

On the contrary, among the fields of knowledge to be included in the
preparational instruction here in question, I would mention the following:

1. So-called *empirical psychology*. Representations of external sensations,
imagination, memory, and other psychic faculties are indeed already in
themselves something so current that an exposition restricting itself to
them would easily be trivial and pedantic. On the one hand, however,
such could be all the more easily dispensed within the University if it were
already to be found in the Gymnasium; on the other hand, it could be
limited to an introduction to logic, whereby in any event this would have
to be preceded by the mention of intellectual activities different in character from thinking as such. Beginning with the external senses, images
and representations, then proceeding to their conjunction or so-called association, and from there to the nature of languages, and especially to the
distinctions between representations, thoughts, and concepts, much of
considerable interest could be adduced, which, moreover, would be of
great use, insofar as the latter subject matter—once the part that thinking
has in intuition [*Anschauungen*] had been rendered apparent—would constitute a more direct introduction to the study of logic.

2. The rudiments of logic, however, would have to be considered the
main object. Excluding its speculative significance and treatment, instruction could be extended to cover the doctrine of concepts, of judgments, of
syllogisms and their modes, and then to the doctrine of definition, division,
proof, and the scientific method, in full accordance with already-established
procedure. Usually, the doctrine of the concept already takes up determinations that more proximately belong to the field of what otherwise is
called ontology; a part of this doctrine is also customarily introduced in the
form of laws of thought. At this point it would be advantageous to introduce an acquaintance with the Kantian categories as the so-called elementary concepts of understanding, leaving aside, however, the remainder of
Kantian metaphysics; yet a mention of the antinomies could still open up
at least a negative and formal perspective on reason and the ideas.

What speaks in favor of linking this instruction to Gymnasium education is the fact that no object is less apt to be judged adequately by the
young in respect to its importance or utility. If such instruction has grad-
ually been abandoned, it is in all probability primarily because this insight
has largely been lost. Besides, such an object is not attractive enough in

general to entice the young into studying logic during their stay at the University, where they are in a position to choose the fields of knowledge—outside of their vocational studies—in which they want to become involved. Moreover, it is not unknown for teachers in the positive sciences to advise students against studying philosophy, which they also probably take to include the study of logic. If this instruction is introduced into the Gymnasium, however, pupils will at least once have the experience of receiving, and thus having, well-formed [*förmliche*] thoughts in their heads. It should be considered a highly significant, subjective effect if the attention of the young can be directed toward a domain of thought for itself, and toward the fact that formed thoughts are themselves an object worthy of consideration—indeed, an object to which public authority itself attaches importance, as indicated by this organization of the curriculum.

The fact that such instruction does not exceed the intellectual capacities of Gymnasium students is attested to by the general experience of the past, and if I may be permitted to evoke my own experience, not only have I daily had before my eyes the ability and receptivity of pupils for such subject matter, since I have been a professor of philosophical propaedeutics for many years, and a Gymnasium rector; in addition, I remember having learned, in my twelfth year—destined as I was to enter the theological seminary of my country—Wolf's definitions of the so-called *idea clara*, and that, in my fourteenth year, I had assimilated all the figures and rules of the syllogisms. And I still know them. Were it not to defy openly contemporary prejudices in favor of "thinking for oneself" and "productive activity," etc., I would not be averse to bringing something of this sort into the proposal for the Gymnasium instruction of this track: for in order to possess knowledge of any sort, including the highest kind, one must have it in memory, whether one begins or ends with this: if one begins with it, one has all the more freedom and occasion to think that knowledge itself. Moreover, in such a way one could most surely counteract the danger that the Royal Ministry rightly seeks to avoid, "That philosophical instruction in the Gymnasium should lose itself in empty formulas or exceed the limits of school instruction."[23]

3. The preceding point joins forces with higher reasons *to exclude metaphysics proper* from the Gymnasium. Yet there is *one* aspect of the previous Wolffian philosophy that could be brought under consideration: what in the *Theologia naturalis* is advanced under the name of *the proofs of the existence of God*. By itself, Gymnasium instruction will be unable to avoid

connecting the doctrine of God with the thought of the finitude and the contingency of worldly things, with the purposive relations within them, etc.; however, such a connection will be eternally evident to unbiased human intelligence, no matter what the objects of critical philosophy may be. However, these so-called proofs contain nothing but a formal analysis of the content that has already introduced itself spontaneously into Gymnasium instruction. Of course, they require further correction by means of speculative philosophy so that they in fact correspond to the content accumulated by unbiased human intelligence along its way. A preliminary acquaintance with the form of that way would be of more immediate interest to all subsequent speculative reflection.

4. In a similar manner, certain just and determinate concepts of the nature of volition and of freedom, of law and of duty, can be brought into the Gymnasium instruction concerning *ethics.* This will be all the more feasible in the higher classes, where instruction will be linked to religious instruction, which runs through all classes and which therefore extends over a period of possibly eight to ten years. In our times it could also seem more urgent to work against the shallowness of insight—the results of which, already manifest in the Gymnasiums, have at times attained public notoriety—through correct concepts concerning the nature of the obligations of citizens and of human beings.

This, then, would be my humble opinion concerning *the extension of the contents* of the philosophical preparatory studies in the Gymnasium, an opinion that I most respectfully place before the Royal Ministry. As to what is still at issue concerning the length of time, and likewise the progression to be followed in exposing such knowledge, nothing more need be called to mind than what has been mentioned regarding religion and ethics.[24] With respect to initiation into the psychological and logical fields of knowledge, it could be specified that, if two hours per week were taken up in one year-long course, the psychological component would be dealt with primarily as an introduction, and hence should be offered before the logical portion. If, keeping the same number of hours, considered as adequate, three or four semiannual courses were devoted to it, more detailed notions about the nature of the spirit, its activities and states, could be taught; in this case it might be more advantageous to begin with instruction in logic, on a level that is simple, abstract, and therefore easy to grasp. This instruction would thereby fall in an earlier period, when the young are more docile and submissive to authority, and are not so infected by the demand that, to merit their attention, the subject matter must conform to their representations [*Vorstellungen*] and to their emotional interests.

The possible difficulty entailed in increasing Gymnasium instruction by two additional hours might best be avoided by reducing the so-called instruction in German and in German literature by one or two hours, or, even more appropriately, by canceling the lectures dealing with the legal encyclopedia, where these occur in the Gymnasium, and replacing them with lectures on logic; all the more so, in order that the *general* formation of the spirit in the Gymnasium—an institution that can be considered to be exclusively devoted to this kind of formation—not continue its apparent decline in favor of a training oriented toward vocational service and alimentary studies.

Finally, concerning the textbooks that can be recommended to teachers for such preparatory instruction, I would not know which of those with which I am acquainted to indicate as preferable.[25] The material can, perhaps, be found more or less in any textbook, but in the older ones it is more complete and defined, and less contaminated with heterogeneous ingredients; an ultimate instruction from the Royal Ministry could put forth the directives designating which materials should be selected.

Reaffirming my beholden respect and obedience to the high Royal Ministry

Hegel
Prof. at the Royal University

Translated by Terry Cochran and Samuel Weber

Philosophy and Its Classes

At a time when no reform plan had yet been published, no document submitted to analysis, no negotiation officially begun, fragmentary indications were from time to time revealed to the press. They concerned only the guiding principles of "legal guidelines for the education system." These principles appear to be fixed. We were therefore aware of the general organization of primary and secondary education in its broad *formal* lines. It was the subject of what the minister called the first "package." Left to commissions, on which the educational "representatives" or, rather, hand-picked nominees remained unknown to us, the definition of the *contents* of education was brutally dissociated and subordinated. That definition will follow one day: as part of a third "updated and reworked" "package," as it is put, again. Everything is happening as if they wanted to remove the project from a true—systematic and critical—examination and to demobilize, with procedural ruses, an opposition they have good reason to fear. The modes of elaboration (or improvisation), of publication (or occultation), of so serious a plan would themselves already call for a vigilant analysis.

Philosophy Repressed

Considering what we do not yet know and what we can already anticipate, the treatment reserved for philosophy deserves particular attention. It is not that the privilege of our attention is required by the sovereign excellence of a discipline that it would once again be a matter of "defending." But the fact is that the teaching of philosophy would be affected more profoundly than any other discipline by the current plan, in conditions that shed light on and determine the entire orientation of the new "education system." The evidence is this. Since the new Terminales are organized according to a totally "optional" system, there would no longer be any required teaching of philosophy in the only class in which, up to this point, it has been offered. Philosophy would be given three hours a week in the "première":[1] about as much, on average, as in the sections of the Terminales that receive the least today. Even before examining the grounds for or aims of such an operation, let's move on to what is irrefutable: the number of hours reserved for philosophy, *for all students*, is massively reduced. Philosophy was already the only discipline confined to a single class at the end of the final year of secondary studies; it would still be contained in a single class, but with fewer hours. Thus an offensive that had proceeded, in recent years, more prudently and deceitfully is openly accelerated: the accentuated dissociation of the scientific and the philosophical, the actively selective orientation of the "best" students toward sections giving less room to philosophy, the reduction of teaching hours, coefficients, teaching positions, and so forth. This time, the plan appears clearly to be adopted. No systematic introduction to philosophy could possibly be attempted in three hours a week. How can one doubt that? Since students will have had no other access to philosophy as such during *their entire studies*, the candidates for the "philosophy" option will be more and more rare. Combined with the technico-economic pressures of a certain market, with a politics of education ruled, more openly than ever, by the law of this market, establishing the so-called "basic" baccalauréat, at the end of the première, will reduce the number of students in the new "Terminale," and later in the university. Already very appreciable, the growing shortage of teaching positions in philosophy will be accelerated and will produce the conditions for its progressive acceleration, discouraging possible candidates for the "philosophy" option and therefore limiting professional prospects. And what we know about "teacher training" confirms this threat. The recruitment of philosophy teachers might even be suspended, it is said, for several years. A machine has therefore been put in place or, rather, has been perfected and finally put on display, a machine that would quickly lead in practice to the evacuation of all philosophy in "general and technical lycées," that would lead to its progressive extinction in the universities. The separateness of the two "ministries" is here a deceptive fiction.

The Defenses of Philosophy

Let's not content ourselves with recalling, one more time, the political impact of what must be called a new "suppression-of-the-philosophy-class." The motivations of the "defense-of-the-philosophy-class" have of course always been more equivocal than we believe in general. This defense must be scrutinized prudently in each historical situation. For example, when, ten years after its suppression, Duruy reestablished the philosophy class under the Second Empire, he did so to retrain bourgeois youth and to protect them from "negative doctrines" ("The true cause of the progress of negative doctrines in some young people has therefore been the reduction of the teaching of philosophy in our lycées. . . . Philosophical studies in our lycées are the best remedy for materialism," V. Duruy). Analogous contradictions can still today inhabit the "defense-of-the-philosophy-class," perhaps even among a certain Left. But if the defence is sometimes ambiguous, the attack, when it comes from those in power, has never been so. The destruction of the philosophy class, since that is what is at issue, is meant to stop most lycée students from exercising philosophical and political critique. Historical critique as well, since history is once again the target associated with philosophy. In the lycées, at the age when one begins to vote, is the philosophy class not, with the exception of history, the only place in which, for example, texts on theoretical modernity, those on Marxism and psychoanalysis in particular, have some chance of being read and interpreted? And there is nothing fortuitous in the fact that the pressure from those in power has become continually more pronounced against this class and certain of its instructors and students since 1968 and the "protests" that developed in the lycées.

The Age of Philosophy

Clinging, tensely and reactively, to the "defense" of philosophy, and especially of *the* philosophy class, assuming it still exists, would, however, give more ammunition to this repression. What would one be defending, in that case? A teaching whose syllabus (an enormous sediment, an eclectic and immutable heritage under a facade of rejuvenations) has never been able to be covered in one year and in which no progress is ever made: the same syllabus reappears at the licence[2] and the agrégation. All the instructors, all the students, know this, which gives rise to the ruses, denials, and shortcuts with which we are familiar. Everywhere one admits to feelings of uneasiness and skepticism. To concentrate the entire teaching of philosophy in one class, at the end of secondary studies, was, first of all, to reserve it for a social class. To a certain extent, this is still true. Establishing the "basic" baccalauréat would risk consolidating this antidemocratic effect. What is more, the "philosophy class" comes at a time when, empirically and implicitly, but very effectively, the "philosophy" of the dominant social forces has already done its work through the other disciplines, notably those which in France are the usual preparation for philosophical training, namely the nonscientific disciplines. A certain teaching of the human sciences, as it is planned before the "première," could, in the spirit of the new "system of education," now play this role of ideological impregnation.

Where, then, did the notion come from that all contact with philosophy was impossible (read forbidden) before "adolescence"? This cunning myth of age and psycho-intellectual maturity reaches back, through all kinds of specific relays, to the most archaic tradition. It can be found again in its dogmatic state in the language of the current minister, who, with the intention of taking into account "pedagogical experience" rather than "sociopolitical analyses," seems to found his whole "educational system" on notions of a "degree of alertness" or "mental age."[3] This occult consensus as regards the natural or ideal age for philosophy has always been one of the untouchable foundations of the philosophy class. It must be analyzed practically; that is to say, its politico-sexual content must be dissolved: the figure of the young *man* who, virgin yet fully grown, ignorant and innocent, yet finally mature for philosophy, would begin to pose, without presupposing any knowledge, or rather begin to let be posed for him, the questions of all questions—between fifteen and eighteen years old, *after* puberty, *before* entering into society. Earlier would be perverse or, because of a natural stupidity, impossible. Later would be useless, ridiculous, or harmful; and the adult philosopher, as people have no doubt never ceased thinking since Callicles in the *Gorgias*, is "un*man*ly and worthy of a beating."[4]

To limit oneself to *defending* the philosophy class would therefore be to try to maintain a very old psychological, sexual, sociopolitical deadlock. A familial, social, political transformation, and, correlatively, a transformation of education, from "primary" school on, should, on the contrary, initiate, long before what we call adolescence, the understanding and practice of philosophy. Such a transformation will go through struggles: *inside and outside* the pedagogical field, *within and outside of* philosophy. It would affect not only the forms of its organization but its contents. It would produce new relations between these: inside philosophy and between philosophy and the other disciplines. In order for philosophy to be teachable, in order for it to be taught differently, long before the première and beyond the Terminale, we will have to avoid (a very difficult task) both atomization (for example, to the benefit of the "social sciences") and traditional onto-encyclopedic hegemony. To accomplish that, we will have to rearticulate new contents with those of other scientific and nonscientific fields. Instructors will thus receive a different (philosophical, scientific, pedagogic) training.

Let's anticipate very quickly the interested objection of those who would like to shrug their shoulders. It is not a matter of transporting to the "sixième" a teaching that is already impracticable in the Terminale, but, first of all, of accepting here, as in all the other disciplines, the principle of a calculated *progressivity* in the introduction to, training in, and acquisition of kinds of knowledge. We know that in certain conditions, precisely those that must be freed up, the "philosophical capacity" of a "child" can be very powerful. The progression would concern questions and texts from the tradition as well as those of modernity. Their alleged difficulty is due essentially to the politico-pedagogical machine that is put into question here. It would be especially necessary to organize critical connections between this teaching of philosophy and the other teachings themselves being transformed. To *reorganize* them, rather: who can doubt in fact that a very specific philosophy is *already* being taught through French literature, the languages, history, and even the sciences? And have we ever worried about the real difficulty of these other teachings? About religious instruction? About moral education? The explicit and critical locating of clandestine "philosophemes," as they are at work in teaching and outside of it, requires training. This training can develop in a specific manner *in* each discipline and in competition with it, at the same time that new philosophical reflections and interventions would be involved in the transformed contents. A single example: since it has to resort to new techniques and new conceptual resources (let's juxtapose the signs, to be brief: modern poetics, semiology, linguistics, psychoanalysis, historical materialism, and all the new theoretical mechanisms that take these into account), the teaching of languages and literatures will have to call for new and specific philosophical debates. We can say as much about the mathematical and physical sciences, about all the "human sciences," about their implicit or explicit epistemology.

That does not mean that a philosophical arbitration over all other disciplines must be reinstituted, but that, after new divisions and a redefinition of the so-called "interdisciplinary" limits and practices, appropriate techniques would be taught to analyze the inevitably politically committed philosophical stakes, whether we recognize this or not, even and especially if something like Philosophy were ever to be put into question.

That cannot be done without a general mutation, from the school to the university, that is to say, first of all, in society. Instead of clinging to the "defense-of-philosophy" or resigning ourselves to a certain "death-of-philosophy" and being bound, in both cases, with the same pathos, to the same interests, must we not work to impose, audaciously and offensively, new programs, new contents, new practices?

The Front Today

Such an extension of philosophy will obviously appear *utopian* today. Translation: there is obviously no chance that the forces supporting those in power today could even conceive of the principle of this extension. Still less would they recognize that such a process is, in any event, already underway.

Those who want to resist the liquidation of philosophy by the new "legal guidelines for the education system" will have to participate in both the critique of the current philosophical institution and the elaboration of these new programs, contents, and practices.[5] Once again, they can do so only through struggles, inside and outside of education, and of the teaching of philosophy in particular. Without ever losing sight of the ultimate stakes of such a transformation, they should, in the short term, join forces with all those who intend to thwart an imminent regression and ally themselves with them on a minimal demand: while considering that in other conditions the required teaching of philosophy in the "première" could constitute a first step, the demand that the required teaching of philosophy be maintained in the Terminales, since the discipline is practically excluded from the whole previous cycle. And philosophy should be obligatory in all the sections of Terminale (scientific, technical, and literary), and occupy at least three or four hours a week.

Divided Bodies: Responses to
La Nouvelle Critique

Question I: We believe the "Haby" Reform contains within it a radical destruction of philosophy. What is your position on this?

—The different consequences of the Giscard-Haby[1] plan—I prefer to give it the proper name of its régime—have already been deciphered. Let's not be in a hurry to single out the fate it reserves for philosophy. To abstract this part from the whole has a demobilizing effect; in the worst of cases, it has a corporatist origin, and it would conceal the systematic scope of the plan, from nursery school to the threshold of the university: a system of political dependencies whose most obvious line connects with "reforms" produced in other ministerial circles (the Royer law,[2] for example, or what is likely to come our way from the Secretary of State in charge of Universities about plugging into the economic needs of the regions, and so forth): All these "reforms" serve the exchanges between teaching and the current state of the capitalist market and practically anticipate, as could be shown with texts in hand, the demands of employers. Demands that have been expressly formulated.

That must not stop us from analyzing every bit of the plan in its most acute specificity. As for philosophy, the plan barely "updates" the most dismal endeavors of the Second Empire and the Vichy government. Yes, it is practically equivalent to suppressing the teaching of philosophy as such, in secondary and higher education. Compressed into a single class, because there are only three hours of it per week, philosophy is effectively excluded from all of what is called mandatory education. And everything is done to reduce the number of possible candidates for the "philosophy option."

This mimicry of freedom is all the more shocking and cynical as everything has been put in place to favor social selection, to increase massively the proportion of students leaving before the Terminale, to make teaching positions in philosophy scarce. Since the plan's publication, this machinery has been described in all of its economico-political implications or aims.

And thus its philosophical implications or aims. I would like to insist upon this point, instead of reiterating legitimate but now well-known denunciations. The Giscard-Haby plan has philosophical aims. I will not say that it literally "contains a radical destruction of Philosophy." Within a field of struggle that extends beyond it and determines it from all sides—and that also includes its own philosophical instance—the plan tends to impose an apparatus capable of inculcating a philosophy or maintaining a certain philosophical type, a philosophical force or group of forces, in the dominant position. Even in its sketchy argumentation and crude rhetoric (Cousin did a much better job in the same vein), the text *Pour une modernisation du système éducatif (For a Modernization of the Education System)*, of which six hundred thousand copies were printed, I believe, is *also* a philosophical text that must *also* be interpreted as such. Striving to contain—insofar as this is possible today—the teaching of philosophy as such, this project aims to reduce the scope of a field of critique and struggle at a time when other philosophical forces were likely to progress, were in reality in the process of progressing, there. The government plan would allow a certain force or coalition of forces to occupy the ground and to resist this progress, which is also political, in other ways: through other kinds of teaching, indeed, systems other than the school system in the narrow sense. One more reason for not keeping the debate enclosed within one discipline or even within teaching, and for recalling that what is at stake is not simply the radical destruction or the unending survival of something like Philosophy. There is nothing radical about the accentuation of an offensive that has been underway for a long time. In particular, its inability or its unwillingness to see that this offensive is not a case of *nonphilosophy* against Philosophy has rendered the traditional defense-of-philosophy unable to recognize its own contradiction or to organize anything more than its own retreat. We cannot retrace here the origins of the teaching of philosophy, not even its foundations in France. We need only remember the most recent episodes and keep in mind the powerlessness of such a defense ever since '68 (the reduction of the hours and coefficients in the Terminale, the reduction of the number of teaching positions, the accentuated dissociation of the scientific and the philosophical, the repression exercised against certain teachers or students in the Terminale, and so forth).

But while there is nothing radically new about it, the reform envisaged proposes a formula of compromise that follows a novel pattern, as far as I know: the elimination of the required study of philosophy and of a necessary set number of hours dedicated to the subject in certain sections of the Terminale, a philosophy requirement for all with a greatly reduced schedule (three hours) in the Première. Fouchet indeed thought of this exploitation of the Première, Fontanet of the "optional" ruse.[3] But the situation was not ripe or not urgent enough, and they had to back down. It is therefore not a question of a "new idea" by Haby—that goes without saying—but the effect of a contradiction, the cobbling together of a compromise formation that was expected, after a very brief analysis, to be acceptable in the end. The field of the exercise of critique had to be reduced, for the reasons I have evoked; the ground of philosophical battles (in the Terminale and in higher education) closed. "A training in a *limited field,* one that traditionally keeps at a distance all controversial domains of knowledge and modes of thought" (Haby's emphasis) had to be guaranteed, and the number of "professional" philosophers, about whom the market could not care less, limited. Professional specialization had to be hastened, and the checkpoints of this specialization made more definitive and pushed forward in time. But at the same time, since the balance of forces did not allow the frank suppression, pure and simple, of the teaching of philosophy as such, the vestige conceded had to retain its traditional form: locked up in a single class, at the end of secondary studies, a cloister for the old "queen-of-disciplines" or for the ceremony of the "crowning-of-studies," a liberal-neutral-objective-secular (see above) reflection on an accepted knowledge. Virginal innocence, questioning and (understandably) taken aback, is not supposed to see the curtain raised on the scene until the moment when family, school, and classes have already consolidated their own preparation. It was thought that this compromise would reassure everyone, even a certain right (and, why not, a certain left) that sees in the philosophy class (in its classical model) a safeguard against the spread outside the institution of philosophies that it considers wild and that it would rather domesticate, reappropriate, frame: this is how Duruy justified reestablishing the philosophy class under the Second Empire. This contradiction (maintaining the status quo without maintaining it) took a specific form that led to tampering (irresistibly, imprudently) with what one still called, for old times' sake, the-philosophy-class, that is, a somewhat sacred place in which for more than a century the same contradiction has been hidden, petrified, and naturalized. It was already a compromise formation, ruled by a—relatively stable—state of the balance of forces. On the one hand, because of the number of hours of teaching, the massive grouping of questions, a quasi-transferential scene, and so forth, the penetration of a certain philosophical type and the exercise of a philosophical critique corresponding to this type were of course possible. But the politico-sexual deadlock remained as tightly secured as ever: a class for one class, bourgeois youth between puberty and their entrance into adult life, with an education that was more literary than scientific, led to consider as natural and eternal a very singular program that is apparently eclectico-baroque but also quite favorable to a particular ideological framework. Of course, given the complex and contradictory structure of this framework, the liberal critique could be deployed against more than one dogmatism, and sometimes, in situations and according to relays or fractions still to be analyzed, against the interests that the institution were massively meant to serve, thus contradicting, as always happens, the simplicity of reproduction. This must be recognized.

The compromise was therefore unstable by definition. Forced by the market to adapt it, the governmental project at the same time revealed that the form of the compromise was not inviolable. It is as though, through a breach that should not have opened, or rather, across a more troubled or troubling representation, the contradiction had appeared as such. We must not hurry to fill in this breach. By tampering with the "philosophy-class," by provoking a virulent national debate on this subject, the Giscard-Haby maneuver brought to light (the compulsive imprudence is here ruled by a necessity that would have to be analyzed in all its consequences, and the worsening repression almost strips bare again, with obscene effects, the very thing it should have concealed, all the structures here being paradoxical and contradictory) that the-philosophy-class was not natural, neutral, and untouchable; from the moment that the-philosophy-class no longer corresponds to a given historico-political transaction, it can be destroyed just as it was constructed. The struggle against the plan therefore threw a very harsh light upon a principal cleavage that also cuts across the teaching body, that is, the set of those who claim to be interested in the practice of philosophy. The struggle for philosophy, in philosophy, around philosophy, in fact cuts through (there is nothing astonishing about this) the entire teaching body, teachers as well as students. The opposition to the Giscard-Haby plan and to the previous reforms already had a considerable history. We can now begin to identify it. We saw that a whole "defense" of philosophy, essentially reproducing Cousin's argumentation (in *Défense de l'Université et de la Philosophie*, 1844), established itself on traditional bases: the preservation of the status quo, an immutable attachment to the-philosophy-class, an apolitical and objectively corporatist, idealistic, conservative critique of a plan considered "threatening," indeed "criminal," regarding, say, a singular corpus, a discipline that is as vulnerable as it is preeminent. What is more, this defense of a pure power of questioning, as crucial as it is impoverished, crucial because it occupies the shotgun seat, finds its objective reinforcement in the partisans of the death-of-philosophy. The pathos is fundamentally the same. This defense in itself has never been very effective, and in any case has never defended what it said or believed it was defending.

In the other camp (I leave aside, *for the moment*, in the analysis of this principal confrontation, differences that another situation might bring to the fore), those who, taking an unequivocal position against the systematic whole of the plan as a political project, demand not only that philosophy as such continue to be taught where it is already taught (in all the Terminales as a required subject), but also and already in previous classes: at least, to begin with, from the Seconde on. Philosophy must no longer be contained in the fortress-prison of one class (the Terminale or the Première). This offensive position has brought together, for the first time, a large number of teachers, students, and pupils from all disciplines. It was elaborated and clearly stated by Greph,[4] in particular, in a call largely approved among the most activist students and teachers. It demands that philosophy be "aligned with the other disciplines, that is, that it be subject to a progressive teaching spread over several years." The thing is to put an end to the false "privilege" ("the glory of French education") in whose name a critical teaching was fenced off in an imperial reserve. By demanding this alignment, we challenge this sort of hegemonic belatedness (a notion that I cannot analyze here), no doubt, but we also give the teaching of philosophy as such the means and the space granted to other disciplines, at least means and space for a critical debate elsewhere, for an articulation of branches of knowledge, and so forth. At least. The issue was not to approve or negotiate the introduction-reduction of philosophy in the Première under the form provided for by the government. On the contrary. Neither in fact or objectively nor is this our intention: rejecting the plan *in its entirety*, Greph proposes:

in the short term, to join forces with all those who intend to oppose the imminent regression and to form an alliance with them on a minimal demand: we believe that the teaching of philosophy in the "Première" could, under other conditions (a transformation of its contents and of pedagogical practice, among others), constitute a first positive component; but we demand that philosophy be maintained as a requirement in the Terminale within a common core curriculum. These minimal demands are meaningful, of course, only within a struggle for a true overhaul of the teaching of philosophy—and of education in general—an overhaul that alone is capable of imposing the idea that there is no natural age for the practice of philosophy and that philosophy should already be taught as early as the Seconde and in technical schools.

By contrast, the traditional defense of the status quo, a demobilized, demobilizing defense that is always already in retreat, in advance finds itself in "concert" with those in power.

Is this surprising? Certain (usually passive) defenders-of-the-philosophy-class, murmuring their protests or requesting useless meetings in ministries, even seats on the committees designed to fill what the minister calls the final "packages" of a reform decided upon without consultation, these defenders, faced with the counterattacks of Greph, turned furiously on us: for we had dared to change terrain; we were so impudent as to suggest that philosophy must, could, be taught not only in the Terminale but outside of and before it! The violence of certain reactions gave an indication of the investments, the passions, and the impulses involved here. All of a sudden the principal target was no longer the government project but the incredible undertaking of Greph! Let us consider here only the explicit objections, whether they directly targeted Greph or the logic of its position.

1. When it "unanimously" "rejected the project of an introduction to philosophy in the Première and the Seconde" and "thought that philosophy ought to take over where French left off," the National Office of the Associations of Teachers of Philosophy in Public Education invoked in advance the following pretext, as though one must never demand anything but what the minister would be happy to give us: the hours taught in the Première and Seconde risked not being added to those in the Terminale. Greph demands, on the contrary, that philosophy be present with more hours in these three classes, in a common core curriculum.

2. Students' alleged "lack of maturity": this argument is not only that of the association I just cited. One finds it everywhere. In conditions and throughout a history that Greph is currently attempting to study, multi-

ple interests and phantasms have cooperated to construct this dogma and to make it pass for common sense. Even if the value of intellectual maturity were not, at this level of generalization, more than suspect, even if there were no way of proving, and in the most convincing way, under certain conditions, the more than sufficient "maturity" of pupils—not to mention their demand for philosophy—why is no one astonished by the fact that disciplines equally "difficult" are taught from the sixième on, and by the fact that, in one way or another, so much philosophy seeps through these other disciplines?

3. It is also said: since philosophy "forms-a-whole," a "structured-system-of-concepts," and so forth, its teaching must be global and be given in one year. Without getting involved in the very difficult problem of such a "systematic-totality," let's accept this hypothesis: But why, then, one year (nine months)? Why this number of hours? (And how many? The number varies from section to section, is being reduced incessantly, and tends more and more to be interrupted.) Why not a month, a week, an hour, the time of a single long sentence or of the wink of an eye? With a logic just as respectfully subordinated to the aforementioned philosophical systematicity, the severest ministerial compression can be supported. But the same logic has another relay: if spread over several years, teaching would be entrusted to "different instructors [*maîtres*]," and this would in some way damage the consistency of philosophical teaching. We are thus referred to what is in fact a very classical concept of philosophical mastery or magistrality. Let's call it, subject to analysis, Socratico-transferential. Not only does it involve all sorts of risks (dogmatism, charismatism, and so forth), it is not even in line with the critico-liberal ethics of the "traditional defense." Logically, it should lead to the uninterrupted presence of the same instructor in higher education (why not present the same request there?), indeed one's entire life, a mentor, guide to wisdom, confessor or director of conscience, the analyst for an interminable training. What, then, is one afraid of when the unity of the philosophy-class or of the teacher-of-philosophy comes into question?

4. Reservations were also voiced about the value of progressivity: Does it not risk provoking an empiricist fragmentation or incompleteness? Or reproducing the traditional teaching, merely making it less consistent, more vulnerable to ideological corruption, exposed to dissolution into non-philosophical disciplines? Or extending the imperium of philosophy, indeed, in this or that historico-political situation, of *a* philosophy, repro-

ducing thus the very thing that must be transformed? This objection is more interesting, and it is the only one that makes a certain labor possible. It must therefore be specified that the value of progressivity belongs, of course, to a very classical tradition of pedagogy. We must not welcome it with tranquil assurance. Still less fetishize the word or slogan "progressivity." It is simply a question, in the very specific phase of a struggle and a strategy, of winning acceptance for the *extension* of the teaching of philosophy over several years, of making it coextensive with other subjects taught, for which progressivity is accepted as completely "natural." By referring to an established norm, we hope to take philosophy out of its narrow pedagogical bounds and to justify a demand (for class hours equivalent to those in the scientific or literary disciplines). Once this legitimate extension is acquired—at the price of a difficult struggle—other debates will be sure to arise to define the contents and forms of the kinds of teaching, their structure, and the communications between them and the outside of the academy. Greph's proposals concerning progressivity appeal—indissociably—to such transformations. Of course if, under the pretext of progressivity, an apprenticeship or even a training (whose ends remain suspect) were reestablished, if the schools were to issue a "training" oriented like a progress toward the harmonious fulfillment of some telos, whatever it be, we would, we will, certainly have to fight against such a reappropriation, whose risk (or security) will always reappear. Other fronts will emerge. But once philosophy is no longer the lot of one class, the broadening of the field will make the work, the critical exchanges, the debates, and the confrontations more effective. This much at least is already certain: to refuse the extension of the teaching of philosophy under the pretext that the motif of "progressivity" does not resolve all the problems and can be reappropriated by what is called the opposing camp is to give credence to a mystifying argument, whether or not it is advanced in good faith. Mystifying and without future, it has been shown.

We must, on the contrary, work from now on to create the conditions for an extension and transformation of so-called philosophical teaching. We must open debates, fashion experiments, join with the greatest number of instructors and students, not only in the "discipline" of philosophy, and not only in school. The process is underway. We have more than one symptom of it. And the ground for struggles to come is already laid out in it. Whatever the immediate fate of the government plan, this regime cannot give itself a "system of education" that does not point out its own contradictions in their most critical and manifest state. Critical and manifest precisely because systematic and philosophical and because education there becomes a more and more fateful stake. The regime will therefore have to pretend to change systems every day or to have several alternative systems always under construction: with a compulsive, convulsive bustle, as though in the hurry of a final phase.

Question II: We believe that philosophy has an irreplaceable function that, in our opinion, includes two fundamental points:
   —putting into place the learning of processes of rational knowledge;
   —learning to conduct an orderly and democratic debate.

Question III: Beyond the simple and insufficient defense of philosophy such as it is, how do you think philosophy should be thought?

—If philosophy in fact has an "irreplaceable function," is it because nothing could replace it were it to die? I believe instead that it is always replaced: such would be the form of its irreplaceability. That is why the fight is never simply for or against Philosophy, the life or death, the presence or absence, in teaching, of Philosophy, but between forces and their philosophical instances, inside and outside of the academic institution.

As to the "two fundamental points" and the third question, I cannot respond here in the same form and according to the same premises, without asking you a lot of other questions in turn, about each of the notions involved. That would demand much more time, more space, at least, and different analyses, different divisions. Let's say that I am trying, that I will try, to respond to them elsewhere.

Philosophy of the Estates General

(I have asked for the floor right away in order to say a few words—and I think this is necessary—about the preparation, indeed, the premises of these Estates General. I do this, of course, in my own name, as one of the members, among many others, of a planning committee whose working sessions were absolutely open and whose participants were even more numerous and diverse than is suggested by the list as first published. As to what preceded and prepared for today's meeting, we owe you some information or explanations. Those that I will propose to you, from my own point of view, are my responsibility alone and, moreover, are my responsibility only insofar as I took part in the initial work.)

These Estates General of Philosophy should mark an event.
After which, as is sometimes said, "nothing will be the same as before."
One cannot set the conditions for events. By definition.
But since, by itself, the holding of these Estates General already has the scope of an event, one can say, beginning right now, and no matter what the future is, that it *will have taken place* on one condition. On at least one condition. Which one?
On the condition that it belong to no agency or instance in particular.
I do not say to no particular person, but to no individual or collective personality, to no nameable figure or configuration, to no group already legitimately or legally constituted, no research or teaching institution, no professional and hierarchical order, no corporate association, no union or political party. The Estates General must constitute themselves and themselves debate their own legitimacy.
I will not remind you here of all the political paradoxes that follow upon

the logic of such a situation. Knowing these paradoxes is our job. Thus, for example, some of us had to be able and believed we were able to constitute ourselves *provisionally* as spokespersons and act as responsible mediators, so to speak, of the appeal that the Estates General would have in a certain sense launched in its own direction and to which certain of us would have been the first to answer. It was indeed necessary, in effect, that certain among us be able to meet, claiming to perceive, understand, and translate *in their fashion* a first appeal. From that point on, they thought they ought to take what is called the initiative or the responsibility for the organization of the Estates General. In part—which was at times a heavy part—this organization remained technical and neutral. But this could only be a part, and it would be frivolous and dishonest to deny that. An interpretation and certain expectations were already at work, and it is on this subject that I would like to venture a few statements. They are brief and schematic, and thus all the more open to discussion.

The planning committee merely tried—this was one of its rules and I believe I can attest to it—to translate in a faithful way the signs of a broad virtual consensus.

To be sure, the members of the committee had their part in this consensus; they themselves gave proof of this, whatever may *elsewhere* have been their philosophy of the Estates General, their philosophy of the consensus or the signs, indeed their philosophy of philosophy.

To do justice to the conditions of this virtual accord, they tried to respect the differences, even the fundamental disagreements [*différends*] that could *in another context* divide all those who would be gathering here.

The shared and implicit certainty was, it seems to me, the following: in the present situation, this consensus could only be affirmed *as such*, could only be put forward as such in practical, effective, and efficacious undertakings to the extent that it made itself by rights independent of the constituted agencies I have just named, whether they be pedagogical, professional, corporative, syndicalist, or political, *et caetera* (and under that "et caetera," you could list whatever individual or group might be tempted to use these Estates General as a base, studio, or staging ground). That these agencies might also, *in another context*, be able to claim competency, legitimacy, even—there is still time—efficacy in this or that specific domain, no one will disagree. It is possible and normal that many among us feel represented by these organizations and that we say so even here. It is desirable—for obvious reasons to which I will return in a moment—that the proposals the Estates General will be led to make tomorrow should receive the approval and then the support of such organizations. It is more than desirable, of course. But it does not seem to me desirable that, de facto or by decision, our proposals be *subordinated, even implicitly,* to the agreement of these organizations. For them as for us, freedom and independence should be, it seems to me, total. This is even the condition of the possible alliances of solidarity which I would consider, for myself and within certain limits, indispensable.

Why? Because the consensus, to give it that name, seems to exceed considerably the borders of these legitimate organizations; it does not find itself to be strictly or fully represented there, particularly as concerns that which demands an *emergency* transformation of an *unacceptable* situation. This consensus, if it is to exist, seems to take shape beyond a certain number of philosophical or politico-ideological divisions.

Is this to say that it remains philosophically neutral or apolitical? Not at all.

It corresponds no doubt to a new position taking, to a new philosophical and political taking sides, even if such a taking sides no longer recognizes itself in the reproduction of codes and still less in common stereotypes. This reproduction would be, on the contrary, the most visible and the most sinister mark of the limits within which some would like to enclose philosophical debate—the debate for philosophy or as to philosophy (in it, around it, inside and outside its institutions)—limits within which some would like to leave us to fight among ourselves and which we want to tear down.

One may want such a consensus, if it exists or if it is still to come, to be very broad, but it will not be unanimity or a general will. It would rather be a matter today of a broad front and another front. At stake perhaps is what has been called in the tradition we know so well "the need of philosophy" or "the interest in philosophy."

Interest in philosophy, interest of philosophy: this does not designate the particular taste for a type of exercise, an expertise, or a discipline, the specialist's vocation, or a cult that is respectful to the point of frightened fetishism for everything that has the name philosophy, for the philosophical tradition, or even for a philosophy. The interest in philosophy, *if there is any,* is an affirmation that *of itself,* in itself, knows *no limit.* If there is any interest in philosophy, it is not conditioned. That is, perhaps, what we must attempt to think here.

Now, in a given historical situation, when social forces, a nation, a state organization, indeed—and we would be seriously mistaken to neglect this today—an interstate organization comes to the point of limiting or, practically, forbidding the affirmation of this interest in philosophy, then it is not that philosophy *in general* is being repressed by nonphilosophical barbarity. Rather, this is the sign of a new conflict among forces, fractions, or alliances of forces. And it is this configuration we must analyze: its major types and its long sequences, as well as its most novel and acutely contemporary traits. Philosophical discourse is always an interested party in these forces and always in different ways. An interested party means at least that this discourse does not simply express, reflect, or represent these forces any more than it sets them in motion. The relation is of another sort.

To analyze or to attempt to transform the situation of philosophy and its teaching, as well as its general context, in France, in Europe, and beyond, we have at our disposal, of course, all sorts of schemas. I will not deduce all of their types, but I will recall that in each of these schemas a philosophy and an interpretation of the philosophical are involved. To comprehend and combat the offensive organized against philosophy in France, conceptual instruments, levers of analysis have been put to the test of certain historical precedents. And, during the past few years, some of us, alone or in research groups, have used them and above all *displaced* them. But I think that these Estates General would be heading for failure if, in the discourses offered here, in the analyses, the practical resolutions, the modes of intervention, resistance, or affirmation, they did not take as their rule the irreducible singularity, the essential novelty of our situation— *both* in its intraphilosophical moment *and* in its general historical space. While in certain respects this moment may recall, as has often been said and rightly so, the stifling of philosophy during the Second Empire or the Occupation, or even analogous manifestations outside of France during identical or different regimes, the situation here clearly differs from them because of certain original characteristics that we must not fail to recognize. Recognizing them, however, is not easy; to do so, one would have to mobilize new socioeconomic analyses, other political problematics, overtures in the direction of objects that professional philosophers have not been trained to study—I am thinking in particular of what is very hastily gathered up under the generic name of "media" and of the "power of the media." Provided one does not content oneself with the theatrical representation, even where it seems to be critical here and there, that the "media" give of themselves through some of their most successful numbers or their most talented champions, one can find in the techno-politics of telecommunications something inescapably at stake, at stake also for philosophy, very new in certain of its forms, its operations, its evaluation, its market, and technology.

Yet, however new and necessary they must be, all of these analyses will not allow us to dispense with an *affirmative* interpretation of the relation to philosophy and of the relation of philosophy to itself, if such a thing exists. In other words, across all the questions that we will have to debate here (institutional, technical, professional, pedagogical, socioeconomic questions), we ought, it seems to me, to hear and let resonate the great questions of philosophy *and* of thought, of the present form of their destination no less than of their beginnings and rebeginnings.

In two words: What is said and done today in the name or under the name of philosophy? And as concerns philosophy? And as concerns thought? What is taught, what ought to be or can still be taught *under this name, in this name and as concerns that which presents itself under this name*?

If the expression "Estates General" quickly suggested itself to us at the moment of naming this event, it is no doubt, more or less explicitly, in order to signal that there was something here to be *inaugurated*.

People will say that the reference to the Estates General is rather traditional: before the Revolution, they were often the place of hierarchized and conservative demands; moreover, in the last few years, certain colloquia have adorned themselves a little too quickly with this title of revolutionary nobility. And yet, despite these risks, it imposed itself on us. Laughing somewhat, we liked the idea of picking up the reference, perhaps out of all proportion, to that great revolutionary upheaval.

Moreover, whatever we might finally think about the *Aufklärung* and the Revolution of 1789, I myself find a certain case being tried against them here and there today (a case that is often confused, hasty, presumptuous) to be one of the signs of the loudspeaker obscurantism about which we are going to have to debate here, overcoming our distaste.

Above all: To call for Estates General, to call oneself by that name, was to avoid a certain number of titles that would all have referred back to the forms of assembly and institutional codes I was talking about a moment ago. The Estates General should be, in fact, neither a protest meeting with speakers and platforms, nor a political convention, nor a conference of specialists, nor the board meeting or general assembly of some constituted, legitimate, and registered body, whatever it may be. If the Estates General of 1789 broke with those that preceded them, it was because they inaugurated something by proclaiming themselves a national and then a constitutional assembly, putting radically in play the order or the orders that had previously constituted them. If there was an event, it was on the order of this eminently philosophical project of self-foundation, which has its initiative only in itself, without any reference to prior guarantees, hierarchies, or legitimacies.

I do not know whether, for philosophy, this gesture has a meaning or a chance today (and at least for the moment, here, I am not going to venture to discuss the bases of this problem). I believe, however, in fact I know that, *mutatis mutandis,* such an idea, the principle of an analogous ambition, is audible in the Appeal for the Estates General of Philosophy.

For example, the word "affirmation" lets it be heard at least three different times.

Now if, over the next two days and beyond these two days, we are not to lose sight of any of the concrete givens, the conjunctural premises, the empirical and tactical necessities of our action, the constraints of all sorts with which we must reckon even in detail, then we will only be able to do so and it will only be worth doing if measured by what I will call traditionally the Idea, the great principle that comes to be affirmed in the Appeal.

While we hear and understand this affirmation, it is not certain that we all hear it in the same manner. Because it is not clear. In a certain manner, it had to be that way. A certain enigmatic reserve had to remain, one that must not be confused with an equivocation to be manipulated. This reserve comes, perhaps, from what remains essentially *undecided* today in the destination of philosophy.

The signs of this indecision are concentrated in the prologue of the Appeal. There is, for example, no indecision in the brief demonstration called "A Tableau Noir" or in the minimal demands formulated in "To Begin With." What is schematically but clearly brought together in these two documents seems to me to derive from objective and statistical demonstration. It is *indisputable* that philosophical teaching and research are declining and will continue to decline in an accelerated manner until they reach atrophy and irreversible asphyxia if the devices put in place by the present government, by those that preceded it, and by the forces, fractions, or alliances of forces that support them are allowed to take over the stage. It is *indisputable* that this process—which signals a serious danger not only for philosophy but for the whole of the educational system and of society—will only be interrupted on the conditions we define, at least for the short and medium term: for example, an increase in the number of instructors and therefore of students and researchers; a redefinition of the "needs" and a minimal staffing per class; the minimal schedule of four hours for all lycée students in all categories; the retention of philosophy and of philosophy professors in the écoles normales d'instituteurs: the *extension* of the teaching of philosophy to every year of the *second cycle* and outside philosophy departments in the university—*extension* with *all* of its consequences, which are not limited either to philosophy or even to education. This last demand—*extension*—is *legitimate, vital, decisive,* and the impressive number of those who subscribed to this Appeal, as well as of those who are participating or are represented at these Estates General, allows one to measure the distance traveled since the moment certain people pretended to judge this extension utopic or dangerous. There is nothing in the two documents accompanying the Appeal that cannot be demonstrated. If we want to be consistent, we will attach to them—resolutely, despite whatever happens—our uncompromising demands and clear-cut determinations.

Naturally, this demonstrative character, this recourse to the most stubborn objectivity, could not characterize the Appeal itself, in particular its prologue. This was, it seems to me, neither possible nor desirable. There, an *affirmation* is put forward, and an affirmation is not demonstrative in the same way. It commits, it decides, it pronounces—in this case, *for philosophy. Yes* to philosophy.

But it can today no longer do that in one stroke, a simple and indivisible stroke. We are no longer young enough, neither is philosophy, for such a militant affirmation on our part to be simple, lighthearted, unruffled, fresh, and untried. If there is reason to reaffirm, it comes at a very singular moment, overburdened with history—the history of philosophy, of this society, of its institutions, and of its pedagogical structures.

We do not forget all the water that has flowed under the bridge called philosophy. It has been a long time since we were ready to be taken for a ride, on whatever boat, and we're not about to treat yesterday's rainwater as something fallen from heaven, especially when it's the old trick of appealing to the purest and most archaic source. A vigilant, rigorous memory, one critical of this history of philosophy, does not necessarily imply that the affirmation I am talking about must be weighed down or broken with age. It can, at least if it has the strength, be just the opposite.

The result is that the Appeal opens with an affirmation *and* an indecision. It thus does not have the same demonstrative character as the two succeeding documents. Whence certain questions, which I would like to try to answer.

The prologue of the Appeal has a somewhat optimistic resonance, even (why deny it?) a triumphant one. It alleges a certain number of signs that could attest to the life, youth, and diversity of the demand for philosophy in this country and throughout the world. Some of us were bothered by this (among those who approved overall our gesture and even among those who, like myself, took a, let us say, active part in the drafting of this text). What bothered them? A certain formulation that might lead one to believe all these signs were cause only for rejoicing, notably the signs coming from *the* publishing industry (by which I mean *in general*), *the* written and spoken press (*in general*), *the* television industry (*in general*).

Now, it goes without saying (we know this only too well) that things are far from being that simple. Today no one, either among philosophers who are somewhat aware or among those who have a little experience of the world and have developed some discernment in these areas (publishing, press, television), would dare testify to philosophical vitality or rigor by invoking a large part, we can say the major part, of what has been exhibited recently on the stage that is most in the public eye, of what noisily proclaims itself to be philosophy in all sorts of studios, where, as of a relatively recent and very determined date, the loudest speakers have seen the loudspeakers entrusted to them without wondering (in the best of cases) why suddenly they were being given all this space and all this air time in order to speak *thus* and say precisely *that*.

If one thinks of what dominates the scene or the market, of what so often (I do not say always, for one would, of course, have to refine, differentiate, multiply the types of analysis, which is what I hope we will begin to do here) can be produced there and can invade everything with its naïve, precritical paucity of thought, ignorant to the point of barbarity, smug and gloating to the point of buffoonery, or even, for us, for me in any case, unforgivably boring—if one thinks of all this, then one may indeed be bothered by the appearance of using it as an argument to prove that philosophy is booming. Such was simply not the intention of the drafters of the Appeal.

Here, in a few words, is the principle of the analysis that convinced me, for my part, to subscribe to this Appeal and to take part in drafting it in this form. To be sure, this form is not perfect; by necessity, it is too brief, elliptical, simplifying. I will not defend it for itself or the letter of it, but only its implicit logic. What is more, the Appeal was not meant to commit the Estates General to anything in advance or to be approved by them a priori; it is right here that it will be submitted to discussion.

In the first place, it was, as you may well imagine, for us not a matter of applauding the content and the quality of all these equivocal signs, notably those that snore or rattle away on the front page of the newspaper or on television. No one is asking for that, and nothing in the Appeal seems to me to invite that. This said, these are signs or symptoms that we would be wrong to neglect, whose scope must be interrogated from all angles, which is to say, from angles and according to criteria and modes of questioning for which we are not all equally prepared. The *intra*-philosophical (others would say the *properly* philosophical) criteria, which, when our sense of humor is on the blink, might often dictate the most ruthless—in fact the most somber and desperate—evaluations when we read or hear this or that performance, these criteria concerning the *philosophical* quality of such messages no doubt do not provide the essential measure of what is happening—and even what is happening with respect to philosophy. In the wake of all sorts of transformations or upheavals in the sociology of education and outside education, in the ideological and philosophico-political landscape of this country and of the world, in the technology of information, the recourse to something that still *resembles* philosophy manifests itself largely in social spaces, in forms and according to norms that largely overflow the space of professional competence, which, moreover, has never been above suspicion in this regard and which also possesses, let us not forget, the old form of powers of evaluation, promotion, selection, and even its little pocket "media"; it thus possesses powers, very concentrated professional and editorial levers, whose critical analysis we ought not to perform sparingly or with indulgence. Who can seriously regret that this space of professional competence has been overwhelmed, and along with it the social space that traditionally supplied the majority of philosophers by profession in France?

Such a regret would be not only sad, reactive, negative, it would also be totally in vain. This process is and must be irreversible. But it does not excuse us from asking ourselves what are the profound and multiple conditions of this enlargement and of the strange effects it is in the process of producing. It would be a serious mistake on our part to ignore the fact that when we are often shocked or made indignant by certain of these effects, it is because, even in our bodies, we live our relation to philosophy behind very selective protecting filters, in laboratories whose social, political, and philosophical conditioning deserves to be interrogated just as much as the one that produces, in newspapers and on television, some philosophy or something that, despite everything, retains a resemblance with philosophy.

I will give you my hypothesis in its raw state, in a few words and nothing more for the moment: it is that of a filiation between the dominant machinery of yesterday and the dominant machinery of today, almost a direct filiation, one that is natural if not legitimate (as one says in families) and in any case essentially largely homogeneous. In the past, processes of evaluation, legitimization, promotion, selection, hierarchization, as well as marginalization would have called for—they do call for because they are still inveterate and concentrated—a critical and relentless vigilance. For my part, I do not believe that the philosophical productions authorized and legitimized by the official apparatuses (yesterday's or today's) constitute, when taken together, of course, an irreproachable reference from whose heights we could look down on what passes for philosophy or what bypasses philosophy outside of the academic enclosure.

It seems to me, therefore, that today, tomorrow, or the next day the Estates General should interrogate from all its angles (philosophical, political, national, or not) the scope of this massive recourse today to something that retains, despite all the gross simplifications, the smugness, and the weaknesses, a distant but certain likeness to something like philosophy.

If, among all the necessary tasks, I insist on the one that concerns the functioning of the market, the techno-politics of the "media," and what the government administers under the title "Culture and Communication," it is precisely because the Appeal referred, more or less prudently, to signs coming from these places.

It is to be hoped that this work on the techno-politics of the media will from now on be given a rightful place, let us repeat, in the "philosophical training" to come. Such work has begun here and there, in very diverse styles and with diverse results. It is advisable, perhaps, not only to extend and systematize this program, to diffuse its results but also to avoid letting it be too easily reappropriated to the point of becoming a source of supplementary surplus value for the device that it itself analyzed and for those who go along with it; for soon we will be seeing work such as this (that is, work that presents itself as a war machine against the techno-politics of the "media") reinvested, overexploited, even gadgetized by the apparatuses, sometimes even by the very agents who find themselves targets to begin with. This is a fairly reliable criterion for measuring the effectiveness of critical work.

Now, as regards all these symptoms, what does the Appeal say?

It speaks of "contrast." Between all the manifestations of a philosophical boom or demand, which include the unfurling in the press of a sophomoric anything-at-all that is never just anything at all, between this glaring abundance outside the school and the university on the one hand and, on the other, the stifling of research and teaching, there is a *contrast.*

Not a contradiction, a contrast.

The hypothesis we can discuss here would thus be the following: Not only is there no contradiction in this, but there are all the signs of a coherent politics, whether or not its cohesion passes by way of conscious representations in the mind of a subject or a group of subjects.

In any case, the effects of this coherence are obvious for us: the control, manipulation, diversion, or reappropriation of discourses will be that much easier outside the academy, through a maximum of telecommunicative trajectories, if the capacities for critical evaluation, for trained discernment, for practiced vigilance are weak or weakly represented in the country (in number and in quality), isolated and marginalized. This law is valid not only for philosophical matters, of course, and we should be careful not to enclose ourselves within these matters. And when I speak of practiced or trained vigilance, I am not thinking only of what could be called the *competence* of philosophers by profession, trained for that purpose, but of all those to whom people would like today to deny an encounter with philosophy, and therefore with quite a few other questions. Briefly put, the more the field of philosophical training is restricted in this country, the less critical competence there will be outside the academy (I am not afraid of the word "competence"; the fact that the word has been put on trial by some should not make us forget that competence can be a weapon of resistance—for example, against all sorts of human rights violations, abuses of police power, and injustice); the less critical formation and information there is, the easier it will be to pass off, even to inculcate, the anything-at-all that is never just anything at all. Thus, I believe it was necessary to call attention to an apparent and all the more symptomatic "contrast" so as to analyze and combat a fundamental complementarity.

I say complementarity, and not (necessarily) connivance or complicity—the latter word refers to a judicial code that I do not like and it is not at all a matter here of incriminating anyone whatsoever. What is more, no one is purely and simply external to this process, even if no one occupies the same place there—far from it, and fortunately so. A profound complementarity, therefore, between an unqualifiable repression of philosophical teaching and research, on the one hand, and, on the other hand, the frantic overexploitation, outside the academy, of philosophical signs and discourses whose weakness, facileness, convenience are the most glaring but also, for the big decision makers, for the great deciding forces of our society, the most acceptable, the most useful, and the most reassuring. One could show that cohabitation can be very harmonious today between, for example, what remains of petty, reactive philosophical powers within educational institutions, of uptight, ossified academicism still clutching the control levers on the one side, and, on the other side, outside the institution, the big philosophical theme park and the amnesiac, gossipy stereotypes that run wild under more or less anonymous, discreet, but effective supervision.

These two types of power neither contradict each other nor get in each other's way in the least, for a reason. Each conditions the other.

For my own part, these last years I have been very aware that the publications billing themselves as philosophy and benefiting, not by chance, from the most diligent and effective, the most assiduous, promotional support, that the publications most likely to be accepted, let us say, are also the most devoid of, the most exempt from, any question, even more so, any critical problematic concerning the official politics of education, the educational and university systems, the publishing and telecommunication systems, the rhetorical normativity controlled by these systems, which is to say, above all, that the majority of said publications reproduce outside the academy the most well-behaved scholarly models. There is here a solid complementarity (although it may sometimes be difficult to read) between the most immobilized, uptight academicism and all that which, outside the school and the university, in the mode of representation and spectacle, plugs almost immediately into the channels or networks with the highest acceptability. It is this complementarity, this configuration—wherever it appears—that one must, it seems to me, combat. One must combat it simultaneously, joyously, without accusation, without putting on trial, without nostalgia, with an uncompromising gaiety. Without regret for the more padded forms that were sometimes (only sometimes) more distinguished, less rowdy, and that will have in part prepared yesterday what we are inheriting today. In part at least—let us discern.

One last word, if you do not mind. I just said "uncompromising." Well, an affirmation, if there is any, must affirm something uncompromising, that is, not negotiable, intransigent. Affirmation, if there is any, is *unconditional.*

During these two days and thereafter, through that which, we must hope, will assure almost everywhere in France a sort of permanent active duty of these Estates General until there can be another large meeting, it will no doubt be necessary to undertake actions, transactions, complex, careful, persevering, minute negotiations with all the interested parties—official, governmental, and even presidential agencies, labor unions and corporative associations, whose support will be essential to us. We will have to define carefully, in all areas, the objectives and the stakes of these negotiations and consultations, as well as their margins.

But we ought also to formulate uncompromisable, nonnegotiable demands. No affirmation without that. Such would be the philosophy of the Estates General. And along this line of the nonnegotiable, which we also ought to trace very concretely (proposals will be made in this direction), the Estates General should, in my opinion, reach decisions in an absolutely unconditioned, autonomous fashion, and invent, so as to accede to this, collective or individual modes of action, intervention, resistance that are its own; one must hope—for nothing will be possible without this solidarity—that these will play an avant-garde role and will set an example to be followed, not only but especially for corporative, labor union, and political organizations.

It has already happened.[1]

(I yield the floor to Roland Brunet. A moment ago I said that the Estates General should belong to no one, be beholden to no one, and I reiterate that. But, perhaps I will contradict myself by saying nevertheless that without Brunet I doubt that these Estates General could have taken place, whether we are talking about the "idea" or the planning of this event. Several of us here could testify to this.)

Appendix

Appeal

The demand for philosophy has never asserted itself in a more lively, youthful, and diverse way. It is everywhere on the move and everywhere it gets things moving, in this country, but also, as recent orientation discussions at UNESCO remind us, throughout the world. Whether or not we are philosophers by profession, we can testify to this and recognize in it a vital necessity. This surge is literally overwhelming: it manifests itself, in effect, through new forms, beyond institutional partitions and academic criteria, in social circles and age groups that have been kept away from it until now. The demonstration is breaking out everywhere—in schools and in the university, in the most diverse kinds of teaching (technical, literary, scientific, juridical, medical, and so forth), but also, in a daily fashion, in the life of publishing, in the press, on radio and television, in all artistic practices, in the debate over the fundamental directions of society, and so forth. Not only the philosophical tradition, but the most novel and adventurous research is everywhere being asked to intervene, to renew the languages of analysis and criticism, or to open new roads for reflection. And those who are undertaking to do so are more and more numerous, even when they do not practice philosophy as a profession.

Between this extraordinary boom and the official politics of education, the contrast is frightening. The government continues to put in place plans that would implacably condemn philosophical teaching and research. We already have withdrawal and atrophy. If we sat back and did nothing, tomorrow things would be more or less dead. But we will not sit back. The seriousness of the stakes is no longer limited to an order of research and teaching, to what is considered to be the body of the discipline, with its competencies, its norms, its profession, and its institutions. At stake as well are the whole educational system and thus, more broadly, everything a society expects from the teaching and research it offers itself. Among ourselves, we may interpret in different ways the offensives against philosophy, but we know that they have always had the most harmful political aims and effects. In the singular context they are developing in France today, these offensives no doubt ought to call forth new analyses and new forms of riposte. These are urgently called for because the will to liquidate has never been so insistent—often arrogant, cynical, obscurantist.

That is why we call on all those who share our concerns, our anger, and our hope to come together as the Estates General of Philosophy, beginning on June 16, 1979. Let it be understood that it will not be a question of merely charting the givens or the sinister perspectives of the official policy (for information in this regard, see "A Tableau Noir,"[2] a document accompanying this appeal). It will not be a matter merely of a trial, a retort, or a fit of indignation in order to safeguard the immediate conditions for the survival of philosophy (other proposals accompany this appeal: our minimal demands "To Begin With"). Within and outside of teaching, we want to undertake for philosophy something more, something better, and something else.

A Tableau Noir

A demonstration is in order and it is easy to do: if left to itself, present policy will see to it that philosophy has the most dismal of futures. We must gather together here a few givens that those in power try to force into oblivion or to disperse in the shadows. We recall that the law to reform the educational system (called the "Haby Reform"),[3] passed in June 1975, set out only a general framework and some pedagogical principles. As for the content of secondary instruction, discipline by discipline and in the hourly distribution, this has been in large part—and at the insistent demand of the government—left to regulatory bodies. It is thus by implementing decrees that the fate of philosophy will be decided in secondary education. Of course, the consequences of this will make themselves felt, inevitably, in university teaching and research. The question of philosophy cannot, to be sure, and ought not to be treated independently of the general economy of a reform. *But, to the extent that, for the moment* (and, we hope, *provisionally*), this reform is imposed on us by law, we find ourselves forced to struggle *also*—and we will do so without ceasing—in the limited and preordained field of implementing decrees. How does this field look?

The reform of the second cycle of secondary instruction will go into effect only at the beginning of the 1981 school year.[4] The ministry [of education] is maintaining a deliberate semi-silence on this subject. It hopes in this way to demobilize opinion, above all, teachers. But the minister's plans (which obviously do not contradict those of his predecessor) are nonetheless known in an unofficial and more or less determined form. A semblance of "consultation" in effect has to be maintained, if only with the office of the Inspection générale.[5]

These plans would be as follows: three *or* four hours of required instruction for all lycée students and, respectively, five or four optional hours. Even though 3 + 5 equals 4 + 4, these two projects are not equivalent. And the choice of optional instruction, although it may have a certain effectiveness when it concerns a discipline students have already begun in prior years, is largely fictive and a hoax when it involves a subject totally unfamiliar to the students. We denounce this deception. Moreover, given that philosophy has the reputation of being a "difficult" discipline, and given the policy under way that accelerates the present rarefaction of teaching positions— which offer the sole professional possibilities for trained philosophers—it is easy to foresee that the choice of an option so spectacularly disadvantaged would be exceptional. Thus, the role of this very contingent optional supplement must be considered negligible. The adoption of the plan that projects four required hours would allow for only a very temporary survival of the teaching of philosophy in lycées, but *it would suspend* for several years the recruitment of professors. One can imagine the consequences of such a suspension and, of course, these would not affect only the corporation of teachers of philosophy. This suspension would cause the majority of philosophy students in the university to disappear; it would dry up research, and so forth. But let's not speak in the conditional. The process is underway: since 1973, the recruitment of philosophy professors has already been reduced by 75 percent for the CAPES and by 70 percent for the agrégation.[6] In one year, from 1978 to 1979, it dropped by almost 50 percent (from 38 to 20 positions for the agrégation). Adding to these brutal measures will be the massive effects of the sinister decision that from now on excludes from the écoles normales d'instituteurs, in a scandalously unjustifiable way, more than 160 philosophy professors.

As for the most unfavorable project (three required hours), it would once again speed up liquidation. Its ineluctable consequences would in effect be the following:

1. "Technical unemployment" (for about 20 percent of the present hourly total) of working professors and immediate layoff of auxiliary teachers [*maîtres auxiliaires*], if there are still any left in 1981. After the redistribution of the shortage, two hypotheses: either *all* professors would have to complete their service by teaching in another discipline or even in an administrative job; or else a certain number of them (the "category of those with the least seniority at the lowest rank," as it is called) would be placed in the situation of being "at the service of the Rector."[7] This is already the case for most newly certified teachers and we are told that it will also be the case for all those certified or admitted to the agrégation for 1979.

2. The proliferation and quasi-generalization of teaching services distributed among several facilities, most often, in several municipalities. This is because a lycée whose "pedagogical structure" includes fewer than five or six Terminale classes—the majority of lycées—will not be sufficient to "fill out" the required service of those certified or agrégés. This scattering of teaching service not only affects the working conditions of teachers and everything not reducible to course time spent in the classroom, it seriously disrupts what is called the "pedagogical relation."

3. The *immediate* halt and suspension for several years of the recruitment of philosophy professors. Once again, this consequence exceeds the space in which professional demands could legitimately be developed. The discontinuation of the CAPES for several years, the transformation of the agrégation into a competition for internal recruitment open only to those certified and to those enrolled in the écoles normales would be followed by a fatal decline in university teaching and in research, which cannot live and develop normally without the needs of secondary teaching. Asphyxia would be inevitable within a kind of academy or academicism: philosophy would be studied like a dead language by a very few specialized anatomists. This is no doubt the dream of those in power; it is not even sure that certain university teachers do not share this dream, more or less in secret. The effects of such a situation are, we know, not only quantitative. That is why our fight should not be corporative. And the circumstantial struggle that is imposed on us (for example, as concerns the num-

ber of positions) in no way implies that we approve in principle the system and content of the competitive exams, less still their scandalous duality,[8] any more than all the conditions of so-called "teacher training" [*formation des maîtres*]. The whole space of teaching, research, and "training" must be changed. But, *to begin with*, we ought to demand certain short- and medium-term transformations.

To Begin With

In the immediate, concerning either teaching or research, the catastrophic process of this dismantling will be interrupted only under the following conditions. They represent a vital minimum:

1. An increase in positions competed for, in accordance with an *immediate* redefinition of needs, based on the maximum number of twenty-five students per class. This demand has been around for twenty-five years, and its pedagogical soundness is universally recognized, including by the ministerial services.

2. A required *minimum* schedule of four hours of philosophy for all students, whether they are in classical or modern, technical or professional lycées.

3. The retention of the positions of the professors of philosophy presently teaching in the écoles normales.

In the medium-term, in order to respond to demand and to needs, the teaching of philosophy will have to be extended to the whole second cycle in the lycées, inclusive from the Seconde to the Terminale (with the possibility of modifying the schedule in the Terminale) and to all lycée students, including those in professional lycées.[9] As several recent experiments have demonstrated, this extension is possible and necessary. It corresponds not only to aptitudes, but to a wide and deep demand among students who are not yet in the Terminale. This has been verified, just as one may also observe such a demand for philosophy instruction at the university coming from students or researchers specialized in other areas. This demand may also be felt outside the educational system. Such an extension should be accompanied by a redefinition of content and methods. It has nothing to do with the caricature represented by the introduction of philosophy in the Première in the abandoned version of the Haby plan.

But beyond this fight for survival, as it has been imposed on us by the

"Haby Reform," only a profound transformation can assure the development of philosophical teaching and research. Only a profound transformation can respond today to a demand, a need, an affirmation as well, the *affirmation* that has not been recognized by all those who would like to submit everything to certain normalizing analyses of techno-economic constraints.

It is this affirmation, however, that will sustain our Estates General. After some information and analysis sessions, after the most open kind of discussions, commitments will be made and actions undertaken.

Whether or not you are philosophers, teachers, researchers, students, join us, distribute our appeal, mobilize, and come out.

The Planning Committee
of the Estates General of Philosophy:

R. Brunet
(Lycée Voltaire, Paris)
D. Cahen
(Eco. Pol., Paris)
F. Châtelet
(Université de Paris-VIII)
J. Colombel
(Lycée Herriot, Lyon)
Ch. Coutel
(Lycée de Liévin)
G. Deleuze
(Université de Paris-VIII)
J. Derrida
(Ecole Normale Supérieure)
J.-T. Desanti
(Université de Paris-I)
E. de Fontenay
(Université de Paris-I)
F. Godet
(Lycée Technique Vauban,
Courbevoie)
B. Graciet
(Lycée de l'Isle-Adam)

M. Hocquet-Tessard
(Doc. Ecole Normale,
Bonneuil)
V. Jankélévitch
(Université de Paris-I)
H. Joly
(Université Grenoble)
G. Kaléka
(Lycée Pothier et IREM,
Orléans)
G. Labica
(Université de Paris-X)
Ph. Lacoue-Labarthe
(Université Strasbourg)
M. L. Mallet
(Lycée Récamier, Lyon)
J.-L. Nancy
(Université Strasbourg)
P. Ricoeur
(Université de Paris-X)
H. Védrine
(Université de Paris-I)

The Estates General are to take place beginning June 16 at the Sorbonne. More detailed information will be available later. We will gladly welcome all proposals. *Signatures* and in general *correspondence* should be addressed to: Roland BRUNET, 11, rue Massenet, 94120 Fontenay-sous-bois (tel.: 875-34-21). Financial support: to the same person, CCP: Lyon 5645 58-Y. Specify (For the Estates General of Philosophy). You can also help us by photocopying this text and distributing it.

In the weeks following the distribution of this appeal, the committee published the following communiqué accompanied by the first signatures (approximately one thousand).

Estates General of Philosophy

The Estates General will be held at the Sorbonne on June 16 and 17.

On June 16, at 10:00 A.M., right after an opening statement by Vladimir Jankélévitch and the planning committee, work and discussion will be organized around the (philosophical and nonphilosophical) problems posed today by the situation of philosophy: its place in society, inside and outside research or teaching institutions, in all categories of lycées, in the écoles normales, in the university.

Without excluding any theme, whether it be a matter of the destiny of philosophy or the present conditions of its pedagogical practice, and so forth, urgency seems to demand that the sessions—of information, analysis, discussion—be directed toward adopting positions, concrete proposals, specific commitments, short- and long-term actions to be undertaken.

It thus seems equally desirable that, in the most diverse forms and under the name of "Grievance Registers,"[10] analyses, notes, depositions, proposals, demands, and so forth, prepare the Estates General, be presented and gathered together here. These "Registers" may now be sent to the planning committee. Participation in the Estates General may be direct and personal, but collective or by delegation, as well.

We ask everyone to distribute this appeal widely, using the local means at their disposal.

It is clear that the success of the Estates General depends above all on the effective mobilization of everyone.

Translated by Peggy Kamuf

Notes

Privilege

A number of notes in the French original were provided by Elizabeth Weber. They are noted below by the designation EW.—Trans.

1. *Right to Philosophy* was first of all the title of a seminar I gave beginning in January 1984 in a rather singular institutional situation. At the beginning of the academic year, I was still, for the twentieth year, maître-assistant at the Ecole Normale Supérieure, and this seminar was given in that place, under its auspices, but also those of the Collège International de Philosophie, which I and others had just founded on October 10, 1983, and of which, that day, I had been elected director. I also knew that I would soon have to leave the Ecole for the Ecole des Hautes Etudes en Sciences Sociales, where I had also just been elected to the position of director of studies (in the branch of studies "Philosophical Institutions"). I have not yet been able to prepare my seminar notes for publication. I merely recall the principal argument of the seminar in this preface. But since I have retained its title, and since this title defines the horizon of this collection, allow me to reproduce here the seminar description, as it was then circulated by the Collège International de Philosophie:

> Right to Philosophy (to destine, to teach, to institute)
> The most open question, that of *destination*, will intersect with the question of foundation or *institution*, particularly the foundation of the *philosophical* institution (school, discipline, profession, and so forth). Is such an institution possible? For whom? By whom? How? Who decides? Who legitimates? Who imposes its evaluations? In what historical, social, political, technical conditions? Beyond an alternative between "internal" or "external" problematics, we will question the constitution of the limits between the inside and the outside of what is called the "philosophical" text, its modes of legitimation and institution. We will call upon certain notions from the so-

ciology of knowledge or culture, from the history of the sciences or pedagogical institutions, from the politology of research. But beyond an epistemology of these knowledges, we will begin to situate their professionalization and their transformation into
disciplines, the genealogy of their operative concepts (for example, "objectification,"
"legitimation," "symbolic power," and so forth), the history of their axiomatics, and
the effects of their place in the institution.

In this too general space, under the title *Right to Philosophy*, are sketched out two
concurrent trajectories:

1. The study of juridical discourse, which, without occupying the foreground,
founds philosophical institutions. What are its relations with social, historical, or political fields? With the structures of the "modern state"?

2. The study of the conditions of access to philosophy, language, teaching, research,
publishing, philosophical "legitimacy." Who has a right to philosophy? Who holds its
power or privilege? What, in fact, limits the alleged universalism of philosophy? How
does one decide that a thought or statement can be accepted as "philosophical"? Even
if this network of questions is not distinguished from *philosophy* itself (if such a thing
exists and claims to be unified), one can still study in specific contexts the modalities
of the determination of the "philosophical," the divisions it implies, the modes of access reserved for the exercise of philosophy: systems of teaching and research in which
philosophy is offered as a principal or secondary discipline, extra-scholastic or extra-
university circles, verbal "supports," whether in books or not. The question of a "support" (speech, book, journal, newspaper, radio, television, cinema) is not purely technical or formal. It also affects content, the constitution and modes of the formation or
reception of the themes and statements, of the corpus of philosophy. Are these the
same once they are no longer given, dominated, and accumulated, in the form of an
archive of books, in specialized institutions, by subjects or communities of authorized
and supposedly competent "guardians"? We will begin with numerous signs of a mutation that has been underway since the nineteenth century at least and in a more accelerated fashion over the last two decades.

The main theme for this preliminary approach: the example of the Collège International de Philosophie. Is this a new "philosophical institution"? The multiple possible interpretations of its origin, its conditions of possibility, its destination.

2. Rectitude, rectilinearity, the "straight path": we know what role these values (which are, moreover, also implied in those of the norm or rule) have played
in the axiomatics of numerous methodologies, in particular that of Descartes.
[On this subject, see J. Derrida, "La Langue et le discours de la méthode," in *Recherches sur la philosophie et le langage*, no. 3, *La Philosophie dans sa langue* (Grenoble: Université de Grenoble 2, 1983).—EW.]

3. Having often dealt with this law of the title, notably in the space of literary
works, I will refer to "Devant la loi" (1982) in *La Faculté de juger* (Paris: Minuit,
1985), as well as to "Survivre" (1977), "Titre à préciser," and "La Loi du genre"
(1979), in *Parages* (Paris: Galilée, 1986). ["The Law of Genre" and "Before the
Law" appear in *Acts of Literature*, ed. Derek Attridge (New York: Routledge,
1992).—Trans.]

4. More directly in "Mochlos—or the Conflict of the Faculties" and "The Wards of the University: The Principle of Reason and the Idea of the University," forthcoming in *Eyes of the University: Right to Philosophy 2*. "Mochlos" first appeared in English in *Logomachia: The Conflict of the Faculties*, ed. Richard Rand (Lincoln: University of Nebraska Press, 1992), 1–34. The same structure was analyzed with another concern in *Otobiographies: L'Enseignement de Nietzsche et la politique du nom propre*, chap. 1, "Déclarations d'indépendence" (Paris: Galilée, 1984); forthcoming in English in Jacques Derrida, *Negotiations: Interventions and Interviews: Interventions and Interviews, 1971–2001*, ed. and trans. Elizabeth Rottenberg (Stanford: Stanford University Press, 2002).

5. "In the proceedings of the meeting of the faculty committee of July 13, 1925, item six, the following comment is made: Benjamin's *Habilitation*. The faculty has decided, given Professor Cornelius's report, to request that Dr. Benjamin withdraw his Habilitation thesis. The faculty has decided, moreover, not to accept Dr. Benjamin's application for the title of doctor should he not follow this recommendation" (Burkhardt Lindner, "Habilitätsionsakte Benjamin: Über ein 'akademishces Tauerspiel' und über ein Vorkapitel der 'Frankfurter Schule' (Horkheimer, Adorno)," in *Zeitschrift für Literaturwissenschaft und Linguistik* 53/54 (1984): 156).

6. I treat this problem more analytically in "Heidegger's Ear (Philopolemology, *Geschlecht* IV)," in *Reading Heidegger: Commemorations*, ed. John Sallis (Bloomington: Indiana University Press, 1993), pp. 163–218.

7. Groupe de Recherches sur l'Enseignement Philosophique (Research Group on the Teaching of Philosophy).—Trans.

8. What is at stake in this question about the question has been identified in *De l'esprit: Heidegger et la question* (Paris: Galilée, 1987), pp. 147 ff.; *Of Spirit: Heidegger and the Question*, trans. Geoffrey Bennington and Rachel Bowlby (Chicago: University of Chicago Press, 1989), pp. 94 ff.

9. As for this "community of the question about the possibility of the question," in which "is sheltered and encapsulated an unbreachable dignity and duty of decision, an unbreachable responsibility," see "Violence and Metaphysics," in *L'Ecriture et la différence* (Paris: Seuil, 1967), p. 118; *Writing and Difference*, trans. Alan Bass (Chicago: Chicago UP, 1978), p. 80.

10. I have always insisted upon this. But faced with some people's obstinate wish to ignore this in order to make a case against me, I refer, at least for the reminder I make of it, to *Psyché: Inventions de l'autre* (Paris: Galilée, 1987), pp. 395–451, *De l'esprit*, pp. 23 ff., and *Mémoires à Paul de Man* (Paris: Galilée, 1988); *Memoires for Paul de Man*, trans. Cecile Lindsay et al. (New York: Columbia University Press, 1989).

11. Forthcoming in *Eyes of the University: Right to Philosophy 2*.—Trans.

12. "Declarations of Independence," forthcoming in *Negotiations*.—Trans.

13. Laurent Fabius was a leading figure in the Socialist Party who worked in various positions in the late 1970s for Mitterand and whom Mitterand (recently

elected President) appointed Minister for the Budget in 1981. In 1983 he became Minister of Industry and Research. Jack Lang rose within the Socialist Party in the late 1970s and was appointed Minister of Culture by Mitterand in 1981. Roger-Gérard Schwartzenberg was Secretary of State for the Minister of Education from 1981 to 1986.—Trans.

14. From this (in fact very philosophical) point of view, one would presume the purity or the untouchable indivisibility of such a limit, the limit that ensures the division between the philosophical itself, philosophy properly speaking and, *stricto sensu,* its "business," *on the one hand,* and, *on the other hand,* everything outside it, however close. This is what was behind Georges Canguilhem's polemical but essential (in fact rigorously essentialist) argument in the clear and vigorous response he made to questions from the *Nouvelle Critique* when the Haby Reform plan menaced: "To this point, many arguments invoked by most of those who have come to the rescue of philosophy without neglecting to put themselves in the spotlight have missed the mark either because of their desire for publicity or because of their routine return to worn out themes. . . . In short, defending the teaching of philosophy, that is, inventing its renewal, is not a matter of one sector. Mr. Haby's entire reform is in question. Philosophy does not need any defenders, insofar as its own justification is its very business. But the defense of the teaching of philosophy would require a critical philosophy of teaching" (*Nouvelle Critique* 84 [May 1975]: 25; see also 239). Let this be said in passing: in 1975, whether its author intended it or not, this final phrase defined at least one part of the project of Greph, *which had never been undertaken in France to that point by any official (individual or collective) representative of French philosophical institutions.* Therefore, how could one not subscribe to it? And how could one not subscribe (this was also one of the principal themes of Greph) to the sentence opposing the "sectorization" of this debate?

That being said, the distinction between philosophy's "business" in its self-justification and "the critical philosophy of teaching" seems to me to be of the most problematic kind. Not only because it contradicts the critique of "sectorization," but because what is "proper" to philosophy is the name of the problem that this affirmation assumes it resolves. This is what is at stake (I no longer dare say it is the stake "itself" or the "very" stakes), one of the inevitable stakes, of deconstructionist thinking. Although "deconstruction"—which has never been a doctrine or a teachable knowledge as such—has never been called to constitute the charter of any institution, in particular of a group as open and diverse as Greph, this group could not, in any case, take such a paralyzing distinction between philosophy's "business" and a "critical philosophy of teaching" as its rule. In its research and *open* struggles (that is to say, necessarily—and fortunately—*public,* which does not mean "publicizing," struggles) and in the very urgency of these struggles (it is not for nothing that they sought the withdrawal of the Haby Reform plan, to take but this example), Greph undertook first of all to connect the two, philosophy's "business" and the "critical philosophy of teaching." Greph intends to demonstrate the necessity of this connection. As for the value of "critique," in the expression "critical philosophy of teaching," I will return to it later.

15. "Popularities: From Law to the Philosophy of Law," forthcoming in *Eyes of the University: Right to Philosophy 2*.—Trans.

16. See, notably, "Signature Event Context," in *Margins of Philosophy*, trans. Alan Bass (Chicago: University of Chicago Press, 1982), pp. 307–30, and *Limited Inc* (Evanston: Northwestern University Press, 1988), pp. 1–24.

17. As for the passage evoked above, I refer here to the Garnier-Flammarion edition of Diogenes Laertius, *Vie, doctrines et sentences des philosophes illustres*, trans. R. Genaille, 1: 242 ff. and 116 ff. [English translations are retranslated from the author's citations.—Trans.]

18. I refer again to *Of Spirit: Heidegger and the Question*.

19. In the seventh of the *Addresses to the German Nation*, Fichte develops an argument of this type. See "La Main de Heidegger (*Geschlect II*)," in *Psyché*, pp. 416–18.

20. This question of idiom was at the center of a seminar I gave over several years on Nationality and Philosophical Nationalism, which was the necessary development of the 1983–84 seminar (Right to Philosophy) whose outline or schema I follow here. I hope to be able to prepare this seminar for publication later.

21. These quotes are from the French *Universal Declaration of the Rights of Man* (1791).—Trans.

22. See R. Balibar and D. Laporte, *Le Français national: Politique et pratique de la langue nationale sous la Révolution* (Paris: Hachette, 1974); M. de Certeau, D. Julia, and J. Revel, *Une politique de la langue: La Révolution française et les patois* (Paris: Gallimard, 1975); R. Balibar, *L'Institution du français: Essais sur le colinguisme des Carolingiens à la République* (Paris: Presses Universitaires de France, 1985).

23. I have attempted elsewhere to expose this topology of the "chiasmic invagination of borders," notably in *Parages*.

24. "Coercion" here translates *contrainte* ("constraint") in order to follow the English translation of Kant more closely.—Trans.

25. See "The Pupils of the University: The Principle of Reason and the Idea of the University," forthcoming in *Eyes of the University: Right to Philosophy 2*.—Trans.

26. The Terminale is the final year of the French lycée before students take the state exam, the baccalauréat.—Trans.

27. See "Mochlos" and "Theology of Translation," forthcoming in *Eyes of the University: Right to Philosophy 2*.—Trans.

28. [See Jacques Derrida, "The Politics of Friendship," in *Journal of Philosophy* 85, no. 10 (November 1988): 632–44.—EW.] See also *The Politics of Friendship*, trans. George Collins (New York: Verso, 1997).—Trans.

29. In the heading to this section, *en direct* means not only "direct" but "live," as in a live radio or television transmission, for example.—Trans.

30. See Austin, "The Meaning of a Word," in *Philosophical Papers* (Oxford: Clarendon Press, 1961), p. 55. See also *Memoires for Paul de Man*.

31. *S'expliquer avec*, not only "to explain oneself" but "to sort out" and even "to have it out with."—Trans.

32. Within the limits of these introductory remarks, I cannot take up in itself the very necessary debate that M. Villey opens—and immediately closes—in particular in his Preface to the French edition of Kant's *Metaphysics of Morals*, trans. A. Philonenko (Paris: Vrin, 1979). The conclusions of this long Preface would no doubt call for a long and meticulous discussion—and perhaps a general recasting of this immense problematic. They discredit without further ado the Kantian doctrine of right, as well as all the philosophical discourses that take it seriously. "For us [jurists and philosophers of law] Kant's *Rechtslehre*, which misses the point on the subject, the aims, the methods, and the instruments of our work, *is not a theory of the law*. It marks the summit of a period of the *forgetting* of the philosophy of law. Kant believed he could speak to us about the law (he was of course the victim of the German habits of the School of Natural Right), while he did something else. If Kant believed he could constitute science from principles, *a priori* foundations, as the *mathematics of right*, he began with a sort of *non-Euclidean mathematics that is essentially foreign to our juridical experience*. Such is, at least, the reaction of one jurist historian of the law—who does not really expect to be followed. There is no chance that philosophers will consent to take our critique of Kant seriously, if all they know of the law they have learned by reading Kant, or Fichte, or Hegel, or other successors of Kant, including Kelsen. . . . No doubt, the success of the *Rechtslehre* can *be explained* in its era. It could, at the beginning of the nineteenth century, have been of service to a particular *politics*, the cause of state control, individualism, bourgeois liberalism. But it has never been the purpose of either judges or the law to put themselves in the service of a *party*," pp. 24–25.

33. This remark is developed in "Popularities: The Right to the Philosophy of Law," forthcoming in *Eyes of the University: Right to Philosophy 2*.

34. Christian Garve, *Vermischte Aufsätze* (Breslau: William Gottfried Korn, 1796), pp. 352 ff.

35. Kant, *The Metaphysics of Morals*, trans. Mary Gregor (Cambridge: Cambridge University Press, 1996), pp. 3–4. I take this allusion to *Logodaedalus* as a pretext to refer, as I should in every sentence, to two great books by Jean-Luc Nancy that clear the way for so many discussions: *Le Discours de la syncope: 1. Logodaedalus* (Paris: Flammarion, 1976) and *L'Impératif catégorique* (Paris: Flammarion, 1983). In the latter work, the fundamental article entitled "Lapsus judicii" must receive here a privilege to which I will return again later. On the pas-

sages from Kant that I cite or evoke at this moment, see in particular the chapter "L'Ambiguité du populaire et la science sans miel," in *Le Discours de la syncope*, pp. 56 ff.

36. See "Popularities," forthcoming in *Eyes of the University: Right to Philosophy 2*.

37. Kant, *The Metaphysics of Morals*, p. 25. The translation has been modified slightly to approach Derrida's French translation more closely.—Trans.

38. *Conscience*, at once consciousness and conscience.—Trans.

39. These motifs have been developed elsewhere: that of *stricture* very extensively in *Glas* (Paris: Galilée, 1974); *Glas*, trans. John P. Leavey, Jr., and Richard Rand (Lincoln : University of Nebraska Press, 1986), notably concerning Hegel's *Philosophy of Right*; that of the relations between being and the law, in the course of a debate with Heidegger, in *Memoires for Paul de Man*.

40. Forthcoming in *Eyes of the University: Right to Philosophy 2*.

41. See note 16, above.

42. On the absolute autonomy of the faculty of philosophy according to Kant, see "Mochlos." It isn't the jurist or the legal advisor as such who has the authority to pronounce the law of law, the truth about the law, what is just and unjust. He can do so no more than the logician can respond to the question "What is the truth?" Having recalled this fact, Kant adds:

> What is laid down as right (*quid sit iuris*), that is, what the laws in a certain place and at a certain time say or have said, the jurist can certainly say. But whether what these laws prescribed is also right, and what the universal criterion is by which one could recognize right as well as wrong (*iustum et iniustum*), this would remain hidden from him unless he leaves those empirical principles behind for a while and seeks the sources of such judgments in reason alone, so as to establish the basis for any possible giving of positive laws (although positive laws can serve as excellent guides to this). Like the wooden head in Phaedrus' fable, a merely empirical doctrine of right is a head that may be beautiful but unfortunately it has no brain. (23)

43. "It would be a definition that added to the practical concept the *exercise* of it, as this is taught by experience, a *hybrid definition* [Bastarderklärung] (*definitio hybrida*) that puts the concept in a false light" (19). In the Appendix to the Introduction to the Doctrine of Right, "equivocal right" (*ius aequivocum*) is deduced strictly and calmly into its two kinds: equity (right without coercion) and the right of necessity (coercion without right). What is the "foundation" of this "ambiguity"?: "The fact that there are cases in which a right is in question but for which no judge can be appointed to render a decision" (27). There is no use in specifying that what is played out in the following three pages is simply dizzying. As was the allusion to the "exceptions" in the realm of virtue.

44. I refer once again to "Lapsus judicii" (in *L'Impératif catégorique*, notably pp. 50–51). There, Nancy remarkably describes the lining or the doubling that

concerns me here: "Such is the *properly juridical* (neither founding, explicative, interpretive, verifying, or sublating—but doubling all these meanings, or, as is said in navigation, bringing them to the surface) meaning of the critical question: 'How are synthetic *a priori* judgments possible?' (51) I think this should be specified: because of this lining or effect of doubling, the hegemony of the juridical consists precisely in the erasure or rather the *re-trait* of the "properly juridical." Or again: if one absolutely wants there to be something *properly juridical* in these conditions, this is on the condition that it would no longer be *strictly* juridical.

45. Kant, *Critique of Pure Reason*, trans. Norman Kemp Smith (New York: St. Martin's Press, 1965), p. 9.

46. "Lapsus judicii," p. 55. Nancy emphasizes the word "privilege," as I discovered in my recent rereading of this text, at the time when I was transcribing this citation. *Privilege* was already the title chosen for these introductory remarks. I am delighted by a coincidence that is so fortunate for me: the singularity of a chance and a justification. Yet another kind of privilege.

47. It is the immense "*philosophical* question of Rome," to take up Nancy's expression. In "Lapsus judicii," he treats it extensively and cautiously, not rushing, in particular, to close the necessary debate with Heidegger on this point. Everything Nancy says in this regard about the accident, the case, and the "case of right" (pp. 36, 37, 41, 43 ff.) is in my opinion a very strong and very new introduction to this problematic.

48. I refer here to "Zur Kritik der Gewalt" (1921); "Critique of Violence," in Walter Benjamin, *Selected Writings*, trans. Edmund Jephcott (Cambridge: Harvard University Press, 1996), pp. 236–52. In *Force de loi* (Paris: Galilée, 1994), "Force of Law: The 'Mystical Foundation of Authority'" (in *Deconstruction and the Possibility of Justice*, ed. Drucilla Cornell et al. [New York: Routledge, 1992], pp. 3–67), which is devoted to this enigmatic text, I try in particular to show why *Gewalt* is difficult to translate, even though it is just as difficult to avoid the inadequate word "violence."

49. Kant, *Critique of Pure Reason*, p. 9.

50. Forthcoming in *Eyes of the University: Right to Philosophy 2*.—Trans.

51. Kant, *Critique of Pure Reason*, p. 11.

52. Putting into question again the (pyramidal and synoptical) hierarchy that, in the name of the question *quid juris*, subordinates sciences or regional ontologies to an absolute logic, to a transcendental phenomenology, or a fundamental ontology was one of the first tasks of the deconstruction undertaken in *Of Grammatology* or in "Différance" (in *Margins of Philosophy*). At issue already was "the very idea of the institution" and of the oppositions into which it lets itself be constructed—therefore remaining deconstructible.

53. In the 1983–84 seminar whose argument I follow here, several sessions were devoted to a questioning, and sometimes detailed, reading of Pierre Bourdieu, *La*

Distinction (Paris: Minuit, 1979), *Distinction: A Social Critique of the Judgment of Taste*, trans. Richard Nice (Cambridge: Harvard University Press, 1984), in particular, what concerns Kant (and a few others) in the "Postscript: Towards a 'Vulgar' Critique of 'Pure' Critique," pp. 485–502 // 565 ff. This reading extended to the rich issue of the *Actes de la recherche en sciences sociales* that had just been devoted to *Education et philosophie* 47/48 (June 1983) (articles by J.-L. Fabiani, L. Pinto, W. Lepenies, P. Bourdieu). Since I can only recall the abstract principle of my questions here, I hope to be able to come back to them elsewhere.

54. Associated with what is also an "undertaking of self-knowledge," the "ethical" concern is often taken on as such by Bourdieu. These words appear, among other places, in an interview with Didier Eribon after the publication of *Homo Academicus* (Paris: Minuit, 1984) (*Nouvel Observateur*, November 2, 1984). As for what connects the theme of "real freedom" or "liberating virtues" to that of the "critical question" and of "objectification," see the most direct text in this regard, "Les Sciences sociales et la philosophie," in *Actes* (esp. pp. 45, 51–52): for example, this passage—which I cite immediately to subscribe to a program (which I would no doubt formulate differently) and to renew an interrogation into the joint motif of freedom and objectivity: "Just the same, how is one not to see the liberating virtues of an analysis of specifically philosophical rhetoric, and notably of the figures of speech and thought that are the richest symbolically in characterizing a writing as 'philosophical' or in attributing a 'philosophical spirit' to its author?" Or again: "One can liberate the thinking of its history on the condition that one knows the history of thought. In fact only a true social history of philosophy can ensure real freedom in relation to social, objective, or corporate constraints." "To objectify the conditions of production of the producers and consumers of philosophical discourse, and in particular the conditions that must be met for this discourse to find itself invested as a properly philosophical legitimacy, is to improve one's chances of suspending the effects of the socially conditioned belief that leads one to accept without examination every unexamined thought that has established itself. A thinking of the social conditions of thinking is possible that would give thinking the possibility of freedom in relation to these conditions."

55. "There is practically no questioning of art and culture which leads to a genuine objectification of the cultural game, so strongly are the dominated classes and their spokesmen imbued with a sense of their cultural unworthiness" (*Distinction*, p. 251).

56. The fold of such a *supplement of objectification* does not add one degree or one notch more in a continuous movement. It not only reorients us in the direction of a genealogical interpretation of the value of objectivity, but marks the differential limit that I have tried, in another context, to formalize on the subject of *thematization* (see "The Double Session," in *Dissemination*, pp. 173–287). One can say about objectivation what was said in this regard about thematization.

Where a Teaching Body Begins

This text first appeared in *Politiques de la philosophie*, texts by Châtelet, Michel Foucault, Jean-François Lyotard, and Michel Serres, collected by D. Grisoni (Paris: Grasset, 1976).

1. See the Appendix to this chapter.
2. Jacques Derrida, *Positions* (Paris: Minuit, 1972), p. 90; *Positions*, trans. Alan Bass (Chicago: University of Chicago Press, 1981), p. 90.—EW.
3. René Haby, former Minister of National Education, whose reform plan for national education is the subject of many of the texts that follow.—Trans.
4. The competitive exam for certification for a teaching position in a lycée or university.—Trans.
5. See the Appendix to this chapter.—EW.
6. André Canivez, "Jules Lagneau, professeur et philosophe: Essai sur la condition du professeur de philosophie jusqu'à la fin du XIXe siècle," Principal thesis for the doctorat d'État, Association des publications de la Faculté des Lettres de Strasbourg, 1965.—EW.
7. *Trois siècles d'enseignement secondaire*, 1936, p. 82.
8. Denis Diderot, *Plan d'une université pour le gouvernement de Russie, 1775–1776*, in *Oeuvres complètes*, chronological edition, vol. 11 (Paris: Société encyclopédique française et le Club français du livre, 1971), p. 747.—EW.
9. Canivez, "Jules Lagneau," pp. 87–88.—EW.
10. *Cours d'études pour l'instruction du prince de Parme*, VI. Extracts from the course on history. Text established by Georges le Roy. Corpus général des philosophes français, Auteurs modernes, vol. 33 (Paris: Presses Universitaires de France, 1948), p. 235.—EW.
11. Canivez, "Jules Lagneau," pp. 90–91.
12. *Poser*, at once "to pose" (a question, for example) and "to posit."—Trans.
13. The name for the arts class preparing the competitive examination for entrance to the Ecole Normale Supérieure.—Trans.
14. The Centre National de Recherche Scientifique and the Fondation Thiers both provide positions for researchers who do not necessarily teach within the framework of these institutions.—Trans.
15. When a collectivity subscribes to Greph's bulletin, we will ask this collectivity for the list of those of its members who desire affiliation with Greph.
16. The new statutes have since been passed.

The Crisis in the Teaching of Philosophy

This paper was originally given at Cotonou (Benin), at the opening of an international conference gathering francophone and anglophone African philosophers in December 1978.—EW.

1. The author here italicizes "*la* philosophie," indicating the unity and uniqueness of the noun.—Trans.

2. Named after René Haby, then Minister of National Education.—Trans.

3. An allusion to the recent electoral failure of the left.—EW.

4. Jacques Derrida, "Réponses à la *Nouvelle Critique*," May–June 1975, reprinted in *Qui a peur de la philosophie?*, collective work by Greph (Paris: Flammarion, 1977), pp. 457–58; translated as "Divided Bodies: Responses to *La Nouvelle Critique*," below.

5. See Edmund Husserl, *The Crisis of European Sciences and Transcendental Phenomenology*, trans. David Carr (Evanston: Northwestern University Press, 1970).

6. See the appendix to the preceding chapter, above.—EW.

The Age of Hegel

This essay first appeared in French, in the volume *Qui a peur de la philosophie*, by Greph, which brought together texts by Sarah Kofman, Sylviane Agacinski, Jean-Pierre Lefebvre, Jacques Derrida, Roland Brunet, Alain Delormes, Bernadette Gromer, Jean-Luc Nancy, Michèle Le Doeuff, Bernard Pautrat, Jean-Pierre Hédoin, Hélène Politis, Michel Ben Lassen, Martine Meskel, and Michael Ryan (Paris: Flammarion, 1977).—EW. It first appeared in English in Samuel Weber, ed., *Demarcating the Disciplines: Philosophy, Literature, Art* (Minneapolis: University of Minnesota Press, 1986), pp. 3–44.—Trans.

1. For this and all subsequent quotes from G. W. F. Hegel's letter "To the Royal Ministry of Spiritual, Academic, and Medical Affairs," April 16, 1822, see the Appendix to the present essay.—Trans.

2. Reference to the texts of the *Philosophy of Right* of Berlin as well as to the political scene of the epoch is a precondition for the minimal intelligibility of this letter. We should therefore specify immediately that it is becoming increasingly clear we must speak of the "Philosoph*ies* of Right" of Berlin. This multiplicity is not simply a matter of revisions, versions, editions, or additions. It is part and parcel of the complexity of the political situation in Berlin, of the over-determinations, stratagems, and occasional secrets of Hegel's political practice or writing. Today we can no longer simplify this multiplicity—as has often been done to the point of caricature—no longer reduce it to the "Prussian State philosopher." As a preface to this letter, and in view of the reelaboration of all these questions (the "Philosoph*ies* of Right," Marx's and Engel's relations to this entire politico-theoretical aggregate, Hegel's effective political writings, etc.), I will indicate at least two absolutely indispensable discussions: Jacques d'Hondt's *Hegel et son temps* (Berlin, 1818–31; rpt. Paris: Editions Sociales, 1968) and Jean-Pierre Lefebvre's preface to his translation of *La Société civile bourgeoise* (Paris: Maspero, 1975). See also Eric Weil, *Hegel et l'Etat* (Paris: Vrin, 1970).

It will also be necessary to read two other texts concerning teaching in the Gymnasium and at the university. They are as yet little known and will be translated soon. The first is the Report to Niethammer, Inspector General of the Kingdom of Bavaria, on the teaching of the philosophical propaedeutic in the Gymnasium (1812). This report constitutes a systematic and important ensemble regarding what can be assimilated at one age or another, regarding the necessity to begin by learning philosophical *content* rather than "learning to philosophize,"concerning the speculative; that is, "the philosophical in the form of the concept," which can appear only "discretely" in the Gymnasium. The second is *On the Teaching of Philosophy at the University* (text addressed to Prof. Von Raumer, Governmental Counsel of the Kingdom of Prussia, 1816). [These two texts later appeared in translation in *Philosophies de l'Université: L'Idéalisme allemand et la question de l'Université* (Paris: Payot, 1979), pp. 331 ff.—EW.]

3. The ENA (Ecole Normale d'Administration) is the training academy for the French administrative elite.—Trans.

4. [Victor Cousin, *La Défense de l'université et de la philosophie* (Paris: Joubert, 1844), p. 123.—EW.] In addressing the correspondence between Hegel and Cousin about all these questions (a correspondence reread, after a manner, in *Glas* [Paris: Galilée, 1974; English trans. John P. Leavey, Jr., and Richard Rand (Lincoln: University of Nebraska Press, 1986)—Trans.]), I have analyzed, in the course of work on the teaching body, the defense of philosophy, ideology, and the Ideologues, Cousin's famous discourse, its content, and its political inscription. Parts of this work will be published later. The same applies to certain writings from 1975 to 1976 about Nietzsche and teaching, *Ecce homo*, the political heritage of Nietzsche, and—since I allude to it later—the question of the ear. [See *Otobiographies: L'Enseignement de Nietzsche de la politique du nom propre* (Paris: Galilée, 1984); "Otobiographies: The Teaching of Nietzsche and the Politics of the Proper Name," trans. Avital Ronell, in Jacques Derrida, *The Ear of the Other* (Lincoln: University of Nebraska Press, 1988), 3–38.—Trans.].

5. Destutt de Tracy, *Observations sur le système actuel d'Instruction publique* (Paris: Panckoucke), 9: 2–3.

6. Cousin, *La Défense de l'université et de la philosophie*, p. 136.

7. In French, *il se raconte*, literally, "he narrates himself."—Trans.

8. Hegel, *Correspondance*, vol. 2, *1813–1822*, trans. J. Carrère (Paris: Gallimard, 1963), pp. 270–71.

9. Hegel, *Briefe*, vol. 2, *1813–1822*, ed. J. Hoffmeister (Hamburg: Felix Meiner, 1953), appendices, p. 495.

10. Hegel to Duboc, July 30, 1822, in Hegel, *Correspondance*, 2: 285.

11. Once again, in order fully to fathom the complexity of this strategy, all the constraints its ruse had to take into account, I refer to Jacques d'Hondt, *Hegel et son temps*, particularly to the section "Les Démagogues" and to the chapter "Hegel clandestin temps."

12. The German word *Beispiel* is translated as "example," but it is composed of the words *bei* (near, with, among, at, during, *chez*) and *Spiel* (play, game, etc.) —Trans.

13. D'Hondt, *Hegel et son temps*, p. 9: "That philosophy which he publishes [makes public], which he exposes to the attacks of his enemies, and which surmounts, barely, being barred by censorship; . . . that one his friends and intelligent disciples read between the lines . . . completing with oral indications, and taking into account the inflections imposed upon him by events and incidents, a legislation that they bear as well. And then . . . the philosophy of right whose maxims Hegel actually follows . . . how he treats the positive institutions whose theory he elaborates: production and profit [*métier et gain*], marriage and the family, civil society, administration, the State—and also, how they treat him."

14. Friedrich Engels, *Ludwig Feuerbach et la fin de la philosophie classique allemande* (Paris: Editions Sociales, 1966), p. 16.

15. Hegel, *Principes de la philosophie du droit*, trans, André Kaan (Paris: Gallimard, 1940), section 75, Note on Contracts and Marriage, pp. 117–18.—EW.

16. Cited by d'Hondt, *Hegel et son temps*, pp. 53–54.

17. Hegel, *Encyclopédie des Sciences Philosophiques*, abridged, trans. M. de Gandillac (Paris: Gallimard, 1970), sections 573, 489.—EW.

18. Hegel, *Philosophie du droit*, pp. 294 and 286.

19. Hegel, *Encyclopédie des Sciences Philosophiques*, section 396, pp. 360–61. —EW.

20. This does not necessarily (or simply) amount to some tendentious movement (via the integral State) toward the "decline" [*dépérissement*] of the State in Engels's "regulated society" or Gramsci's "State without a State." But I will try to return to these difficult "limits" elsewhere . . .

21. Hegel, *Correspondance*, 2: 308.

22. The English translation of this letter is based on G. W. F. Hegel, *Berliner Schriften, 1818–1831*, ed. J. Hoffmeister (Hamburg: F. Meiner, 1956), pp. 543–53.

23. *Addendum from the rough draft*: "The knowledge of logical forms would be expedient not only in the aforementioned respect, insofar as the treatment of such forms entails an exercise that also includes the treatment of abstract thoughts themselves—but also insofar as these logical forms are themselves already presupposed as the material that then is treated by speculative thinking in its own way. Speculative philosophy's dual task—on the one hand, bringing its material, the general determinations of thoughts, to consciousness and raising it to a level of familiarity; and, on the other, linking this material to the higher idea—is limited to this latter aspect by the fact that knowledge of the forms is presupposed. Anyone who is so prepared and then moves into philosophy proper finds himself on familiar grounds."

24. *Variant in the rough draft*: "As to what merely concerns the older natural theology, its exposition would be entirely taken up in the instruction of religion,

where the matter will already appear for itself and only its formal aspect need be added; but this knowledge would have to be given only in a wholly historical manner, rather than projecting a modern contempt upon forms that (since Anselm— *deleted*) come from Catholic theology and even from ancient times, and which have always been venerated."

25. *Addendum from the rough draft*: "Not as if I held none of the present textbooks to be suitable, but because every book fair presents us with new compendia and I am not in the habit of following up this literature; in my experience those that I have seen are nothing more than more or less elaborate repetitions of the older manuals, augmented with useless innovations. Without attempting to anticipate, in my view the entire aim and mode of this instruction would require teachers to refer to previous textbooks, on the whole to those belonging to the Wolffian School, with perhaps the single modification of replacing the Aristotelian category-table by the Kantian.

Philosophy and Its Classes

This is the complete version, under its original title, of the text "La réforme Haby," which appeared in *Le Monde de l'éducation*, no. 4, March 1975. Reprinted in Greph, *Qui a peur de la philosophie?* (Paris: Flammarion, 1977).—EW.

1. The final years of lycée instruction before the baccalauréat are called "Seconde," "Première," and "Terminale."—Trans.

2. A three-year university degree.—Trans.

3. Cited by Yves Agnès, "Le libéralisme pédagogique," *Le Monde*, December 13, 1975.

4. Gorgias, 485c. Plato, *The Collected Dialogues*, ed. Edith Hamilton and Huntington Cairns (Princeton: Princeton University Press, 1961), p. 268.

5. This is the goal of the recently established Greph. Cf. *Le Monde de L'Education*, January 1975.

Divided Bodies

This essay first appeared in *La Nouvelle Critique*, 84–65 (May–June 1975). Reprinted in Greph, *Qui a peur de la philosophie?* (Paris: Flammarion, 1977)—EW.

1. Named for Valéry Giscard d'Estaing, then President of France, and René Haby, Minister of National Education.—Trans.

2. The *loi Royer* (Royer Law) is the common name for the "law on commerce and artisanry" ("loi d'orientation du commerce et de l'artisanat"). Passed in December 1973, it sought to equalize large-scale and small-scale traditional commerce. In modified form it still exists.—Trans.

3. Joseph Fontanet was Minister of Education from 1972 to 1974. He was assassinated in 1980. Christian Fouchet became Minister of Education in 1962 and initiated secondary school and higher education reforms. He became Minister of the Interior in 1967 but quit his post in the wake of the events of May 1968. He continued in various political positions and died in 1974.—Trans.

4. The Research Group on the Teaching of Philosophy (Groupe de Recherches sur l'Enseignement Philosophique; Greph) organizes and coordinates work on the apparatus of the teaching of philosophy. Teachers and students participate in it. Although its aims are not only theoretical critique within some seminar reproducing the critical self-repetition of philosophy, Greph intends to intervene according to a specific mode that would not be that of a corporative association, a union, or a party, even if common actions appear to it to be necessary in this or that situation. For information, contact the provisional office of Greph, 45, rue d'Ulm, 75005 Paris.

Philosophy of the Estates General

Read at the opening of the Estates General, which was attended by more than twelve hundred people at the Sorbonne. The text was published in *Libération*, June 20, 1979, and then in *Etats généraux de la philosophie (16 et 17 juin 1979)* (Paris: Flammarion, 1979). On the planning and premises of the Estates General, see the Appendix to this chapter.

1. The provisions of the "Haby Reform" challenged by the Estates General were subsequently dropped or never implemented. Two years later, the Socialist Party and François Mitterrand were elected on a platform that specifically included several of the proposals of Greph and the Estates General concerning the extension, rather than the curtailment, of the teaching of philosophy in secondary schools.—Trans.

2. Blackboard, but also a black picture.—Trans.

3. Named after René Haby, then Minister of National Education.—Trans.

4. The second cycle refers to the final three years of pre-baccalauréat instruction, called respectively Seconde, Première, and Terminale.—Trans.

5. The administration of central education. There is an inspecteur d'académie for each département in France.—Trans.

6. National competitive exams that certify for a teaching position in a lycée or university. CAPES: Certificat d'aptitude professionelle d'enseignement secondaire.—Trans.

7. Each of the académies or regions of the French national education system is administered by a Rector. It should be noted that agrégés and those receiving the CAPES are civil servants and, in principle, are guaranteed a teaching position for the duration of their careers.—Trans.

8. The agrégation and the CAPES exams are almost equally difficult and competitive; nevertheless, the first is considered more prestigious and carries with it more privileges.—Trans.

9. In professional lycées, students complete what is known as the short second cycle. They do not do a Terminale year and they earn a professional degree (the "brevet d'études professionelles") rather than the baccalauréat.—Trans.

10. *Cahiers de doléances*: the traditional name of the lists of grievances drafted by different groups and committees for presentation to the Estates General.—Trans.

MERIDIAN

Crossing Aesthetics